ENDANGERED PEOPLES
of Europe

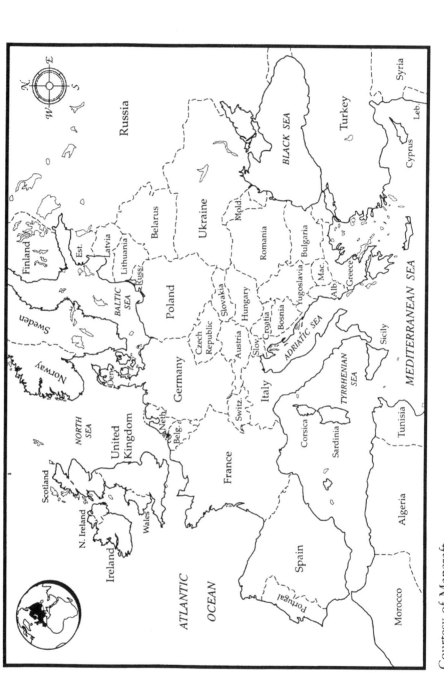

Courtesy of Mapcraft.

ENDANGERED PEOPLES
of Europe

Struggles to Survive and Thrive

Edited by Jean S. Forward

The Greenwood Press
"Endangered Peoples of the World" Series
Barbara Rose Johnston, Series Editor

GREENWOOD PRESS
Westport, Connecticut • London

Library of Congress Cataloging-in-Publication Data

Endangered peoples of Europe : struggles to survive and thrive / edited by Jean S. Forward.
    p. cm.—(The Greenwood Press "Endangered peoples of the world" series, ISSN
1525–1233)
    Includes bibliographical references and index.
    ISBN 0–313–31006–8 (alk. paper)
    1. Minorities—Europe—History. 2. Europe—Ethnic relations. I. Forward, Jean
S., 1948– II. Series.
    D1056.2.E85   E63   2001
    305.8'0094—dc21   00–034140

British Library Cataloguing in Publication Data is available.

Library of Congress Catalog Card Number: 00–034140
ISBN: 0–313–31006–8
ISSN: 1525–1233

First published in 2001

Greenwood Press, 88 Post Road West, Westport, CT 06881
An imprint of Greenwood Publishing Group, Inc.
www.greenwood.com

Printed in the United States of America

The paper used in this book complies with the
Permanent Paper Standard issued by the National
Information Standards Organization (Z39.48–1984).

10 9 8 7 6 5 4 3 2 1

Every reasonable effort has been made to trace the owners of copyright materials in this book,
but in some instances this has proven impossible. The editor and publisher will be glad to
receive information leading to more complete acknowledgments in subsequent printings of
the book and in the meantime extend their apologies for any omissions.

Contents

Contents

Series Foreword

Barbara Rose Johnston

Two hundred thousand years ago our human ancestors gathered plants and hunted animals in the forests and savannas of Africa. By forty thousand years ago, *Homo sapiens sapiens* had developed ways to survive and thrive in every major ecosystem on this planet. Unlike other creatures, whose response to harsh or varied conditions prompted biological change, humans generally relied upon their ingenuity to survive. They fashioned clothing from skins and plant fiber rather than growing thick coats of protective hair. They created innovative ways to live and communicate and thus passed knowledge down to their children. This knowledge, by ten thousand years ago, included the means to cultivate and store food. The ability to provide for lean times allowed humans to settle in larger numbers in villages, towns, and cities where their ideas, values, ways of living, and language grew increasingly complicated and diverse.

This cultural diversity—the multitude of ways of living and communicating knowledge—gave humans an adaptive edge. Other creatures adjusted to change in their environment through biological adaptation (a process that requires thousands of life spans to generate and reproduce a mutation to the level of the population). Humans developed analytical tools to identify and assess change in their environment, to search out or devise new strategies, and to incorporate new strategies throughout their group. Sometimes these cultural adaptations worked; people transformed their way of life, and their population thrived. Other times, these changes produced further complications.

Intensive agricultural techniques, for example, often resulted in increased salts in the soil, decreased soil fertility, and declining crop yields. Food production declined, and people starved. Survivors often moved to new regions to begin again. Throughout human history, migration became the common strategy when innovations failed. Again, in these times, culture was essential to survival.

For the human species, culture is our primary adaptive mechanism. Cultural diversity presents us with opportunities to draw from and build upon a complicated array of views, ideas, and strategies. The Endangered Peoples of the World series celebrates the rich diversity of cultural groups living on our planet and explores how cultural diversity, like biological diversity, is threatened.

Five hundred years ago, as humans entered the age of colonial expansion, there were an estimated twelve to fourteen thousand cultural groups with distinct languages, values, and ways of life. Today, cultural diversity has been reduced by half (an estimated 6,000 to 7,000 groups). This marked decline is due in part to the fact that, historically, isolated peoples had minimal immunity to introduced diseases and little time to develop immunological defenses. Colonizers brought more than ideas, religion, and new economic ways of living. They brought a host of viruses and bacteria—measles, chicken pox, small pox, the common cold. These diseases swept through "new" worlds at epidemic levels and wiped out entire nations. Imperialist expansion and war further decimated original, or "indigenous," populations.

Today's cultural diversity is further threatened by the biodegenerative conditions of nature. Our biophysical world's deterioration is evidenced by growing deserts; decreasing forests; declining fisheries; poisoned food, water, and air; and climatic extremes and weather events such as floods, hurricanes, and droughts. These degenerative conditions challenge our survival skills, often rendering customary knowledge and traditions ineffective.

Cultural diversity is also threatened by unparalleled transformations in human relations. Isolation is no longer the norm. Small groups continually interact and are subsumed by larger cultural, political, and economic groups of national and global dimensions. The rapid pace of change in population, technology, and political economy leaves little time to develop sustainable responses and adjust to changing conditions.

Across the world cultural groups are struggling to maintain a sense of unique identity while interpreting and assimilating an overwhelming flow of new ideas, ways of living, economies, values, and languages. As suggested in some chapters in this series, cultural groups confront, embrace, adapt, and transform these external forces in ways that allow them to survive and thrive. However, in far too many cases, cultural groups lack the time and means to adjust and change. Rather, they struggle to retain the right to simply exist as other, more powerful peoples seize their land and resources and "cleanse" the countryside of their presence.

Efforts to gain control of land, labor, and resources of politically and/or geographically peripheral peoples are justified and legitimized by ethnocentric notions: the beliefs that the values, traditions, and behavior of your own cultural group are superior and that other groups are biologically, culturally, and socially inferior. These notions are produced and reproduced in conversation, curriculum, public speeches, articles, television coverage, and other communication forums. Ethnocentrism is reflected in a language of debasement that serves to dehumanize (the marginal peoples are considered sub-human: primitive, backward, ignorant people that "live like animals"). The pervasiveness of this discourse in the everyday language can eventually destroy the self-esteem and sense of worth of marginal groups and reduce their motivation to control their destiny.

Thus, vulnerability to threats from the biophysical and social realms is a factor of social relations. Human action and a history of social inequity leave some people more vulnerable than others. This vulnerability results in ethnocide (loss of a way of life), ecocide (destruction of the environment), and genocide (death of an entire group of people).

The Endangered Peoples of the World series samples cultural diversity in different regions of the world, examines the varied threats to cultural survival, and explores some of the ways people are adjusting and responding to threats of ethnocide, ecocide, and genocide. Each volume in the series covers the peoples, problems, and responses characteristic of a major region of the world: the Arctic, Europe, North America and the Caribbean, Latin America, Africa and the Middle East, Central and South Asia, Southeast and East Asia, and Oceania. Each volume includes an introductory essay authored by the volume editor and fifteen or so chapters, each featuring a different cultural group whose customs, problems, and responses represent a sampling of conditions typical of the region. Chapter content is organized into five sections: Cultural Overview (people, setting, traditional subsistence strategies, social and political organization, religion and world view), Threats to Survival (demographic trends, current events and conditions, environmental crisis, sociocultural crisis), Response: Struggles to Survive Culturally (indicating the variety of efforts to respond to threats), Food for Thought (a brief summary of the issues raised by the case and some provocative questions that can be used to structure class discussion or organize a research paper), and a Resource Guide (major accessible published sources, films and videos, Internet and WWW sites, and organizations). Many chapters are authored or coauthored by members of the featured group, and all chapters include liberal use of a "local voice" to present the group's own views on its history, current problems, strategies, and thoughts of the future.

Collectively, the series contains some 120 case-specific examples of cultural groups struggling to survive and thrive in a culturally diverse world. Many of the chapters in this global sampling depict the experiences of indigenous peoples and ethnic minorities who, until recently, sustained their customary way of life in the isolated regions of the world. Threats to survival are often linked to external efforts to develop the natural resources of the previously isolated region. The development context is often one of co-optation of traditionally held lands and resources with little or no recognition of resident peoples' rights and little or no compensation for their subsequent environmental health problems. New ideas, values, technologies, economies, and languages accompany the development process and, over time, may even replace traditional ways of being.

Cultural survival, however, is not solely a concern of indigenous peoples. Indeed, in many parts of the world the term "indigenous" has little relevance, as all peoples are native to the region. Thus, in this series, we define cultural groups in the broadest of terms. We examine threats to survival and the variety of responses of ethnic minorities, as well as national cultures, whose traditions are challenged and undermined by global transformations.

The dominant theme that emerges from this sampling is that humans struggle with serious and life-threatening problems tied to larger global forces, and yet, despite huge differences in power levels between local communities and global institutions and structures, people are crafting and developing new ways of being. This series demonstrates that culture is not a static set of meanings, values, and behaviors; it is a flexible, resilient tool that has historically provided humans with the means to adapt, adjust, survive, and, at times, thrive. Thus, we see "endangered" peoples confronting and responding to threats in ways that reshape and transform their values, relationships, and behavior.

Emerging from this transformative process are new forms of cultural identity, new strategies for living, and new means and opportunities to communicate. These changes represent new threats to cultural identity and autonomy but also new challenges to the forces that dominate and endanger lives.

Introduction

Jean S. Forward

The continent of Europe is the homeland for many diverse cultures struggling to thrive and survive into the twenty-first century. When readers think of indigenous peoples and their homelands, it usually brings to mind a picture of some exotic "other," a culture belonging to "them." This volume focuses on the struggles of a variety of ethnic groups in Europe who are faced with a range of threats to them and their cultures, from ongoing wars to commercial expansion.

"Us" and "them" are cultural constructions studied by anthropologists and other social scientists when they analyze identity and what it means to belong to one specific culture. What does it mean to be European? More or less than it means to be Greek, Catalan, Slovak, Northern Irish, Serbian, Macedonian, Basque, Rusyn, Armenian, French Algerian, Tyrolean, Cypriot, Scottish Highlander, or Bosnian? Each group has various lengths of "traditional" residence in areas that they call "home," some niche on the European continent. The length of time that cultural communities claim to have resided in particular locations varies considerably, but there is always a linkage between territory and culture. "Homeland," therefore, is not an abstract idea, but a very specific and powerful symbolic geography.

While much intermarriage, migration, and general mixing of the gene pool has consistently occurred within the human species, the notion of us as a specific, culturally homogenous group of people tied to a homeland is perpetuated through what anthropologists call enculturation. Enculturation is the process of learning one's own culture, who "we" are. Learning how to talk, how to eat, how to sit and dress, who is a relative, whom one can marry, whom one should pray to, and how to obtain food are all parts of that culture and that identity.

Ethnic identity is regarded in this book as the badge that defines a person and her or his cultural heritage. Ethnicity is a constantly changing category of people who see themselves as related through common ancestry, real or fictitious. This category—actually more of a process—has fluid boundaries. Today's Tyrolese, for example, do not necessarily behave, dress, or travel as their ancestors of 500 years ago did. Who does? The impacts of technological and environmental changes affect the content and processes within an ethnic identity. The modern construction of national cultures emphasizes the dominant ethnic identity while other ethnicities usually of less populous groups exist within the boundaries drawn for each nation-state. The process of nation building in Europe is perceived here as a threat to the majority of ethnic groups.

The end of the fifteenth century is an arbitrary time to use in discussing nation-building in Europe, but it is a dramatic one because Western Europe was on the cusp of the push to create homogenous nation-states. A teacher once described it to me as the time of the change from the king of the Franks to the king of France—a subtle, but significant, distinction. In 1493 the Ottoman Turks conquered Constantinople, renaming it Istanbul, and undertook a major expansion of the Ottoman Empire. Also in 1493, the English king expanded control over marginal areas of the British Isles and outlawed any independent (read indigenous) Gaelic kingdom in the Scottish Highlands. In another consolidation of control, Maximilian became the Hapsburg emperor.

An important colonizing, nation-building year for the Iberian Peninsula was 1492. Isabel, queen of Castile, married Ferran (Ferdinand V), the king of the crown of Aragon, thereby creating "a collection of several independent kingdoms under a common monarch" (DiGiacomo, chapter 3). The laws of individual kingdoms were to be respected as long as they were Roman Catholic. The Jews were expelled (those who converted were allowed to stay), and the last Moorish stronghold on the Iberian Peninsula was conquered. Castile colonized vast areas of the globe in pursuit of significant resources, as evidenced by the resulting language situation in South America.

The expulsion of the Jews from Spain is one of many examples of threats to European Jews that occurred after Christianity became the dominant religious force in Europe. The Holocaust is another. The continual persecution of Jewish people in Europe is a clear example of attempts to make Europe a homogenous Christian "us." While Christ lived and died in the Middle East, it is Europe that is regarded as the Christian homeland. Armenians from east of Turkey identify themselves as Christians and as Europeans. Jewish people are regarded as "others" with a homeland elsewhere and are thus ousted from Europe even though they are generally viewed as being European.

Another significant event, which began in 1492 and aided the formation of Spain as a Catholic nation-state, was the Inquisition, a search for heresy as defined by the Catholic Inquisitors. Suspects were questioned (especially for the names of co-conspirators) and, if they survived the questioning, were publicly tried and executed. Most of the people executed were "witches" (women) who had to pay for their own questioning, trial, and execution. The rest of their assets were seized by the state. The church and the state in Spain, as in other European countries, were one and the same and they grew steadily wealthier together.

Nation-state formation requires access to vast quantities of natural resources. Colonies can provide the resources needed to build nation-states. As states grew, more and more colonies were needed to support the ever-increasing needs of the ever-expanding states. Again, in 1492, Spain, through the exploration of Christopher Columbus, made a legal claim to the entire Western Hemisphere, an uncharted territory ripe for the expansion of Christendom and commercialism through colonization or other means of political subordination. Columbus earned 10 percent of all the profits gained from the resources exported from these new colonies back to the mother state, including slaves, gold, silver, and foodstuffs. Commercial expansion was a driving force; restricted, controlled access to resources for the elites at the apex of European Christendom was the goal.

Christianity taught that European Christians were at the top of "civilization" morally, socially, economically, and politically. It also taught that the pope and divinely appointed kings and queens were the elite class of Christianity and that they were the links between the people and their God. When Henry VIII of England broke with Roman Catholicism and established his own church with himself at the top, there was a change in English identity, but not a change in the power structure.

When "others" converted to Christianity, they were never considered as good as the European Christians. They always constituted a low socioeconomic class. The Spanish court spent forty years deciding whether the indigenous peoples in the Western Hemisphere had souls that could be missionized. Unfortunately for the indigenes, the Spanish decided that they could and should be missionized during their assimilation into civilization as a working class. The English and French also sent missionaries to their colonial territories armed with varying styles of persuasion in their conversion efforts. English images of devil-worshiping savages persist in stereotypes of North American Indians to this day.

Homogeneity, everyone alike, theoretically means that everyone will be willing to fight and die for their national homeland. Homogeneity in national identity can include many classes. Nation-states strive to reinforce nationalism with national holidays, full of ceremonies and symbols. As nation-states attempted to become homogenous, the states became more and more involved in the education of the youth, a persistent and continuing trend in the process of state formation. Priests were frequently also teachers. Most people were illiterate. The language and rules of the elite class dominated, and those who could afford a formal education could dominate the elite class. Language became a weapon in the wars of dominance. Nation-states reinforce national language dominance by conducting government business only in the dominant national language. National languages unite a nation-state and oppress minority languages and groups within their arbitrary political boundaries.

Obviously, cultural, ethnic, and political boundaries do not always coincide. They are also always changing. For hundreds of years, many changes within Europe resulted from the process of colonization, expulsions, and forced migrations of nondominant groups to marginal environments. States expanded from the establishment of colonies on the European continent first. The trade that developed supported military dominance and religious proselytization. This pattern for colonization was first practiced in Europe and then spread across the globe.

Many readers of this volume may find it difficult to understand the dominance of the Christian religion in Europe from the fifteenth through the nineteenth centuries. In the past, as already shown, some nations established Roman Catholicism as the national religion, some Eastern Orthodox, others demanded Presbyterianism or the Anglican church, but all identified as Christian. Religion was commanded. Religious control was strong. The conflict within Christianity in the last few centuries between the various sects relates to the long-standing conflict between Spain and England and shows us a wider European "civil war" that lasted for generations (Reformation and Counter-Reformation). The twentieth century, for a variety of reasons, has seen religion treated as a matter of choice, not ascription. The world is more secular today.

Technological development increased alongside commercial and colonial expansion, creating a further need to extract more resources (from tall white pines for sailing masts to whalebone for women's corsets, minerals for machine making, and furs for fashion). Much of this development has depended on and depleted nonrenewable resources. Ireland is a startling case of deforestation. In many areas, ecological decline paralleled the economic growth, which is linked to technological, especially industrial, "advances." For example, the push for Eastern Europe to catch up in the area of industrialization in the twentieth century has made the Blue Danube brownish-black from intense factory development. The change in the river affects the lives and lifeways of the resident population, their culture, and their identity.

A constant need to increase profits pushed this industrial, capitalist, and imperialist system. It was reinforced by Christian, especially Protestant, values of hard work, rational planning and profit taking, simple tasks, an ascetic lifestyle, stability, trustworthiness, sobriety, yet a willingness to take calculated risks. Divine favor is bestowed upon *individual* accomplishment.

Profits are the prime motivation. Over time, the state and religion separated more distinctly than in the United States, and the values of hard work, stability, sobriety, and loyalty were assigned to a good citizen, a key political invention of the modern era.

Work was increasingly defined as what one is paid wages for. Before this time, everyone (extended family households, clans) worked together for the benefit of the whole group of "us." As the fifteenth century progressed to the twentieth century, the definition changed to work for wages, another encouragement for individualism. An emphasis on individual achievement placed the individual above the ethnic group, the family, the clan, and it rewarded individuals who made more money with higher social and political status and with more access to resources. Taxes are paid by individual citizens. One person excels at the expense of others, but much of the profits (taxes) are for the development of the state.

In the bigger picture, being and belonging to an identity, national or kin, and the rights and responsibilities that this confers on individuals and groups are always being contested. Class interests can oppose ethnic interests. National identity competes with smaller group identities. Full rights to citizenship are denied through the manipulation of identity variables such as religion or occupation or "race" (an arbitrary social construction in itself). And everything is a commodity on the international market.

If we view it all as interacting systems, it is easier to see the interconnections, the loosely configured wholes responding to and acting on global economic and ecological forces. We can begin to understand how ethnic identities survive and, sometimes, even thrive, despite the various threats to their persistence. Slovaks and Scots and Kosovars acquire more national control but still feel threatened. Serbs and Turks feel threatened by the Greeks, and the Greeks feel threatened by the Macedonians even though the different groups have lived closely together for generations or even centuries, often in considerable harmony (Jews in medieval Spain, Greeks in Turkey). These changes are ongoing, a continuing process.

This volume is a sample of the diversity of ethnic and cultural groups that illustrates the broad range of cultural constructions, their accompanying cultural and ethnic identities, the ways and means that the diverse cultural systems interact with each other and the environment, and the various threats they face as well as their responses.

Our focus is on the margins and the whole. A wider view of the complicated process of use of the land and people by the merchant/industrial system is invoked—a view that encompasses all ethnicities, skin colors, religious boundaries, and categories; a view that indicates that profit taking keeps control of the world economic systems in the hands of the profit takers; a view that goes from the bottom up, politically, economically, and environmentally, in a very linear system.

Herein is a brief outline of the contents of the volume. Kyriacos C. Markides and Joseph S. Joseph have worked for many years on the island of Cyprus, observing the growth of Cypriot identity. Who draws the boundaries? How are they taught and perpetuated? Unifying forces threaten and are threatened by dividing forces on the island. Where are the boundaries between ethnic identity and nation-state on Cyprus? Cypriots, both Greek and Turkish, have lived together in relative harmony in recent history. How has this changed? Who is directing the change? Similar questions can be asked in each chapter. Should, could, or can nation-states be ethnically homogenous? This question is critical.

Kathleen Young provides a view of competing ethnicities, each vying for increased access to resources in a limited world. Religion is manipulated in this competition. Roman Catholic Croats compete with Bosnian Serbs (Muslim) and Eastern Orthodox Serbs (a national religion). Each group wants that industrial quality of life held up as the goal of all civilized persons. We see this process of economic competition tied to religious identity and political processes over and over again, resulting in armed conflict as described in chapters 1, 4, 7, and 12. Resulting political policies attempt to squelch any diversity and enforce homogeneity. Thomas Taaffe's description of Ireland shows this quite clearly as does Loring M. Danforth's description of the Macedonians in Greece. The Scottish Highlanders, the Catalans, and the Basques have long been the targets of political policies designed to assimilate and absorb minority groups.

Beyond military and legal measures to encourage homogeneity, there is another force, in some ways a stronger and more insidious one—globalization. The Tyrolese, the Armenians, the Rusyns, the Slovaks, the Scottish Highlanders, and the French Muslims all confront this threat to their identities. At the same time, new global technologies supply the possibilities for coalitions which cut across clan, national, and cultural lines, coalitions which could empower small groups.

Global industrialization threatens the environments in which we all live; however, new cultural identities are always developing in response to new threats, and humans are ever creating new strategies to face new challenges. This volume tries to present the whole picture through a sampling of situations.

Chapter 1

The Armenians of the Western Diaspora

Susan Pattie

CULTURAL OVERVIEW

It is significant that today Armenians around the world continue to celebrate a defeat suffered in 451 C.E. Vartanants, one of the traditional year's major events, commemorates a battle fought to protect the Armenians from the Persian army. Though the Persians won, it was a Pyrrhic victory; that is, they lost so many of their own soldiers in battle that they were unable to accomplish their goal of converting the Armenians to Zoroastrianism from Christianity. Armenians throughout history, and particularly in this century, have considered themselves to be under threat as a people and as individuals, and such symbolic occasions are used to remind themselves and each other that one must continue to struggle, despite any setbacks and against all odds.

The People

Though the sense of what it means to be Armenian has changed and, like the identity of any group of people, is continually changing, their presence has been noted for more than 2,500 years. The first mention of Armenians by name came in 518 B.C.E., and linguistic evidence indicates there were Armenian speakers before this time. In the first century B.C.E., King Tigran the Great ruled an Armenian kingdom which stretched from the Mediterranean Sea to the Caspian Sea. The people then and now call themselves "Hai," the land "Hayastan," and the language "hayeren." Haig and Aram or Ara, early mythical figures, are very popular names still today. "Aram" is connected to the words used by outsiders to describe the people,

1

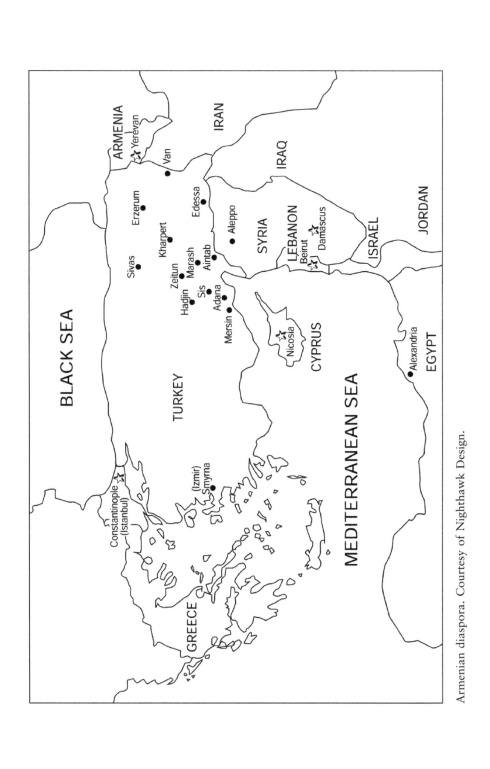

Armenian diaspora. Courtesy of Nighthawk Design.

their land, and the language (*Armina* in ancient Persian; *Armenian, Armenia* in English, for example). The language, which is Indo-European, branched off quite early from its neighbors. It shares root vocabulary most closely with ancient Greek and Persian. The alphabet, constructed around 400 C.E. by Mesrob Mashdots, a priestly scribe, contains thirty-six letters. Read from left to right, it is phonetic. Classical Armenian (*Grabar*) continues to be used in the church liturgy, and the vernacular language is divided today into two mutually intelligible dialects—eastern (the Republic of Armenia and Iran) and western.

The Setting

Armenians are often called a mountain people because the land is a series of plateaus crosscut by mountain ranges. The climate is continental with harsh changes in temperature in eastern Anatolia and the Caucasus but milder in the western-most parts around the Mediterranean. This is a volatile earthquake region but also a land bridge between east and west. Consequently, competing empires have battled over the area for centuries, with Armenians being torn between them or living in a permanent buffer zone.

Here we consider the situation of the "western" Armenians, those who speak the western dialect, whose recent ancestors lived in the Ottoman Empire, and who suffered most directly during the deportations and genocide at the end of that empire. The survivors of that period scattered around the world, and today roughly half of the world's six million Armenians live in diaspora. The diaspora also includes Armenians living in Iran and the former Soviet Union. These people, like those living in the Republic of Armenia (former Soviet Armenia), are also affected by and influence the issues to be discussed below.

Traditional Subsistence Strategies

At the turn of the twentieth century, the majority of Armenians in the Ottoman Empire were peasants who worked the land in eastern and central Anatolia and northern Syria. Crops included wheat and wheat products, fruits and vegetables, sericulture, cotton, and some tobacco. Sheep and goats were kept. Many people lived in larger towns, such as Adana, Mersin, and Erzerum, where they worked in a wide variety of trades and skilled crafts. In Constantinople (now Istanbul) Armenians also worked in the civil service of the empire and as architects for the royal court. A very visible network of Armenian traders and merchants established an early diaspora in which family members lived in faraway commercial centers to facilitate buying and selling. In the countryside and city, throughout the last half of the nineteenth century, Armenians became increasingly interested in edu-

3

cational opportunities for both boys and girls, and a significant number of young people went on to become doctors, nurses, and teachers. By the time of the genocide in World War I education was seen by many intellectuals as the way to reclaim and reform Armenian identity.

Today very few diaspora Armenians till the soil. There is an important dried fruit production in Fresno, California, and in the Middle East there are a few farming villages such as Kessab in Syria and Anjar in Lebanon. Instead, Armenians have become known as merchants, traders, and skilled artisans, and in the Middle East as photographers and musicians. Like other diaspora peoples, Armenians pursue a host of other mobile professions, increasingly varied as generations pass. Education remains highly desirable, and one of the problems discussed below is the tension between the pressure for traditional Armenian language–based schooling and a more Western-oriented, often English based, education which is regarded as providing more sophisticated job opportunities.

Social and Political Organization

The Armenians' political structure consisted of a network of princely families (*nakharars*), with kings as first among equals. This feudal system continued through the Middle Ages, though centers of power changed frequently. In 1080 the kingdom of Cilician Armenia began nearly 300 years of independent rule, some 600 miles south of earlier centers. An alliance followed with the invading Crusaders, and the last king of Cilicia is buried in France. After this time, Armenians had no ruling class of their own. They became minority peoples within successive empires, divided between east and west. Under the Ottomans and Persians, because their rulers were enemies, contact between Armenians living on either side of the shifting border decreased, but never ceased.

Social and political structures are necessarily loose and overlapping in a diaspora context. The cement of diaspora life is the family network within which some connection to being Armenian is established and nurtured. The family may have lived in small nuclear units or shared housing with brothers or parents (usually of the husband but not always), but the extended family was of paramount importance. Marriage traditionally was between two families as well as between two individuals. The families of the bridal couple also had social obligations to each other, potentially helpful in times of need, which generally formed a social network. In earlier times, young people were pressured to choose an Armenian spouse from a particular town and often a particular family.

The Armenian family of the last century and earlier is often thought of as "patriarchal," or having its authority based in the male line and the father figure. Certainly public life was male dominated. Many people, men

4

and women, however, speak of having been influenced by the strength of female relatives. In a world where the home and family were the focus of life, power was shared by women working within and men working outside for the home and the shared life of family. This shifted radically with dispersion and uprooting and also with the rapid adaptation to modern life with its emphasis on the individual and personal satisfaction and, in the realm of work, the accumulation of capital. The role of women within the home became secondary and this source of power much diminished. The size of the family network decreased as did the amount of time spent with family. The definition of family continues to evolve but its importance remains and interdependence is encouraged, though to a lesser degree than before.

The Ottoman Empire was a Turkish empire that dominated much of eastern Europe from the 16th century until World War I. In the Ottoman Empire, the population was divided into millets, which were administered by their own religious leaders. This system consolidated power within the Apostolic Church and encouraged an identity based on religion, locale, and family ties. Since the demise of the empire, that power has been contested by secular political parties formed at the end of the nineteenth and early twentieth centuries—first the Hnchakian Revolutionary Party (Hnchak) (1887) followed by the Armenian Revolutionary Federation (Dashnakstoutiune or Dashnak). Both began by proposing reforms to the imperial system but soon started to organize demonstrations and consider resistance to the increasing destruction of Armenian villages and towns. The third major party, the Ramkavars (Armenian Democratic Liberal), opposed their methods and urged rapprochement. Since the genocide and dispersion, these parties have continued to work in the diaspora, but took opposite sides during the Cold War. Their bitter rivalry turned bloody at times but usually remained at the level of rhetoric. The Dashnak party, to some degree, considered itself a government in exile. Having led the Republic of Armenia through a brief independent period following World War I, they were opposed to the Soviet takeover and became associated with the West. The Ramkavar party was pro–Soviet Armenia and anti-Dashnak, and the much reduced Hnchak party usually fell into this camp. With the independence of the Republic of Armenia in 1991, the parties retain their diaspora bases and activities but have turned their attention to the state.

There are also numerous "cultural" organizations, most of which are associated with or sympathetic to one of these parties, for example, the Armenian General Benevolent Union, a nonpolitical charity but until recently overlapping with Ramkavar membership. The Dashnak party and cultural organizations in its circle, such as the Hamazkaine and Armenian Youth Federation (AYF), have by far the largest and most active membership. Much to the dismay of political activists on every side, the most popular community events are dinner-dances, picnics, and bazaars. These activities bring together people who in earlier times would have shared a neighborhood, but now are scattered around large cities or regions.

Religion and World View

In 2001 Armenians will celebrate 1,700 years of Christianity, and they are proud to have been the first kingdom to convert to that religion. The Armenians broke away from the early church following the Council of Chalcedon in 451. Thereafter the Armenian Apostolic Church became known as a monophysite church, as it retained the early doctrines maintaining that the divine and human elements are made one in the body of Christ. The theological implications are little known or understood; more important are the social and political ramifications of that early decision, which resulted in the independence of the Armenian church.

The church is important to Armenian identity because it provides a link with the ancient past and preserves the classical language; because its political role, solidified during the Ottoman Empire, continued through the twentieth century; because it is a link to Europe through shared Christianity; and because the structure connects people throughout the diaspora. It is also important as a social center in most communities, a place where newcomers can find other Armenians and contacts are maintained. Each of these have contentious aspects. It is important to note that there are two small but important religious minorities within the Armenian population: the Protestants and the Roman Catholics.

THREATS TO SURVIVAL

There has been an Armenian diaspora for more than 1,000 years, as a result of trade routes, forced emigration under the rule of various empires (including Byzantines and Persians), and the fleeing of survivors in the wake of successive invasions of the region (Seljuks, for example). The diaspora of the twentieth century is radically different from this earlier network of people both in its nature and in its numbers. At the close of the twentieth century, other changes affect the diaspora, but first we will consider the rupture in Armenian life at the close of the Ottoman Empire.

At the end of the nineteenth century, the Ottoman Empire, formerly a mosaic of different peoples and religions, was in decay and crumbling. Some portions of the empire, such as Greece and Bulgaria, had already won their independence. The Ottoman rulers refused demands for reforms made by the remaining population, including Turks and minorities. Instead the Turkish majority grew, putting the remaining minorities at great risk. Armenians suffered periodic massacres throughout the 1890s, especially in 1895. Some began to organize political and later armed resistance. Their numbers were small, but the impact was significant because the Ottoman leaders regarded this as an indication of danger within. The beginning of World War I, and the alliance of the empire with Germany against the Allies and its neighbor Russia, increased this sensitive position. Armenians were seen as potential traitors with ties to their compatriots over the border in Russian Armenia. This was used as an excuse to herd together whole towns and villages of Armenians and force them onto a long march into the Syrian desert. Of the nearly 2 million Armenians living in the Ottoman Empire then, 1.5 million were uprooted, and well over 1 million were killed. Homes, schools, churches, and businesses all were looted and destroyed.

Survivors of the massacres congregated in relatively safe areas such as Aleppo or escaped farther away, if possible. Some fled to Russian Armenia, others farther south to Jerusalem and Egypt, and others to the Americas and Europe. Around the Middle East, orphanages were set up by aid societies and missionaries. Everywhere there was sickness and starvation. Some people returned to their former towns and villages, especially those outside the borders of the newly founded Turkish state, and tried to rebuild their lives and homes. Others initially thought they would be returning when the political crisis was over. Instead, further problems followed and people continued to leave, particularly in 1921 and 1922 during the Smyrna (Izmir) crisis and when the French ceded a further portion of Cilician Armenia to Turkey. The historic western homelands were virtually emptied, and the numbers living in diaspora soared.

It is not an exaggeration to say that nearly every family living in the western diaspora has been directly touched by loss and trauma from the genocide period. The immediate aftermath of the destruction found the survivors rebuilding and concentrating on a new life. However, the psychological burden of what these people had witnessed and experienced remained with them and was passed on to the next generations in a variety of ways. Some survivors were unable to communicate what they had seen or believed that no one else could possibly understand and so kept silent. Some were bitter. Many took their own survival as a message that they must work hard for those who had died. The notion of sacrifice took on special significance because it was believed that those who died were martyrs and now the survivors must sacrifice in order to rebuild communities and families quickly. In the third generation, young people are still pushed hard to achieve, and most consider it important to remember the genocide and demand recognition from Turkey, the successor state. Turkey continues to insist that the Ottoman government did not organize either genocide or ethnic cleansing but rather that any deaths that occurred among Armenians were part of the general consequences of war, disease, and banditry at that time.

The genocide is significant for the obvious reason that the population was decimated, historic and personal property were lost, and local belongings were destroyed. Its continuing threat to survival is in turn due to the consequent dispersal of survivors but also to the ways in which it has overshadowed most of twentieth-century Armenian life, both public and private. It has been suggested that Armenians have a root paradigm of an endangered people. This means that they live as if they as individuals and a group are constantly threatened. Meanwhile, a focus on genocide issues and the related fostering of hatred of Turkey and all things Turkish is itself debilitating. Sadly, as elsewhere, former neighbors and friends cannot see over this wall and thus far the passing of time has only helped new generations to forget former ties and deny mutual influences. However, it is impossible to begin reconciliation without recognition.

Throughout the twentieth century, other events have nourished the concerns over security. Until the 1970s, the Middle East was the core of the western diaspora and, with Iran, was home to the majority of Armenians outside (then Soviet) Armenia. As a result of the Lebanese civil war, the revolution in Iran, the war between Iran and Iraq, and the communal troubles in Cyprus, thousands of Armenians migrated to Europe, Australia, and the Americas. An earlier exodus had followed unrest in Istanbul, Egypt, and Palestine, but many of these people had moved elsewhere in the Middle East, only to be uprooted again. In addition to these conflicts, the devastation of the earthquake in Armenia, in December 1988, when some 25,000 people were killed, contributed to this feeling of constant danger and insecurity. Though Armenians in the diaspora were not harmed, they seemed to absorb this, as well as the pogroms held against Armenians in Azerbaijan during that period, as part of the larger configuration of threats to the Armenian people as a whole. This in part explains the eventual support of many in the diaspora for the independence of Nagorno Karabakh (Artsakh in Armenian) from Azerbaijan.

Living in the Middle East had allowed people to remain quite close to their original homes and the historic lands. They were familiar with the Arab and Turkish worlds and felt part of them, although they were connected to Europe through their Christian faith and, increasingly, through education. These migrations from the Middle East, farther west, meant a further transformation of the diaspora, and a new form of insecurity. Assimilation or, as the Armenians call it "white massacre" (*jermag chart*), replaced physical survival as the main concern in the stable western environments. During centuries of living with mostly Muslim neighbors, Armenians maintained friendly social relations with them, but religious differences prevented nearly all intermarriage. In Christian or, equally important, secular settings, this changed and barriers were considerably lessened. In addition to an increase in marriage to non-Armenians, there was a marked increase in participation in activities and organizations outside the Armenian community sphere. Again, in the Middle East, there had been less opportunity for such an expansion of personal networks.

Also, speaking Armenian became the norm in the Middle East and Armenians regularly speak several languages. However, in many Western countries, monolingualism is normal and young Armenians have followed this pattern. Learning Armenian means attending Saturday or Sunday schools, or a private day school, but even after such efforts are expended, it remains difficult to practice the language on a daily basis. Readers and writers of Armenian literature are decreasing rapidly.

As noted, family relations also change in the Western countries whereas Arab, Persian, and Turkish neighbors shared many of the same values and reinforced those of the Armenian communities there. In the West there is an emphasis on the individual which is at odds with the traditional focus on the family unit. Higher education and diverse professional jobs have also encouraged a focus on the individual and his or her personal satisfaction. Ties with one's family become narrower and, with the community, more tenuous.

Ironically, the identification with Europe (and by extension the United States) comes from sharing the Christian religion, but Armenians have found themselves in an increasingly secularized West. While still proclaiming that the Armenian Apostolic Church is one of the cornerstones of Armenian identity, the population is increasingly abandoning the church in all practical terms. The identification with Europe also has another important side effect—that of rejecting the Muslim world and distancing themselves from the past.

Finally, at the end of the twentieth century, a new development compounded the threat to Middle Eastern and diaspora Armenian identity: the independence of the Republic of Armenia. Although dreamed of and wished for, the republic has thus far proved to be quite different than imagined in its role as a homeland for all Armenians. Following glasnost, and especially beginning with the rebuilding following the earthquake, diaspora funding has been channeled away from its own institutions and toward Armenia. For some, the existence of a free Armenia means there is no further need for a diaspora public life. Armenia should serve as anchor and focus of all future Armenian life. This overlooks the very different historical and contemporary experiences of the western diaspora and assumes that the political agenda and cultural attitudes of the state are similar to those of the diaspora. Instead they are often quite far apart or even opposing. The republic itself recognizes this and has thus far been reluctant to offer dual citizenship to diaspora Armenians for fear of obstruction of internal affairs by those without the experience of and commitment to life on that land.

RESPONSE: STRUGGLES TO SURVIVE CULTURALLY

There are public and private responses to the concerns about survival, just as the concerns themselves are both about personal identity and communal continuity. On every level, these interact with each other. Private responses begin with the encouragement to accomplish as much as possible. This is presented in terms of making up for those who were lost in the genocide and letting the world know about this small group of people who would otherwise be ignored. Nuclear families act as a resource for their own children but also for an extended network of advice and personal aid on both husband's and wife's sides, whether people live nearby or elsewhere around the globe. In times of crisis, this may mean sending goods or financial help or even sponsoring people to emigrate. Diaspora Armenians also respond with aid on a communal level by joining fund-raising campaigns to send goods and services. Immediately following the earthquake in northern Armenia, for example, political differences were temporarily dropped, and many Armenians who had previously drifted far from the active communities returned to take part or create new initiatives to help.

Certain aspects of home life have continued to anchor new generations in a sense of belonging to a people called the Armenians, though their own lives may not often intersect with many other members of the group. The most obvious among these is food and the importance given to hospitality and the sharing of food on a daily basis within the family. Like others around the Middle East, Armenians always welcome guests with a heavily laden table. Reciprocal hospitality is a way of binding people together, whether they are in the same community or the many who pass through. Networks of family and friends are large and widespread, and it is common to have visitors or houseguests from abroad. In this way, as well as by telephone, post, and e-mail, Armenians maintain contact with each other. Children grow used to meeting many new people and through them are introduced to political problems around the world in a very direct manner. This then ties in with the sense of precariousness they begin to associate with being Armenian.

Although the pressure to marry other Armenians has decreased recently, it still exists. This has been internalized for many who seek an Armenian partner; others fear rejection by their families. Rejection is uncommon now because the outsider (*odar*) is usually absorbed into the family and, if cooperative, is incorporated as an honorary Armenian. The hope is that the children will grow up feeling a connection to the Armenian world. There is no rule concerning the line of descent—one can be an Armenian if one's mother or father was considered Armenian. However, with increasing intermarriage, there is less chance of a household creating the connections described above, whether through food or other means. In addition to the family network including many non-Armenians, it may be that the non-

Annual feast day and community meal for Armenians at the Nareg Armenian Elementary School and Surp Asdvadztsatsin Church in Nicosia, Cyprus. Courtesy of Susan Pattie.

Armenian spouse does not enjoy the constant rounds of hospitality and visiting that are considered normal.

The institutions of diaspora life are struggling to come to terms with the kind of response appropriate to the new and changing environments. Established in another place and in another time, they have generally been slow to change and have missed out on the impact that Western (or Westernized) educational systems have had on the new generations. However, political parties, churches, cultural organizations, and clubs continue to be active and provide a framework for amorphous and floating family networks. As mentioned, these institutions are interconnected as, for the most part, the Armenian diaspora has been divided throughout this century on an axis between Dashnak and anti-Dashnak, with organizations, including the churches, falling within one sphere or the other. This is changing today as young people are much less interested in the bitter internal political battles of the past. Active party membership has always been relatively small, but until recently, many more in all communities were drawn into questions of allegiance. The Dashnak party demanded a "free, independent Armenia" and wished to free Armenia from Soviet rule and the western historic homelands from Turkey. They continued to fly the flag of the short-lived pre-Soviet republic and taught their young people revolutionary songs. The leadership feared the infiltration of the Soviet system into the hierarchy of the church since the supreme head (*Catholicos*) was based in Etchmiad-zin, Armenia. Historically, there is another independent head, based in the western diaspora, who administers churches in the Middle East. The Dash-naks expanded the role of this center, which they brought into their own sphere of influence, and formed a parallel system of churches in the New World, particularly in the United States. To this day, most American Ar-menian communities have two churches, one affiliated with Etchmiadzin, the other with Antelias, outside of Beirut.

The anti-Soviet fervor of the Dashnak side was met with equally ardent sentiment against the Dashnaks themselves. The Ramkavars, and their sym-pathetic clubs and organizations, took an opposite stand regarding Soviet Armenia. They believed that Armenia should be supported, no matter who ruled it. Though a few were Communists, the great majority were not. They chose to ignore the increasingly obvious political and economic problems in the republic and emphasized its assets, such as the use of the Armenian language in everything from opera to nursery schools. This view maintained that the diaspora would soon die out through assimilation and physical threats and that the republic was the only viable solution for an Armenian future. These organizations regularly hosted guests from Soviet Armenia, whether visiting artists, academics, or political speakers. Teachers went there for training, and some students went there to attend the university. The Dashnak side was appalled at what they saw as naïveté and false hopes while the anti-Dashnaks reviled the others as traitors. The two sides envi-sioned very different futures, though both believed they were working to-ward the only possible longterm solution.

The two sides also differed on the role and importance of the diaspora itself. While both focused on a vision of homeland and believed that di-aspora was ideally a temporary phase, the Dashnak idea of homeland was more in line with the practical and personal longings of the people. They spoke of returning not to a land they had never seen, but to their own villages and towns. This direct emotional tie brought out an electrifying response when large groups gathered. Both sides agreed that Turkey must recognize the genocide carried out against the Armenians by the Ottomans. Turkey's continuing denials have energized what is called the "Armenian cause" (*Hai Tad*): political efforts to extract an admission of genocide. In the late 1970s and early 1980s, small but very visible groups (from both sides) turned to terrorism to make their case heard, and a number of Turk-ish diplomats were killed or wounded. This ended with internal fighting and a diaspora divided over methods. It has been suggested that these groups were equally motivated by the desire to awaken what they called a "sleep-walking" diaspora to political activism on a larger scale.

Each year all those who died during the genocide are commemorated on April 24, the day in 1915 when intellectuals, priests, poets, and artists were arrested in Istanbul by the Ottomans and nearly all killed. The services and events range from a church mass to evenings with speeches and poetry and music to protests and marches in front of Turkish embassies. In some communities, where young people have tired of hearing the political speeches, new activities have begun, such as organizing blood donations for current victims of ethnic cleansing and massacres. In some communities, these are jointly sponsored events; in others, the political divisions continue and each side organizes its own. The purpose of such events is threefold: to remember the dead, to put pressure on Turkey, and to forge ties among dispersed people.

While public issues surrounding the genocide are most visible, there are other responses to the sense of endangerment expressed by Armenians in diaspora. One of these has been the establishment of a number of chairs of Armenian studies in universities throughout the United States (for example, University of California at Los Angeles and Fresno, the University of Michigan, and Harvard University). The motivation for this is to encourage further learning and research, particularly in history and literature, to legitimize the field and make academic links, and to reach as many Armenian students as possible. The fact that the great majority of American Armenians do not attend Armenian schools responds directly to the distress that the new generations know nothing about their past and to the fear that Armenians are being forgotten by the world: "No one knows about us."

Since the last century, education has been important, and in the Middle East, most children attend Armenian schools at least at primary level. Elsewhere in diaspora, such schools are available only in certain cities and neighborhoods. In earlier times, children may have had no other educational opportunity, but today the purpose of the Armenian school is to provide a specifically Armenian education, emphasizing language and history. It also might provide an environment the parents believe is "safe" from drugs, gangs, and assimilation. Other parents feel strongly that their children must learn how to function fully in the host culture and that local rather than ethnic schools are the key to that process. In recent years, e-mail and the Internet have had a great impact on communication and education. News agencies provide instant information, and many young people who would never subscribe to the ethnic press follow events regularly. Equally important, new Web sites emerge daily on a wide variety of subjects, some representing organizations, others individuals. One of the most creative is Narod which links Armenian schools around the diaspora and the republic with interactive projects.

Throughout this century, the Apostolic Church has been regarded as a key symbol of survival and continuity. The church itself has emphasized this, and sermons are frequently heard praising the resurrection of the people following their trials and urging the congregation to go forward as soldiers for the nation. This has resulted in a national church which some have accused of focusing on the survival of the ethnic group rather than focusing on religious messages. It has become a national museum for many. In Europe, the secularization of society in general continues to grow; in the United States, however, a very different social environment prompts changes in other directions. Some have emphasized education for children or introduced English into part of the mass to try to reach the third and fourth generations. There is great tension surrounding any such changes. The church is caught in a double bind of representing continuity and links with the past in its seemingly "unchanging" structure, while losing people because they say it does not speak to their present needs.

Through political rhetoric, poetry, novels, sermons, newspaper editorials, and other means, the intellectual elite of the diaspora (of all political shades) have tried to counter the problems of dispersion and mobility by shaping a new identity that is not based on locale or kin. The "real" Armenian in this version is someone who speaks the language, knows the history, is a member or supporter of the Apostolic Church, and shows an active commitment to the perpetuation of the culture in the wider community. This response has alienated those who do not fit into such categories but who consider themselves Armenian. The public image of "Armenian-ness" as an unchanging core does not fit easily with the flexible, changing realities of lived experience. Anny Bakalian, in her 1993 study, documents the drift from an identity that is taken for granted to one that is more conscious, situational, and symbolic.

FOOD FOR THOUGHT

The term "endangered peoples" in the Armenian case fits very closely with the experiences and concerns of people in many cultures, whether genocide, communal wars and troubles throughout the Middle East, or reverberations of the earthquake in Armenia. However, it also conjures up an image (fostered by the nationalists) of a previously unchanging essential core of identity that masks the variety of ways of being Armenian in earlier times.

When we talk about a diaspora, we usually include ideas about a homeland. This may or may not include a dream of actual return. In the western Armenian case, there have been several visions of homeland, the most potent having been the homes that were left behind during the genocide, now in eastern Turkey. With the establishment of an independent Armenia in 1991, the focus is beginning to change to an idealized homeland on that soil. As with Israel and the Jewish diaspora, relations between homeland and diaspora reflect differences between their historical experiences, current political situations, and expectations of each other. In the future, the Republic of Armenia will increasingly become a kind of standard of Armenian-ness, which again, those living in diaspora will find unfamiliar.

Diaspora life fits well with the mobility and flexibility required by globalization and modern life. Ironically, both the lack of physical threats in the West and the easy fit of globalization produce another danger, that of further dispersion and assimilation.

In 1939, while he was preparing to invade Poland, Adolf Hitler asked, "Who remembers the Armenians?" It is crucial to the future of healthy plural societies to remember not only the Armenians but all minority peoples at risk from more powerful neighbors.

Questions

1. How does one accommodate private and public visions of identity?

2. What does "homeland" mean?

3. In the diaspora, is it possible to be a good, active citizen of one country while engaging in a network of diaspora relations (and possibly with the homeland as well)?

4. Given the physical traumas of survivors, in what ways is psychological trauma passed on through generations? How can memory be honored without forever defining future relations?

5. How can one live with the mobility and flexibility required in modern life and still retain a connection to family, community, and the past?

RESOURCE GUIDE

Published Literature

Armenian International Magazine (AIM). 207 South Brand Blvd., Suite 203, Glendale, California. 91204. E-mail: aim4m@well.com.

Bakalian, Anny. *Armenian-Americans: From Being to Feeling Armenian*. New Brunswick, N.J.: Transaction Publishers, 1993.

Hovannisian, Richard, ed. *The Armenian People: From Ancient to Modern Times*. 2 vols. New York: St. Martin's Press, 1997.

Kasbarian, Lucine. *Armenia: A Rugged Land, An Enduring People*. Parsippany, N.J.: Macmillan, 1998.

Miller, Donald E., and Lorna Touryan Miller. *Survivors: An Oral History of the Armenian Genocide*. Berkeley: University of California Press, 1993.

Pattie, Susan Paul. *Faith in History: Armenians Rebuilding Community*. Washington, D.C.: Smithsonian Institution Press, 1997.

Films and Videos

Egoyan, Atom, director. *Calendar*. Eg. Film Arts, 1993. The director stars as (Canadian) diaspora photographer working in Armenia exploring his identity and ambivalent feelings, contrasted with his (Middle Eastern) wife's more obvious comfort there.

Holmquist, PeA, G. Gunner, and S. Khardalian. *Back to Ararat: A Forgotten Genocide: A Dream of Return.* Sweden: HB PeA Holmquist Film, 1988.

WWW Sites

Largest Armenian web site.
http://www.cilicia.com

An introduction to Armenian art from medieval to contemporary times.
http://www.roslin.com

Lively, educational, and colorful introduction to Armenian language, stories, and projects.
http://www.narod.com

Recordings

Kotchnak: Chants Populaire Armenians. "Al Sur." Paris: Media 7, 1997.
MEG Recordings. P.O. Box 412, Cambridge, MA 02238. Fax: 617–489–1094. Variety of Armenian music from sacred to folk, instrumental and voice.

Organizations

Armenian General Benevolent Union
55 East 59th Street
New York, NY 10022
E-mail: agbuny@aol.com

Armenian National Institute
122 C Street NW, Suite 360
Washington, D.C. 20001
E-mail: ani@aaainc.org

Armenian Youth Federation (AYF)
Western America branch: 818–507–1933

Chapter 2

The Basques
Linda White

CULTURAL OVERVIEW

Identity is a mercurial concept, heavily dependent on self-examination and the establishment of relationships between an individual and certain characteristics of the group with which one identifies. For the Basque people of Western Europe and for Basque emigrants around the world, the nature of Basque identity and the definition of what it means to be a Basque have changed from century to century.

The People

The Basques call themselves *euskaldunak* and their language is *euskara*.[1] They are often called the "mystery people of Europe" because no one knows for certain where they came from. Theories abound, however, ranging from the mundane to the highly fantastic. There are those who believe the Basques have inhabited their land since Cro-Magnon man evolved, and thus the Basques are direct descendants of those early peoples. At the other end of the spectrum are advocates of the Atlantis theory (the Basques were the survivors of the lost continent of Atlantis and took refuge on what today is known as the Iberian Peninsula). Others claim that the Basques are the descendants of Tubal, the grandson of Noah, and that their language was spoken everywhere before the Biblical incident at the Tower of Babel.

Regardless of their origins, the *euskaldunak* were described 2,000 years ago by the Greek geographer and historian Strabo (63? B.C.–A.D. 21?), and

17

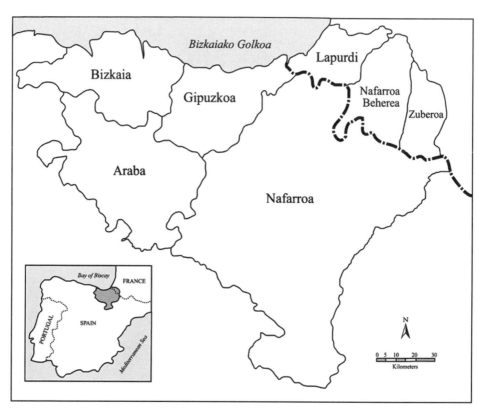

Basque country.

they still occupy the same territory (albeit considerably reduced) as they did then.

The Setting

The geographic homeland of the Basques is Euskal Herria. This small region, about the size of the state of Rhode Island, is situated in and around the Pyrenees and straddles the border between France and Spain. Today the area comprises seven provinces, four in Spain (Gipuzkoa, Bizkaia, Araba, and Nafarroa) and three in France (Lapurdi, Zuberoa, and Nafarroa Beherea), hence the misnomers "Spanish Basque" and "French Basque." While it is true that natives of the region are citizens of either France or Spain, the Basques have always considered themselves to be a separate nation.

Euskal Herria is composed of seacoasts and mountains, green valleys and golden plains, oak and pine forests, and a climate humid enough for dry farming, that is, farming without irrigation. The sea is the Gulf of Bizkaia (Bay of Biscay). Beneath the water, the continental shelf extends only a few miles, then plunges to a depth of nearly 10,000 feet, making a variety of fauna more accessible to the Basque coast than to other areas. Sardines, anchovies, bonito, and different types of mackerel migrate to the warm summer waters of the Basque coastline and share the sea with lobster, shrimp, clams, sea bass, grouper, mullet, sea bream, and sole.

Although fine beaches are available (and are very crowded in the peak tourist season), most of the Basque coast is rocky and precipitous. Numerous rivers and estuaries, including the Bidasoa, the Urumea, the Oria, the Urola, the Oca, and the Butron, provide refuge for migrating birds, and the Bidasoa River is the last remaining home to such species as sea trout and shad.

The mountains were the home of the major figures of Basque mythology, sheltering Basajaun, lord of the forest, and the female spirit Mari, known by many other names as well. Individual peaks are well known in the Basque country, and people speak fondly of Gorbea, Aitzkorri, and Aralar.

The Basque country also boasts a variety of woodlands. Holm oak, Kermes oak, chestnut, alder, ash, and beech are examples of the variety of forestation still growing in the region. However, these old forests have been harvested over the years, and today Basques replace them with pine trees, considered a cash crop in Euskal Herria. Small single-family farms also produce fodder for livestock, such as alfalfa, turnips, or clover, and food for the residents as well, such as apples and corn.

In the south the mountains give way to the plains of Araba where cereals, olives, and grapevines grow. To the east, in Nafarroa, the landscape is drier and flatter.

Traditional Subsistence Strategies

The Basques were famed for shipbuilding. Christopher Columbus' vessels were built in the Basque country, and much of his crew was Basque. The Basques were deeply involved in whaling long before other nations ever attempted it. The first historical evidence of Basque whaling appeared in 1199 when a tithe was paid on two whales. During the thirteenth and fourteenth centuries Basques monopolized the industry.

By the sixteenth century whales were scarce in the Bay of Biscay, and the Basques were forced to seek them elsewhere, first along the coast of Spain, then to Scotland and finally to Newfoundland.

A Basque named Martin Sopite from Lapurdi invented a process for melting down whale blubber on board ship. Other nations learned quickly from the Basque fishermen. Stiff foreign competition and the surrender of Newfoundland to the British by the Treaty of Utrech (1713) eventually drove the Basques off the high seas.

Basque seafarers turned their energies to pirating. Basque corsairs were the scourge of European shipping. The port of Bayonne was headquarters for pirates with Basque names like Dihiart, Dargaignaratz, Destibertcheto, Etchebaster, Hiriart, and Garat. Today the pirates are gone, but many coastal residents still make their living as fishermen.

Because of the limited size of the Basque country, family farms or *baserriak* were passed down to one child. The other children had to go elsewhere for a livelihood. They could marry into a family with land; become soldiers, priests, or nuns; enter the king's service; or emigrate. Many came to the New World, and some of those established hardy reputations in the American West as sheepherders after the Gold Rush.

Many Basque immigrants intended to stay in their new country only long enough to make their fortunes. Once they built up a substantial stake, they planned to return home, buy some land, open a business, or simply retire. Often, however, the immigrants waited too long to return, or they married and had children in the new land.

Social and Political Organization

Today Euskal Herria comprises three different political entities. On the French side of the border, the area known as Iparralde (the north) includes the provinces of Lapurdi, Nafarroa Beherea, and Zuberoa. On the Spanish side, the large province of Nafarroa is one autonomous community (Navarra in Spanish), and the provinces of Araba, Bizkaia, and Gipuzkoa form another, the Comunidad Autónoma Vasca (Basque Autonomous Community) or CAV.

Lapurdi, Nafarroa Beherea, and Zuberoa are part of the Département des Pyrénées Atlantiques. Although the three Basque provinces have no official recognition in France, the bucolic hills of Iparralde harbor Basque culture and language while the cities wear a very French face. To the south, the Basque language was lost in most of Nafarroa, except for the most northerly and easterly areas. In the CAV, the conflict between the Basque nation and the Spanish state is still a part of daily life, and the area is officially bilingual (Spanish and Euskara). The CAV is popularly referred to as Euskadi, a name invented in the early twentieth century by the founder of the Basque Nationalist Party, Sabino Arana Goiri.

The name Euskadi has taken on social nuances because speakers use it to refer to the CAV while at the same time implying the inclusion of Iparralde and Nafarroa within its borders. Needless to say, the political reality of life in the Basque country is complex and intricate, a multilayered fabric of current events heavily embroidered with past visions and future dreams of what it means to be Basque.

Religion and World View

The Basques embraced Christianity in the tenth century. Although they were the last group in Europe to be Christianized, once they accepted the Church, they did so thoroughly. Protestantism gained a foothold in Iparralde, and the need for scripture in the vernacular prompted the first translation of the Bible into Basque. In the south, the Roman Catholic Church is still the single greatest religious force in Basque lives.

Even as Basques cling to old traditions—the Church, their language, and such cultural expressions as *bertsolaritza* (an art form in which Basque troubadours extemporize verses and sing them before an audience)—they do not see themselves as a small nation cut off from the world. Because of emigration, Basques have relatives scattered around the globe, and they have played large roles in the history of Spain and other states. The Internet affords them rapid communication with Basque communities and gives them a means of acting and interacting globally. Basques often joke that Euskal Herria is the center of the universe.

THREATS TO SURVIVAL

Basques have been a minority people since the dawn of recorded history, and Euskara has been a minority language. The importance of the language to Basque identity is evident in the word *euskaldun* (a Basque person) for its literal meaning is "possessor of the Basque language." The greatest threats to their survival as a people and a nation have been invaders who came and settled at different periods and brought their own languages and cultures with them.

The Basques maintained their language and culture in the face of the Roman occupation of the Iberian Peninsula. Popular myth ascribes ferocious warlike qualities to the Basque population of that time and attributes their durability to guerrilla tactics used in fighting off the Romans, who were also discouraged by the mountainous regions of the Basque country. It is likely that the Basques survived as an ethnic unit after the fighting ended because of their ability to coexist with the Romans who, receiving no provocation from the Basques, were content to leave them alone. The Romans and the Basques coexisted, but the presence of the Roman language, Latin, was a serious threat to the survival of Euskara. Latinization contributed hundreds of loan words to the Basque language. Only the arrival of other invaders (and the subsequent ousting of the Romans) saved the Basque language and culture from obliteration.

After the Romans came the Germanic tribes, then the Goths and the Franks.

In 711 Arab forces crossed the Strait of Gibraltar and invaded the Iberian Peninsula. Formerly enemies, the Basques and the Goths united and rallied their forces against the invading army, but all was lost. Within a few short years, the Arabs controlled the entire peninsula, capturing the Basque city of Pamplona in 718. The rest of the Basque area, however, was not occupied. The Arabs were more interested in sacking cities than in controlling the forests and fields of the Basque country. Once again the Basques survived because of their ability to coexist with a majority culture.

In 824 a coalition of Basque warlords recognized one of their own, Eneko Arista (Aritza in Basque), as the king of a rebuilt Pamplona and established the kingdom of Navarra.

Geographically, the kingdom of Navarra covered much more territory than present-day Basque country. It included all of the Pyrenees, Vasconia as far north as Bordeaux (in France), and all of Old Castilla. Navarra's power peaked during the reign of Sancho el Mayor (1000–1035), but by 1200 Gipuzkoa and Araba were under the control of the Castilian king Alfonso VIII, dividing the Basque country, leaving Bizkaia (to the west) and Navarra (to the east) isolated from each other. To the north, Lapurdi and Zuberoa were under English rule until the English suffered reversals in the Hundred Years' War and lost their authority in Europe, at which time the northern Basque provinces came under French rule.

Although the glory of the kingdom of Navarra was over, the Basques did not consider themselves a conquered people. Araba and Gipuzkoa agreed to ally themselves with the king of Castilla, but only if he would respect their old laws (*fueros*) and customs. According to the *fueros*, the kings of Castilla had to travel to the Basque country to the holy Tree of Gernika and swear to uphold the old Basque laws and privileges. Only then would the Basques condescend to be ruled by him. Basques commanded special privileges, such as nobleman status for every Basque citizen. During the fifteenth to the eighteenth centuries only titled nobility were allowed to be officers in the army and hold government posts. The Basques used their status to become colonial governors in Latin America, to captain ships of exploration, and to participate more fully in the world-shaping activities of that era. For example, Simón Bolívar was Basque, and when Ferdinand Magellan died in the Philippines, Elcano, a Basque, took command and became the first man to circumnavigate the globe.

Demographic Trends

The loss of the Basque *fueros* during the nineteenth century left the Basque people demoralized and frightened, concerned that soon they might lose their language and culture as well.

Many Basques today still think that their language is the most endangered aspect of their culture. The geographic reach of the language has grown smaller every century. The encroaching Spanish and French cultures to the south and north, respectively, combined with a history of lost wars and political oppression, have greatly reduced the area in which Basque is the language of everyday existence. During the Spanish Civil War (1936–1939), the Basque Republican army was defeated by Francisco Franco's forces, and when General Franco became the dictatorial leader of Spain at the end of that war, he took active steps to eradicate the Basque language. The fledgling Basque University (created in 1936) was shut down, books written in Euskara were burned, and the language was prohibited in schools, public places, newspapers, and on the radio. All official documents had to be translated into Spanish, and citizens were not allowed to put their Basque names on birth certificates, death certificates, or any other legal paperwork.

As a result, many Basques lost the language after 1939. The pendulum of identity swings back and forth between those who feel Basque blood is the most necessary attribute and those who feel that the language is the paramount issue. Sabino Arana, founder of the Basque Nationalist Party at the end of the nineteenth century, united the two issues by claiming Basques were unique as a race because their language was unique.

Although the Basque country is politically divided between Spain and France, Euskara is not related to any of the Romance languages; it is not even Indo-European. Linguists categorize Euskara as a language family unto itself. The difficulty of learning Euskara is legendary. According to Basque folklore, the devil once came to the Basque country where he lived for seven years. During that time, he learned to say only *bai* (yes) and *ez* (no), and upon leaving the region he forgot even those small words.

Current Events and Conditions

Since Franco's death in 1975, great strides have been made to reeducate Basques about their mother tongue, but today even optimists claim that only 25 percent of the inhabitants of the Basque country speak the language; the pre–civil war estimate was 50 percent.[2]

Ironically, now that the CAV is established and doing well, a growing number of Basques believe that the major reason for learning Euskara has disappeared. These individuals viewed speaking Basque as a manifestation of their opposition to Franco, and now they see no need to continue with the language.

Finally, the growth of a non-Basque immigrant population threatens to overwhelm the small Basque region with new residents from other parts of Spain, making the use of Spanish even more necessary in the interactions of daily life, even though today Euskara is on equal legal footing within the CAV. However, the Spanish Constitution of 1978 makes it very clear that Castilian Spanish is the official language of Spain, and the Basque language is limited to usage within the Basque region, just as Catalan and Galician are restricted to their regions. To further complicate the language issue, the Basques must also deal with the ubiquitous influence of English.

Environmental Crisis

The Basque people are very aware of how small their region is. Activists both inside and outside the Basque country periodically protest against nuclear reactors, most recently against the Spanish government's waste disposal plans for the Garoña plant in Burgos, close to the CAV border. In the 1980s numerous major demonstrations were held in the Basque country against nuclear power plants. The pro-independence group ETA (Euskadita Askatasuna, or Basque Country and Freedom) joined with thousands of citizens in demonstrations and coordinated electrical blackouts. High-tension pylons and distribution stations were bombed and lives were lost. In 1982 construction was stopped on the two reactors being built at Lemoiz (near Bilbao, a major urban population center), and later the projects were phased out by the Spanish government.

The environmental group Gurelur (Our Land) fights the dumping of toxic industrial waste into the waters of Basque rivers on both sides of the Spanish-French border. Eguzki (Sun) is another grassroots ecological group on the lookout for damage to the fragile Basque environment. After the damage done to the region by Franco's questionable economic policies (which encouraged many thousands to move to the Basque country to work but provided no money to counteract the impact of such an influx on the region's infrastructure and ecology), the politicization of the ecology movement in Euskadi comes as no surprise.

24

Basque painted protest on wall, in Bilbao, 1998. Photo by Susan Thompson. With permission from University Studies Abroad Consortium.

RESPONSE: STRUGGLES TO SURVIVE CULTURALLY

The Basques have maintained their culture and language by suiting their responses to the threats at hand. In the case of invaders, from the time of the Romans, they have fought when necessary and coexisted whenever possible.

The loss of Basque citizens to emigration has spurred ongoing efforts by the current autonomous governments of the CAV and Navarra (Nafarroa) to reestablish and nurture contact with ex-patriot communities around the world. Organizations such as the North American Basque Organization (NABO) and the Federación de Entidades Vasco Argentinas (FEVA) assist in these efforts by coordinating Basque clubs and their activities. Links to the Old World are maintained through personal visits, electronic mail, conferences, publications, and the media. Basque government dignitaries also attend events sponsored by the clubs, such as the National Basque Festival held in Elko, Nevada, over the Fourth of July weekend.

Efforts to recover and maintain the language are ongoing. On the Spanish side, organizations such as HABE (Helduen Alfabetatze eta Berreuskalduntzerako Erakundea, or the Institute for Adult Literacy and Basque Reeducation) and AEK (Alfabetatze Euskalduntze Koordinakundea, or the Coordinating Body for Literacy and Basque Education) were created to "re-Basqueify" the Basque country by offering adult education classes in

25

Basque at all levels, from beginner to advanced. After Franco's death the Basque University was reinstated. Basque children can now be educated in Euskara from preschool through university. On the French side, schools where children can study in Basque are quite rare. In Iparralde there are fewer Basque speakers every decade.

A Basque Academy of Language (called Euskaltzaindia) sets standards for Basque and decides what will be included in the man-made unified dialect, Batua.

The influx of non-Basque workers was a motivating factor in rethinking the criteria of Basqueness. In the 1960s nationalist rhetoric shifted course to make the language the key element of Basque collective identity. Thus, the children of immigrants can attend Basque schools, become fluent in Euskara, and self-identify as Basque, regardless of their parents' ethnicity. If a child is born in the Basque country and acquires the language but is not Basque by blood, is the child Basque? Many Basques today say yes. Thus, especially within the CAV (Araba, Bizkaia, and Gipuzkoa), people who self-identify as Basque run the racial gamut from those with pure Basque blood for several generations (who may or may not speak the language) to those who have no Basque blood but feel Basque due to cultural assimilation and place of birth (even though they, also, may or may not speak the language).

FOOD FOR THOUGHT

The Basque people have managed to survive as a culturally and linguistically unique nation in the face of a long history of subjection by various majority cultures and states. Only twice in recorded history have they existed as an independent state: once during the Middle Ages (the kingdom of Navarra) and once in 1936–1937 when the anti-Franco Republican government granted the Basques autonomy. They named their new country Euzkadi (note the different spelling). Nevertheless, the Basques have played major roles in shaping the history of not only Spain and France but the world as well.

In the twentieth century, the organization known as ETA used any means they could to promote their nationalist goal of an independent Basque state. In the 1990s, however, an entire generation of post–Franco era babies reached the age of majority without experiencing the dictator's oppression firsthand. A movement for peace, specifically the cessation of ETA-generated conflict with the Spanish government in Madrid, took root through organizations such as Elkarri, and by 1998 a pro-peace slate of candidates was elected in the CAV, culminating in a cease-fire declared by the ETA in the fall of 1998.

Basques are now regenerating their cities and redefining what it means to be Basque within the European Community.

Questions

1. If a Basque leaves Euskal Herria, is he or she still a Basque? What about children born in other countries? How does emigration affect a person's identity?
2. How many different names are used to refer to the Basque country from Roman times to the present? Which Basque provinces are included in each name? Which name traditionally includes all seven provinces?
3. Search the Internet for sites devoted to Basques. Pick five sites and compare them for content. Which Basque attributes are touted on the sites you chose? How much of this chapter is reflected on these Internet sites? What differences in content did you find?
4. Should minority languages like Euskara be preserved? What value does language have in establishing a person's identity?
5. How does your native language affect the way in which you see the world? Would you be a different person if you grew up speaking a minority language?

NOTES

1. The names of languages are not capitalized in Basque, but they are in English, so within the text you will see Euskara. Also, the spelling used here is the official orthography of the Academy of the Basque Language, but other frequently used spellings are *euskera* in Spain and *eskuara* in France.

2. Census figures for 1991 put the number of Basque speakers for the three provinces in the Basque Autonomous Community (CAV or Euskadi) at 543,617 (Tejerina "Language" 232; MacKinnon 98). Ros and Cano say 27% of the population of the CAV speaks Basque (89). The figure above (543,617) refers to native Basque speakers. The same census included another category of quasi-Basque speakers that would add another 410,536 to the total, if we wish to count those who are not native or fluent. This would put the number of Basque speakers at all levels in Euskadi at 954,153 (MacKinnon 98).

RESOURCE GUIDE

Published Literature

Bard, Rachel. *Navarra*. Reno: University of Nevada Press, 1982.

Clark, Robert P. *The Franco Years and Beyond*. Reno: University of Nevada Press, 1979.

Douglass, William A., and Jon Bilbao. *Amerikanuak*. Reno: University of Nevada Press, 1975.

Gallop, Rodney. *A Book of the Basques*. Reno: University of Nevada Press, 1970.

Laxalt, Robert. *A Cup of Tea in Pamplona*. Reno: University of Nevada Press, 1985.

MacClancy, Jeremy. "Bilingualism and Multinationalism in the Basque Country."
    In *Nationalism and the Nation in the Iberian Peninsula: Competing and*

Conflicting Identities, edited by Clare Mar-Molinero and Angel Smith, 207–220. Oxford, England: Berg, 1996.

MacKinnon, Kenneth. "Minority Languages in an Integrating Europe: Prospects for Viability and Maintenance." In *Language Minorities and Minority Languages in the Changing Europe*, edited by Brunon Synak and Tomasz Wisherkiewicz, 93–108. Gdansk: Widawnictwo Uniwersytetu Gdanskiego, 1997.

Parot Zubimendi, Mila. "Ecological Disaster in Basque Rivers." *Euskal Herria Journal*, on-line edition. (http://www.contrast.org/mirrors/ehj/html/eco71299.html) Accessed 1/20/2000.

———. "Ecologists Demand Closure of Garoña Nuclear Power Plant." *Euskal Herria Journal*, on-line edition. (http://www.contrast.org/mirrors/ehj/html/nuclear.html) Accessed 1/20/2000.

Ros, Maria, and J. Ignacio Cano. "Language and Intergroup Perception in Spain." In *Language and Ethnic Identity*, edited by William B. Gudykunst, 87–103. Philadelphia: Multilingual Matters, 1988.

Tejerina Montaña, Benjamin. "Language and Basque Nationalism: Collective Identity, Social Conflict and Institutionalisation." In *Nationalism and the Nation in the Iberian Peninsula: Competing and Conflicting Identities*, edited by Clare Mar-Molinero and Angel Smith, 221–36. Oxford England: Berg, 1996.

Videos

Basque Tree Carvings: Legacy in Nevada. (1992) Produced by Instructional Media Services of the University of Nevada, Reno. Surveys the carvings left on aspen trees by Basque sheepherders working in the American West. Highlights the research of Professor Jose Mallea. Available from Basque Studies /322, University of Nevada, Reno, NV 89557–0012.

Song of the Basques. (1995) Produced by Julian Nava and Edmund Penney. Presents a modern vision of the Basque people and region. Narrated by John Forsythe. 47 minutes. Available from Professor Julian Nava, Department of History, California State University, 18111 Nordhoff Street, Northridge, CA 91330–8250.

WWW Sites

Basque studies
http://www.scsr.nevada.edu/~bstudies

North American Basque Organizations (NABO) for information about Basque clubs, language lessons, culture, dancing, music camp, and links, links, links
http://www.naboinc.com

The Buber pages (Blas Uberuaga's site about Basques)
http://students.washington.edu/buber/

For opportunities to travel and learn in the Basque country, try the University Studies Abroad Consortium
http://usac.unr.edu

Basques

To read about the Basque Country in English, see the *Euskal Herria Journal*
http://.www.contrast.org/mirrors/ehj/

To view a magazine in Euskara or see what is happening in the Basque country from day to day, visit *Argia* magazine's site.
http://www.argia.com

To discover whether you have a Basque last name, search for surname sites on the web. Many free sites provide onomastic information by ethnic group.

Organizations

The Basque Studies Library
University Library/322
University of Nevada, Reno
Reno, NV 89557–0012
Telephone: (702) 784–4854
Fax: (702) 784–1355
E-mail: basque@unr.edu
Web site: http: //www.library.unr.edu/~basqlib/

Society of Basque Studies in America
19 Colonial Gardens
Brooklyn, NY 11209
E-mail: Ramon Cengotitabengoa (sbsa@gte.net)
Web site: http://www.naboinc.com/club-studies.htm

Courtesy of Mapcraft.

Chapter 3

The Catalans

Susan M. DiGiacomo

CULTURAL OVERVIEW

During the 1992 summer Olympic Games held in Barcelona, Spain, American readers of *Time, Newsweek*, and the *New York Times*, like European readers of the *International Herald Tribune, The Times* of London, *Le Monde, Stern*, and others, opened their newspapers and magazines to find an unusual two-page advertisement placed by the Generalitat, the autonomous government of Catalonia. It consisted of two maps, the first a blank square in bright yellow, showing only Barcelona as a point. The caption below read, "In Which Country Would You Place This Point?" Readers turned the page to find a second map, this time an outline map of Western Europe with no political boundaries except for Catalonia, highlighted in bright red, Barcelona now visible as its capital. The answer to the question—"In Catalonia, Of Course"—was followed by a short text explaining that Catalonia is "a country in Spain with its own culture, language and identity."

A country in Spain? What does that mean?

Catalonia was incorporated into the Spanish state in the late fifteenth century, when Isabel, the queen of Castile, married Ferran (Ferdinand V), the king of the crown of Aragon. Catalonia's relationship to the state has taken many different forms over the past 500 years, but even during periods of absolutist rule or military dictatorship it never lost its distinctive character. Most of Catalonia is *in* Spain, but not quite *of* it.

The Setting

The autonomous community of Catalonia is defined in law as the four provinces of Barcelona, Girona, Lleida, and Tarragona in northeastern Spain, a triangle of territory that is commonly referred to as the Principat (Principality) because the early medieval Catalan rulers preferred the more modest title of prince to that of king. Administratively, it forms one of seventeen of the autonomous communities into which Spain is now divided. Autonomous communities have powers similar to those of American states or Canadian provinces in democratic Spain.

Catalonia is bounded by the Pyrenean mountain range on its northern side, the Mediterranean Sea on its eastern side, and the Ebro River on its western side. Its total land area is 12,432 square miles, roughly the same as the state of Maryland. Catalans themselves, however, recognize a kinship through language to the people of Valencia, the Balearic Islands, the tiny Pyrenean country of Andorra, Rosselló (Roussillon) in southeastern France, and the inhabitants of the Sardinian city of L'Alguer (Alghero), where local dialects of the Catalan language are spoken. Some of this linguistic unity is the product of conquest and colonial expansion, as in the case of the Balearic Islands, Valencia, and L'Alguer, while Rosselló and Andorra formed part of Catalonia's original core. Together, they have come to be known as the Països Catalans, or the Catalan lands.

Catalonia is a small country with a geography remarkable for its variety and contrast. The Pyrenees form both a barrier against, and a bridge to, the rest of Europe. Mountain fastnesses permitted resistance to invaders of many kinds—Greeks, Romans, Visigoths, Arabs, Franks—while mountain passes permitted the regular movement of people between what is now Spain and France, long before either of them existed as states, and many families living in mountain villages have relatives on both sides of the border. Dairying and transhumance—the seasonal movement of livestock from lower pastures in the colder months to the higher, cooler slopes in summer—were traditional ways of life in this ecological zone, along with the banditry and smuggling celebrated in legend and folksong. Two smaller mountain chains extend southward from the Pyrenees. One runs parallel to the Mediterranean shore, creating a coastal landscape that begins dramatically in the north with steep cliffs punctuated by small inlets and gradually widens into broad, sandy beaches, finally ending in a great, flat, marshy delta at the mouth of the Ebro River, where short-grain rice has been grown since the Arabs introduced it. Another mountain range passes through the interior, creating systems of river valleys where Catalonia's industrial economy was born of the energy of running water, and the fertile plains that produce olives and wine, wheat and fruit.

Catalonia's political character was formed in the context of the physical nature of the landscape as labyrinth, refuge, and corridor (*terra de pas*).[1]

Catalonia's best image of itself is that of a country open to influences from other lands; enterprising in spirit; endowed with practicality, realism, and common sense (*seny*); capable not only of compromise (*pactisme*) but also of combat, of measured response and response out of all measure (*rauxa*), as circumstances require. This is not an argument for environmental determinism, but a recognition of the reciprocal relationship among space, place, and people.

Origins

Catalans are passionately interested in their own history in a way Americans may find difficult to understand, and the important place of historians in Catalan life has no real equivalent in the United States. Theirs is a history that has often been erased by the master narrative of the Spanish state, and Catalans experience the erasure of their collective past as a very real threat to their survival as a people. Telling their own national story in their own language has been an act of resistance in times of political repression and a necessary affirmation of nationhood under conditions of greater liberty.

Catalonia, like other European societies, emerged out of successive experiences of contact, commerce, conquest, and conflict. In the sixth century B.C., the Iberian peoples inhabiting Catalonia's northern coast encountered the first colonists, the Greeks, who traded with them and founded a market town, Emporion (Empúries), which gave its name to Catalonia's heartland, the Empordá. Four centuries later, Roman settlement would leave a much deeper impression on Catalonia, incorporating it into pan-Mediterranean cultural and trade networks, a form of early globalization. Barcelona—the Roman garrison town of Barcino—was established late in the first century B.C. Modern visitors to the excavated Roman remains that form part of the Barcelona city museum can see production and storage facilities for the local winemaking and olive oil industries, as well as a factory for the processing of *garum*, a fermented fish paste that was a staple in the Roman diet.

By the middle of the fourth century A.D., the structure of Roman rule was disintegrating on the peripheries of the empire. Wave after wave of invading Germanic tribes from northern Europe crossed the Pyrenees into Iberia, and during the fifth century one of these tribes, the Visigoths, drove out the others and set up their court in Barcelona. They eventually established their capital in Toledo, south of where Madrid now stands. The Visigoths had little in common with the people of Roman Hispania except for Christianity, to which they had converted.

Visigothic rule was thus a fragile edifice that came tumbling down in the eighth century, when Arab armies crossed the Strait of Gibraltar and rapidly advanced as far as the foothills of the Pyrenees. Peasants fled from the vulnerable coastal settlements and plains to the deep northern valleys that made resistance possible. From these peasant communities a new society began to crystallize. This was the Hispanic march that separated Christian Europe from the Islamic world, and it was the origin of the territory of *La Catalunya Vella*, Old Catalonia, the crucible of the Catalan national character. These independent mountain dwellers willingly placed themselves under the protection of the Frankish kings—Charlemagne and his successors—in return for free and full possession of the land they worked, and they fought the Muslim armies alongside them.

In 801 the Arabs were driven out of Barcelona. During the 870s, Guifré el Pelós (Wilfrid the Hairy), the first count of Barcelona, repopulated and asserted Frankish control over what is now central Catalonia. He is, however, revered less for his historical deeds than for his legendary ones. In the year 878, as the story goes, Guifré was badly wounded in battle against the Arabs on behalf of the Frankish king, whose name, by amusing coincidence, was Charles the Bald. As Guifré lay in his tent, the king came to offer him a reward for his loyalty. Noticing Guifré's gilded shield, bare of any device, the king dipped four fingers in the blood flowing from Guifré's wound and drew them down the shield: the origin of the Catalan national flag, four red bars on a gold field.

The truth behind the legend is that when Guifré died in 897, his sons, without waiting for the king to designate one of them as the successor, divided their father's lands among themselves and governed them as if they had inherited the right to do so. Thus a process leading to Catalan independence was set in motion by the beginning of the tenth century, even though it was not recognized in law until the Treaty of Corbeil, signed in 1258 by the Catalan King Jaume I and King Louis IX of France.

Social and Political Organization

Catalans speak of themselves as a nation, not as an ethnic group or a region. Their choice of words is not accidental, and it emerges from their awareness of a collective heritage that includes a long history of political independence; a well-defined territory; a language (not a "dialect" of Spanish); and a distinctive social structure, economy, and culture.

The medieval Catalan state came into being in the twelfth century through a dynastic marriage that joined Catalonia to the neighboring kingdom of Aragon. The Catalan-Aragonese confederation preserved the autonomy of each of its components, and the arrangement lasted until the end of the fifteenth century, with the dynastic marriage of Isabel of Castile and Ferdinand of Aragon. The political institutions that gave medieval Catalonia its form and substance include a parliament, the Corts, founded in the early thirteenth century and based on the form of Barcelona's municipal government, the Council of One Hundred (Consell de Cent). While not democratic institutions in the modern sense, they were representative ones. The Corts and its standing executive committee, the Generalitat, included members of the nobility, Church, and middle class. The more populist Consell de Cent included tradesmen and skilled workers as well as professionals, merchants, and aristocrats. Its composition reflected an urban society whose wealth was generated by manufacture and commerce, enduring characteristics to which the interest of the present-day Generalitat in establishing international trade relations can be traced.

These institutions were regulated by laws: the Consolat de Mar, the oldest international law of the sea; and a kind of feudal constitution or bill of rights, the Usatges (Book of Usages). Like the English Magna Carta, which it predates by almost a century, the Usatges opened the path to a bourgeois society in Catalonia, placing townsmen (*ciutadans honrats*, "honored citizens," meant any man not a serf) and nobility on an equal legal footing and providing the means for settling disputes through negotiated agreements rather than through appeal to a higher authority. This is the historical source of the Catalan talent for negotiation and compromise (*pactisme*). The Usatges form the basis of the Catalan civil law code in use today. It is distinct from Spanish civil law in a number of important aspects, one of which is the status of women, whose right to retain control of their own property after marriage was first set down in the Usatges.

The dynastic marriage of Ferdinand and Isabel created not a centralized Spain, but a collection of several independent kingdoms under a common monarch. Spanish kings renewed yearly their promise to uphold Catalonia's laws and institutions of government. Naturally, there were periodic tests of this principle. In 1640, when Spain was at war with France, the Spanish court violated Catalan law by issuing an order requiring the people of Catalonia to feed and quarter the soldiers. Resistance to the order escalated into guerrilla warfare, and the Spanish authorities retaliated by imprisoning the president of the Generalitat, Pau Claris, and several members of Barcelona's Council of One Hundred. The prisoners were liberated when 1,500 Catalan peasants, armed with their harvesting sickles, stormed the jail—an event commemorated in Catalonia's national anthem, "Els Segadors" (The Reapers). Eventually matters were settled by a compromise from which Catalonia emerged with its laws and institutions of government largely intact, if not its territory: Rosselló (now Roussillon) was ceded to the French in the Treaty of the Pyrenees.

Sixty years later, King Charles II died without issue. His will named a French heir, whose claim to the throne was challenged by an Austrian pretender, and the outcome was the Spanish War of Succession. Catalans, fearing an absolutist French ruler who would end Catalan self-government, supported the Austrian archduke, along with England and Holland. But the English and the Dutch, tired of war, eventually abandoned their Catalan allies. Barcelona, besieged for fourteen months by Spanish and French forces, finally fell on September 11, 1714.

Catalans paid heavily for betting on the losing contender. The Generalitat, the Corts, and the Consell de Cent were dissolved immediately. An entire section of Barcelona, the working-class waterfront quarter of La Ribera, was razed to the ground to make way for the building of an immense new fortress, the Ciutadella (Citadel). From here, and from the newly enlarged castle perched atop Montjuïc, which loomed above Barcelona's harbor, the occupying Spanish army was in a position to crush any spark of resistance. The Decree of the New Plan (*Nueva Planta*) promulgated by the victorious King Philip V in 1716 introduced a centralized system of military control, civil administration, and taxation similar to the plans of other centralizing absolutist monarchs in France, where Louis XIV had used similar means to subdue rebellious Bretons, and in England, which sought to break Irish and Scottish resistance.

The intellectual and cultural life of Catalonia suffered, too. Catalan universities were closed, and the official use of the Catalan language was outlawed. But, in fact, the language's public and literary use in the cities of Valencia and Barcelona had already begun to decline in the sixteenth century, as the center of political and economic gravity began to shift away from Catalonia and toward Castile and its new capital, Madrid. The emerging urban aristocracy differentiated itself from its social inferiors by adopting Castilian (Spanish), the language of the royal court. In smaller towns and villages far from the cities, however, Catalan remained the language spoken by local society. Most Catalans, like most people in eighteenth century Spain, could not read or write, and simply went on speaking their own language. Illiteracy, oddly enough, had unexpected benefits.

THREATS TO SURVIVAL

Military Rule: The Primo de Rivera Dictatorship, 1923–1930

The turn of the twentieth century was a time of violent class confrontation in many parts of Spain, but especially in Barcelona. An increasingly conservative Catalan industrial bourgeoisie was unable to reach an understanding with the more moderate sectors of Catalonia's labor movement, whose leadership then passed to the more radical sectors, and the result was a vicious cycle of terror and repression. Bombs were thrown at representatives of the Church and the Spanish state and in the Liceu (Barcelona's opera house), the prime architectural representation of elite power and society. During the many general strikes, factory owners hired pistol gangs to patrol the streets and shoot union members; labor leaders, naturally, armed their militants in turn. During the week from July 26 to August 1, 1909—the Tragic Week—what began as a general strike to protest the conscription of soldiers for an unpopular colonial war in Morocco became a rebellion in which workers burned and looted convents, churches, and parochial schools all over Barcelona and in neighboring towns.

The Catalan bourgeoisie, desperate to have the masses restrained, welcomed the military dictatorship of General Miguel Primo de Rivera, installed with the approval of the Spanish monarchy in 1923. Political parties and labor unions were outlawed, but during the seven years of military rule, Catalans found cultural rather than political ways of resisting. Folk dancing and Catalan music became expressions of political defiance. Record numbers of books were published in Catalan, and Catalan-language plays were performed. Private schools were established in which Catalan was the language of instruction. And every point scored on the soccer field by the Barcelona Football Club against the Madrid team was a political victory. All of these strategies would again become important instruments of social and political mobilization during the more brutal, much longer dictatorship of General Francisco Franco after the Civil War of 1936–39.

After the Primo de Rivera dictatorship had run its course, Spaniards were in no mood for a return to monarchical rule. In 1931, monarchist political parties were swept out of power all over Spain in the municipal elections. In Catalonia, a socially progressive republican nationalism appealed successfully to a broad cross-section of Catalan society from peasants and workers to shopkeepers to middle-class professionals, and it won an electoral victory so complete that it nearly brought a fully independent Catalan republic into being. A negotiated settlement between the new Spanish government in Madrid and the Catalan political leadership produced a compromise: Catalonia would remain part of Spain, but it would have substantial powers of home rule. The new autonomous government adopted the name of Catalonia's medieval governing body, the Generalitat.

The Spanish Civil War, 1936–1939

Both Catalan autonomy and the Spanish Republic were to be short lived. In July 1936 a group of Spanish military officers, under the leadership of General Franco, revolted against the legitimate government of the republic, which precipitated a three-year civil war. Part social revolution and part dress rehearsal for World War II, the Spanish Civil War was a confrontation between the traditional agrarian Spain of idle and privileged landlords and landless agricultural laborers, which was in the hands of the fascist generals; and the Spain of peasant proprietors and of industry, which sided with the republic. The war also divided Republican Spain against itself. The radical labor unions, whose militants wanted to win the social revolution first, then use its momentum to defeat the fascists, found themselves pitted against the more moderate left, which saw the principal aim of the war as the defeat of fascism. This war within a war is an important reason why the republic lost. There were, of course, other reasons as well: Benito Mussolini and Adolf Hitler sent weapons and troops to aid the fascist forces, while the Western democracies refused to intervene in an "internal matter," even to the extent of selling arms to the republic.

The Postwar Repression of Catalonia and the Franco Dictatorship

Catalonia was Republican territory from the beginning, and remained so until it was overrun by the Franco forces in January 1939. Thousands of Republican soldiers and civilians crossed the Pyrenees on foot in the snow. Most of them were to remain in exile for decades; many died before it was possible for them to return. As in 1714, Catalans paid a heavy price for their defense of the republic and their own national liberties. Spanish fascism had very little ideological content; it was primarily a backward-looking patriotic traditionalism that feared "red separatists" (*rojoseparatistas*)—the Catalans and Basques—above all else. Accordingly, as soon as the war ended, the victorious General Franco, as the new military dictator of Spain, began a remarkably thorough linguistic purge in Catalonia that touched every aspect of public life and many aspects of private life as well. Barcelona was plastered with posters commanding, "If you are Spanish, speak Spanish"; "Speak the language of the Empire" (even though Spain had long since lost its colonial possessions abroad); and even "Don't bark; speak Christian." Not content with this, the fascists prohibited Catalan parents from entering their children's names in the Civil Register in any language except Castilian. Newspapers were forbidden to publish death notices in Catalan, and the use of Catalan inscriptions on cemetery monuments was outlawed.

The persecution of Catalonia was not limited to language. The victorious General Franco immediately abrogated the Catalan Statute of Autonomy and dissolved the Catalan parliament and the Generalitat. Especially during 1939 and 1940, there were mass arrests and summary executions. Police spies were everywhere. The president of Catalonia, Lluís Companys, was arrested in exile in a French village and handed over to the German Gestapo, who delivered him to the fascist authorities in Spain. He was imprisoned, tortured, tried by court martial, and executed in secret on October 15, 1940. The new regime thought it had solved its Catalan problem.

RESPONSE: STRUGGLES TO SURVIVE CULTURALLY

Language: The Key Symbol of Catalan National Identity

Historical linguistics places the emergence of spoken Catalan at about A.D. 800, roughly the same time that other Romance languages were forming as a result of contact between Latin and local languages. Catalan is not a derivative or a dialectal variant of Castilian (Spanish), nor was it simply an oral vernacular. Catalans often refer to *la nostra llengua mil lenària*— our thousand-year-old language—and proudly point to the earliest surviving written texts in Catalan: the Homílies d'Organyà, a collection of sermons that dates to the twelfth century. Catalan developed a distinct literary standard and an extensive history of literary use that began not with poetry, as in the case of most Romance languages, but with prose. The thirteenth-century novels and theological works of the philosopher Ramon Llull (in English, Raymond Lully) are among the earliest examples. At its height, the Catalan literary tradition produced such masterpieces as *Tirant lo blanc* (The White Tyrant), a novel of chivalry, in 1490. Its greatness was recognized even by the most important writer of the Spanish Renaissance, Miguel de Cervantes. In the first part of his book *Don Quixote*, the priest who conducts an inquisition over the contents of the knight's library chooses *Tirant lo blanc* as the only book of its kind to be spared from burning, praising it as a "rare treasure of delight . . . for its style it is the best book in the world" (Cervantes 1604 [J. M. Cohen, trans. 1950], p. 60).

By the sixteenth century, however, Spanish began to predominate as the language of the educated classes, and Catalan literary production slowed dramatically. Almost 300 years would pass before Catalan was again used regularly as a literary language. The revival of literary Catalan was fueled by the energy of Catalonia's industrial revolution. The old patrician class, which had gravitated toward Madrid and the Spanish court, was displaced by the new industrial elites whose wealth transformed the city of Barcelona into a cultural capital that rivaled Madrid and a financial and manufacturing capital that far surpassed it. The restoration of Catalonia's national literary heritage is conventionally dated to 1833, when the poet Bonaventura Carles Aribau's ode "La Pàtria" was published. Aribau's romantic vision of his "Fatherland" evokes the glories of medieval Catalonia, of troubadours and kings, and it helped to inspire yearly public poetry competitions of medieval origin, the Jocs Florals (Floral Games), established in 1859 under the sponsorship of the Barcelona city government.

In the early twentieth century, the political wheel finally turned in Catalonia's favor. In 1914 the four provincial administrations (*diputacions*) of Catalonia were consolidated into a single administrative unit called the Mancomunitat (Commonwealth) under the leadership of Enric Prat de la Riba. The forerunner of the restored Generalitat (the modern Catalan autonomous government), the Mancomunitat embarked on a broad range of social, cultural, and infrastructure programs that included educational reform, road and railway construction, modernization and expansion of technical colleges, and an ambitious design for a health care system that included up-to-date psychiatric services.

But the Mancomunitat is best remembered by many Catalans for its support of the Institut d'Estudis Catalans (Institute of Catalan Studies), which commissioned and published the linguist Pompeu Fabra's *Orthographic Dictionary* (1917) and *Catalan Grammar* (1918). These works, which established a generally accepted standard for modern Catalan usage, spelling, and grammar, are still the foundation on which later dictionaries and models of usage have been constructed. Fabra set out not to resurrect a medieval language, but to reconstruct a natural process: the twentieth-century Catalan language that would have come into being had its development not been arrested, had it not been impoverished and fragmented by centuries of subordination to Castilian. Fabra envisioned a standard Catalan flexible enough to be a language of science and government as well as of poetry, and for this reason he kept it as close as possible to *el català que ara es parla* (the Catalan we speak now)—the Catalan spoken by workers, peasants, artisans, and shopkeepers. The Primo de Rivera dictatorship of 1923–1930 suppressed the Mancomunitat, but Fabra's work continued. The Institut d'Estudis Catalans published Fabra's *General Dictionary of the Catalan Language* in 1932, the same year that Catalonia's political institutions—the Generalitat and Parliament—were restored through the Statute of Autonomy under the Second Republic, and language planning began in earnest, only to be halted by the Civil War and the military dictatorship of General Franco (1939–1975).

From Cultural Resistance to Political Resistance

As they had under the dictatorship of Primo de Rivera in the 1920s, Catalans used their language, culture, and organizational ability to resist the Franco regime. To speak Catalan in the street could mean arrest, and it was forbidden to assemble more than twelve people for any purpose, so as early as 1940, small Catalan language classes, poetry readings, and literary and scholarly discussion groups were held secretly in private homes. In 1942 the Institut d'Estudis Catalans, sustained by private contributions, resumed clandestine activity. Catalan publishing houses began to operate underground, and by 1945 a few were able to operate above ground; the first nonclandestine Catalan literary prizes were awarded shortly thereafter. This was not mere sentimentalism. Continually pushing the envelope of official censorship in a police state meant risking not only one's personal safety, but also that of one's family and friends.

The Catholic Church in Catalonia was another early site of resistance to the regime. The Church was the only institution exempt from censorship, and the abbey of Montserrat took full advantage of the loophole, publishing a literary magazine entirely in Catalan. The Catholic scouting movement became a training ground for many members of Catalonia's future political leadership.

The Catalan tradition of music as a vehicle for social and political protest originated in nineteenth-century workers' choruses. In 1947 the Coral Sant

Requiring steadiness, perseverance, strength and teamwork, the raising of human towers (*castells*) has come to be a metaphor for the best qualities of Catalan national identity. Here, a group of *castellers* takes part in the annual celebration of Catalonia's patron saint on April 23, St. George's Day (Sant Jordi). Photo by Susan M. DiGiacomo.

Jordi (named for Saint George, Catalonia's patron saint) was founded. The group sang not only the traditional repertoire of choral works, but also music by Catalan composers, both historical and contemporary, and choral arrangements of Catalan folksongs. In this way it helped to transmit a body of Catalan folk culture in the Catalan language to those born after the end of the Civil War, who might not otherwise have come into contact with it. A new form of popular music, the *nova cançó* (new song) movement, emerged in the late 1950s and early 1960s. Its nearest equivalent in the United States is the folk/protest genre of singer-songwriters like Woody Guthrie, Pete Seeger, and Joan Baez, and it had the same broad appeal. The *nova cançó* singers set the verses of the great Catalan poets, both medieval and modern, to music, and wrote their own songs as well. The Franco regime's censors took every opportunity to delete songs from concert programs, or to ban concerts altogether, but the movement proved unstoppable.

These seemingly nonpolitical activities brought like-minded Catalans together regularly, and they were an important part of the organizational basis for reconstructing political opposition to the dictatorship. When Franco died in November 1975, and Spain entered an eighteen-month period of preparation for its first democratic elections in forty years, fully formed political parties seemed to emerge out of nowhere. But they had been taking shape for many years around dinner tables, at concerts, on mountain hikes, in church, and in many other unlikely places.

National Reconstruction and Language Planning

By the late 1960s, the laws against the public use of the Catalan language were no longer being enforced as thoroughly as they had been in the years immediately following the Civil War. Still, by the end of the Franco regime in 1975, two generations of Catalans had grown up in a society in which the only language of school, workplace, business, the mass media, and government was Castilian. Many had learned to speak Catalan at home but found it much easier to read in Castilian because it was the language in which they had learned all their subjects at school. Hardest of all, for many people under age fifty, was writing Catalan correctly. And after decades of avoiding arrest for the crime of speaking Catalan in public, many people found it difficult to break the habit of automatically addressing any stranger in Castilian.

Moreover, Catalan society had changed significantly since the war. Hundreds of thousands of people fled the grinding poverty of southern Spain to seek factory jobs and a better life in the industrial north: first in Catalonia and the Basque country, and later in Madrid as well. By 1970 well over half the population of the greater Barcelona area (a total of roughly 3 million people, half of Catalonia's total population) had been born outside Catalonia. The Franco regime's prohibition on the public use of Catalan ensured that these "immigrants," as they were generally called, had little opportunity to learn Catalan. The language barrier between natives and newcomers was reinforced by the fact that it paralleled lines of social class. Castilian-speaking immigrants tended to be working class, and the Catalan natives tended, more often than not, to be middle class.

When Franco died, his regime died with him. It was clear to all that the transition back to democracy in Spain would have to mean the restoration of political autonomy for Catalonia, and for the Basque country as well. It was less clear how to bring these "other Catalans," who were neither ethnic Catalans nor Catalan speakers, into the process of Catalan national reconstruction, which could not succeed without their votes and their support.

Most immigrants to Catalonia, by contrast with those who had gone as "guest workers" to German, French, and Swiss factories intending to return home in ten, fifteen, or twenty years, had made a permanent move. While they often used their vacation time to visit relatives still living in the Andalusian villages where they were born, they quickly became aware during these visits of how much they had been changed by living in Barcelona. Their clothes, their mannerisms, even their accents marked them out as "different." Andalusia was no longer "home" in the same sense for them, and it was not home at all for their Barcelona-born children. Some of them had become politically active through their participation in neighborhood associations that struggled to bring adequate city services—public transportation, schools, sidewalks, streetlights, even grass and trees—to the newest and poorest neighborhoods, where many immigrants lived.

Catalonia was now their country, too, and the country their children would inherit. And although some of them would never learn to speak Catalan themselves, most of them wanted their children to learn it. Even during the Franco regime, when its public use was severely limited, Catalan had never lost its social prestige as the language of educated and cultivated people. Learning Catalan would help their children rise out of the working class and into the middle class. In 1977, the year of the first elections since 1936, they were ready to hear what the Catalan parties on the left side of the political spectrum told them: All who live and work in Catalonia are Catalans. At the same time, the definition of the working class was also broadened to include many Catalans in white-collar occupations: The working class consists of all those who sell their labor in exchange for a wage. Teachers, doctors, and secretaries now had important things in common with mechanics, bricklayers, and factory workers, and they elected as their representatives in the new Spanish parliament leaders who promised to work both for social justice and for the restoration of Catalonia's national life.

The main task of the newly elected government was to prepare a new Spanish constitution, which was approved the following year and provided the mechanisms for restoring Catalan and Basque autonomy, as well as instituting home rule for fifteen new autonomous communities in a decentralized state structure. In the fall of 1979, a new Catalan statute of autonomy was passed by referendum, and in the spring of 1980, Catalans elected representatives to their own parliament. A law of linguistic normalization, first passed by the Catalan parliament in 1983 and updated in January 1998, has allowed the Catalan language to engage in the process of regaining the social space it lost during the forty years of the Franco dictatorship, and to claim new spaces opened up by the media, the Internet, and the European Union.

The Present and the Future

All children in Catalonia, regardless of the language they speak at home, now learn Catalan in school, and for some it is also the language of instruction in other subjects. There are Catalan-language newspapers, magazines, and novels; Catalan-language television and radio broadcasting; Catalan street and shop signs; and Catalan menus in restaurants. Catalan speakers have the right to a translator during legal proceedings, and to have legal documents drawn up in Catalan. It is quite common to hear bilingual conversations in which one person is speaking Catalan and the other is speaking Castilian. Catalonia's people, like the citizens of other European countries, do not consider it a burden to speak two languages, and often they become proficient in a third by the time they complete high school.

This is not to say that all the problems have been solved. Many of the old ones are still around, and new ones have emerged. Catalans continue to debate the merits of bilingual education, as do Americans. They wish more foreign films were dubbed or subtitled in Catalan as well as Castilian, and they argue about how "correct" the language of Catalan television, radio, and the press should be. They would like to be able to buy products labeled in Catalan, since they can now buy products imported from all the countries of the European Union, labeled in French, English, German, Dutch, Italian, and Greek. They worry that all the institutional supports for the Catalan language have given people a false sense of security about its survival in a world where English has become the new lingua franca. As new immigrants arrive from Africa and Asia, Catalans are again pondering the question of who is Catalan, and they are struggling to devise new answers for a society that is increasingly becoming racially as well as linguistically diverse.

The European Union has given a role and greater visibility to small countries. Ireland combines the revival of its ancient language, Gaelic, with a dynamic modern economy; Scotland, a stateless nation like Catalonia, elected representatives to its own parliament in 1999, Britain's first important step toward decentralized government. Like the Irish and Scots, Catalans feel comfortable as part of a Europe that respects minority languages and peoples and offers the opportunity for cultural exchange.

The experience of Catalonia offers some important lessons. Its present population is of mixed origin, but there are no long-standing ethnic hatreds of the kind that produced the tragedy of Bosnia, or violence against immigrant communities such as the Turks have suffered in Germany. The meaning of being Catalan has changed in the course of the twentieth century. To take just one example, every spring, the Andalusian ethnic community of greater Barcelona organizes the April Fair, a festival modeled on the famous April Fair of Seville. It has become a part of the Catalan cultural landscape, and no Catalan politician misses the opportunity to attend. In 1999 it drew more than two million visitors, about a third of Catalonia's total population.

Third World immigrants from north and equatorial Africa, India and Pakistan, and the Philippines are changing this cultural landscape in new ways as Catalonia enters the new century and the new millennium. While their presence causes a degree of anxiety about their cultural impact—will they prefer to learn Spanish instead of Catalan?—and concern about the strain their substantial needs may place on social services, Catalan society is also becoming alert to the dangers of racism. Both the Generalitat and the Barcelona city government have supported efforts to develop an international perspective. They sponsor transcultural music festivals, art exhibitions, and conferences. Nongovernmental organizations, such as SOS Racisme, are actively working to promote a genuinely multicultural society.

Every year on September 11—the date of the fall of Barcelona in 1714—Catalans celebrate their national holiday. It may seem odd that they are celebrating a crushing military defeat, rather than a declaration of independence, as Americans do on July 4, or a revolutionary victory, as the French do on Bastille Day (July 14). For Catalans, their national celebration is a reminder of the extraordinary bravery with which their ancestors resisted an enemy that far outnumbered them. And it underlines a lesson that all democratic societies must learn: Freedom is not something that is achieved once and for all in a single decisive battle or a declaration of principle, but must be won again and again, in ways both large and small.

FOOD FOR THOUGHT

Catalonia is a small society in southern Europe which is linguistically, socially, culturally, politically, and economically distinct from the rest of the Spanish state, into which it was incorporated at the end of the fifteenth century. An independent country in the Middle Ages, it developed a manufacturing and commercial economy and representative institutions of government that set it apart from all other Iberian kingdoms and most

European ones. These characteristics set it on the path toward the emergence of a modern class structure and industrial economy in the nineteenth century, when the rest of Spain was still an agrarian society dominated by a privileged aristocracy. The main threats to its survival have been absolutist rule and, in the twentieth century, military dictatorship. Now an autonomous community within a decentralized and democratic Spain, Catalonia is a multiethnic society that continues to be proud of its historic openness to other cultural influences while retaining a sense of its own identity.

Questions

1. Many writers who grew up in post–Civil War Catalonia, or came to live there as adults, have produced books that draw their inspiration from Catalan realities, but are written in Castilian. Catalans themselves are of different opinions concerning whether these books are part of Catalan literature, or should be thought of as Spanish. What do you think?

2. After the Civil War ended in 1939, many Catalans spent years, even decades, living in exile, mostly in Mexico and other Latin American countries. Exile raises the question of the relationship between language and culture in a different way. Are the foreign-born and Spanish-speaking children of exiled Catalan parents still Catalans? Would their first trip to their parents' homeland be a homecoming for them, or a visit to a foreign country?

3. The Catalan government's language policy and planning initiatives have taken the form of a linguistic affirmative action program for Catalan. Some Spanish political leaders have criticized this as a kind of reverse discrimination against Spanish speakers living in Catalonia. What do you think?

4. Why is history so important to Catalans? How is their sense of their own history different from Americans' relationship to their history?

5. In the countries of southern Europe, as in the states that share a border with Mexico, there is rising concern about large numbers of undocumented Third World immigrants. Some Catalans say that racism is an American problem, not a European one. Do you agree, or disagree? Why?

NOTE

1. Pierre Vilar, *Catalunya dins l'Espanya moderna*, vol. 1 (Barcelona: Curial Edicions Catalanes and Edicions, 1979), 62.

RESOURCE GUIDE

Published Literature

Alba, Victor. *Catalonia: A Profile.* New York: Praeger, 1975.
Hughes, Robert. *Barcelona.* New York: Knopf, 1992.
McDonogh, Gary Wray. *Good Families of Barcelona: A Social History of Power in the Industrial Era.* Princeton, N.J.: Princeton University Press, 1986.
Peffer, Randall. "Catalonia: Spain's Country Within a Country." *National Geographic* 165, no. 1 (1984): 95–127.
Woolard, Kathryn A. *Double Talk: Bilingualism and the Politics of Ethnicity in Catalonia.* Stanford, Calif.: Stanford University Press, 1989.

Films and Videos

"Barcelona." A film by Robert Hughes, broadcast on PBS in 1992 as part of the series *Travels.*
Barcelona: Archive of Courtesy. Museum City Videos series, available from V.I.E.W., Inc., 34 East 23 Street, New York, NY 10010. Tel. (212) 674–5550.
The Spanish Civil War. 6 hours on two videocassettes. Granada Video, available from The VideoFinders Collection, National Fulfillment Center, P.O. Box 27054, Glendale, CA 91225–7054. Tel. 1–800–799–1199.

WWW Site

North American Catalan Society (NACS)
http://www.indiana.edu/~nacs

Organizations

Casal dels Catalans de California
P.O. Box 91142
Los Angeles, CA 90009

Center for Catalan Studies
Dr. Josep M. Solà-Solé, Director
The Catholic University of America
Washington, DC 20064
E-mail: solasole@cua.edu

Fundació Paulí Bellet
P.O. Box 9481
Washington, DC 20016

Gaspar de Portolá Catalan Studies Program
Institute of International Studies

251 Moses Hall
University of California, Berkeley
Berkeley, CA 94720
E-mail: mataro@violet.berkeley.edu

North American Catalan Society
Dr. Kathleen McNerney, President
Department of Foreign Language
West Virginia University
Morgantown, WV 26505

Chapter 4

The Cypriots

Kyriacos C. Markides and Joseph S. Joseph

CULTURAL OVERVIEW

Culturally, Cyprus is part of Europe and enjoys one of the highest standards of living in the Mediterranean region. In 1997 it had a per capita income of about $15,000, compared to $4,400 in neighboring Egypt.[1] For this reason the Republic of Cyprus is qualified for, and is being considered for, full membership in the exclusive club of the European Union. However, Cyprus is a troubled society plagued, during the last forty years, with external threats and ethnic conflict between the Greek majority of 80 percent of the population, who are Orthodox Christians, and the Turkish minority of 18 percent, who are Moslems. A formula has yet to be found to enable the entire population of about 750,000 to live together in peace and security within the same society.

The People

The origin of the Greek Cypriots goes back to about 1400 B.C. when large numbers of Mycenaean Greeks arrived on the island and set up their cities and kingdoms. With their arrival, Greek civilization and culture were established on the island. Because of its strategic geographic location, however, Cyprus came under the control of all the empires that ruled the Eastern Mediterranean: Assyrians, Egyptians, Persians, Romans, Byzantines, Franks, Venetians, Turks, and finally the British succeeded one another, each leaving their mark on the island. Greek Cypriots find pride in the fact that, despite the island's long history of being ruled by one conqueror after another, it remained fundamentally Greek and Orthodox Christian in re-

49

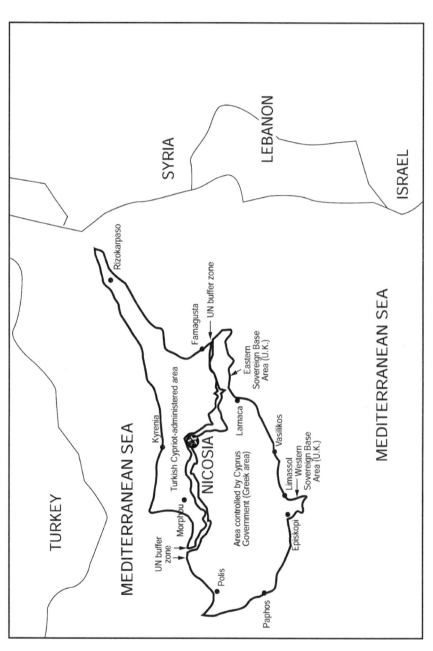

Cyprus. Courtesy of Nighthawk Design.

ligion. Greek Cypriots are fond of pointing out the archaeological evidence supporting the Hellenic character of the island. Tourist brochures, for example, mention that, according to Homer, Aphrodite, the goddess of love, was born out of the foams of the Cypriot sea near the town of Paphos. Until Saint Paul's arrival on the island, the town hosted yearly religious festivals in honor of the goddess. Saint Paul, with his disciple Saint Barnabas, a Cypriot Jew, turned the pagans into Christians, among the first to embrace the new religion that originated in the nearby Holy Land. The long centuries of Byzantine rule (fourth to twelfth century) sealed the cultural configuration of the island, which became famous for its many monasteries and Orthodox saints.

The Ottoman Turks came to Cyprus in A.D. 1571 after they had conquered it from the Venetians. It was the beginning of the emergence of the Turkish community on the island. The Ottomans ruled Cyprus during the following three centuries until 1878 when the British, after an agreement with the Ottoman sultan, took possession of the island and turned it into a British colony. The island gained its independence from Britain in 1960 and has ever since been a full member of the United Nations and other international organizations.

The Setting

Cyprus is located near the northeastern corner of the Mediterranean Sea, at the crossroads of Europe, Asia, and Africa, about 100 miles west of Lebanon, 40 miles south of the Turkish coast, and 600 miles east of the mainland of Greece. Its area of 3,572 square miles, stretching 160 miles from east to west and 60 miles from north to south, is about half the size of New Jersey. It is the third largest island in the Mediterranean after Sicily and Corsica.

The island's topography is dominated by two mountain ranges, the Kyrenia range, which covers the northern coast from east to west, and the forested Troodos mountains, which occupy much of the central landmass. Between the two mountain ranges, there is the Mesaoria plain, in time past the "bread basket" of the island. Although considered to be the warmest island of the Mediterranean, Olympus, the highest peak of Troodos, rises up over 6,000 feet and, in a normal winter, it is covered with snow, making skiing possible and supplying spring runoff that keeps the island relatively green. In fact, one of the advertising mottos for attracting tourists is that during a certain period of the year it is possible to ski in the morning and swim in the afternoon at one of the island's sandy beaches.

The capital city, Nicosia, has a population of about 200,000 people. Situated approximately at the center of the island, it is the seat of government and the main business center. The second largest city, Limassol, is a major port, with about 150,000 people. Smaller cities are Larnaca and

Paphos. The coastal eastern city of Famagusta, once the thriving port and tourist center of the island, is today a barbed-wired "ghost city," abandoned by its inhabitants in 1974 for reasons that are explained below.

Economic Opportunities

Cyprus is a fertile Mediterranean island which, in spite of chronic droughts, produces and exports such items as wines, citrus fruits, grapes, watermelons, potatoes, and a variety of other fruits and vegetables. In ancient times it was a center of copper production from which, it is said, the island acquired its name. Today, however, with its mines depleted, Cyprus relies heavily on tourism for its economic prosperity. In 1999, for example, there were about 2,500,000 visitors to the island. Income from tourism represented about half of its total foreign income. Because of its location and first-class banking, transportation, and telecommunication systems, the island has become a center for the operation of thousands of foreign, "offshore" companies which add substantially to its prosperity.

Confrontational Politics

It is important to point out that the differences between Greek Cypriots and Turkish Cypriots are not religious but political. There are no theological conflicts between them, such as, for example, whether Jesus was the Son of God or whether Mohammed was the Seal of the Prophets. However, since religion is at the core of their ethnic identities, in an indirect way it has contributed to keeping the two groups apart, for example, by preventing intermarriage.

Most troublesome for Greek Cypriots is the July 1974 Turkish invasion of the island republic and the capture of 36 percent of its territory. Over 165,000 Greek Cypriots, or about one-third of the total population of 600,000 at the time of the invasion, became refugees in their own country. They fled to the southern part of the island when Turkish troops landed on the northern coast near the town of Kyrenia.

The invasion was triggered by a military coup instigated by the dictatorship that ruled Greece from 1967 to 1974. The aim of the coup appeared to be the eventual union of the island with Greece, a prospect fiercely opposed by the Turkish Cypriots and by Turkey only forty miles away. With the forcible partition of the island, the Turkish Cypriots were moved to the occupied northern part and, along with thousands of settlers from Turkey that began arriving after the invasion, they were housed in the abandoned homes of Greek Cypriot refugees. The only place that has not been settled as yet remains the port city of Famagusta.

"Cyprus," wrote Henry Kissinger, the former U.S. secretary of state, in reference to the 1974 crisis, "was the forerunner of conflict between ethnic

The city of Famagusta before the Turkish invasion. Now it is a ghost town surrounded by barbed wire. Photo by Edwards and Sons.

groups, which has become increasingly common and threatening in the
decades since. . . . Cyprus initiated the United States into the archetypal and
as yet unfamiliar drama of ethnic conflict."[2] One can also add that the
tragedy of Cyprus exemplifies another troubling phenomenon, that of "ethnic cleansing," a term that became widely used in reference to another
European state, Yugoslavia. As explained below, the conflict in Cyprus that
resulted in the forcible separation of Greek Cypriots and Turkish Cypriots,
who lived side by side in intermixed villages and towns for 400 years, is
threatening the longterm survival and viability of both ethnic groups.

Social and Political Realities

For the Greek Cypriots, the arrival of the British in 1878 was a form of
liberation. It raised their hopes that at last the island would eventually be
ceded to the "mother" country Greece, a friend and ally of England. But
the British Foreign Office had other plans. Cyprus was a prized strategic
island near the oil wells of the Middle East. It soon became apparent to
the frustrated Greek Cypriots that England had no intention of giving up
Cyprus. Consequently, Greek Cypriot nationalism began to emerge with
increasing intensity. It found its expression in *Enosis*, a movement, led by
the Greek Orthodox Church, to unite Cyprus with Greece. *Enosis* opened

the way to an underground guerrilla campaign in 1955 (the EOKA movement, which the British considered "terrorist") to force the colonial government to abandon Cyprus and hand it over to Greece. But the violent campaign to overthrow British rule in retrospect had disastrous consequences for both Greek and Turkish Cypriots.

What the advocates of *Enosis* did not take into consideration was the violent reaction of the Turkish minority which, emboldened by Turkey's close proximity, under no circumstances would accept the union of Cyprus with Greece, the traditional adversary of Turkey. Ethnic passions were ignited leading to riots and atrocities committed by extremist elements on both sides. Instead of *Enosis*, there was a forced compromised solution, the establishment of an independent republic, the product of the "Zurich and London agreements." The constitution, however, which was based on a formula that the Greek Cypriots felt gave excessive privileges to the Turkish minority (veto over basic legislation and 30 percent representation in government—although they accounted for only 18 percent of the population) collapsed in 1963, three years after independence. The government at that point came completely into the hands of the Greek Cypriots, and a large portion of the Turkish Cypriot population lived in fortified enclaves that they controlled with clandestine military support from nearby Turkey. Repeated attempts between 1964 and 1974 for an accommodation failed, thus paving the way to a Greek coup on July 15, 1974. The coup, which overthrew the Cyprus government, was organized and carried out by the Greek military junta that at the time ruled Greece. It was the result of sharp divisions within Greek Cypriot society. A minority of extreme nationalists started a campaign against the government of President Makarios (who was also the archbishop) whom they accused of betraying the cause of *Enosis* by promoting Cypriot independence. Their allies were the Greek military junta. The Turkish invasion took place five days after the coup with the presumed goal of restoring "constitutional order" and for the "protection" of the Turkish minority.

Since those tragic events, which cost the lives of thousands of civilians, the island remains de facto divided. The northern part is still in the hands of Turkey in spite of repeated United Nations resolutions that call for the withdrawal of all foreign troops from the island.

THREATS TO SURVIVAL

A Heavily Militarized Island

An index of the magnitude and complexity of the political problem of this small and vulnerable island republic is the fact that it has on its territory six different armies controlled by different states and military establishments: the Greek Cypriot National Guard with about 10,000 soldiers;

the Turkish Cypriot militia with about 4,000 men, the Turkish occupation forces including 35,000 soldiers, the British army which is stationed at the two sovereign military bases that were established as part of the 1960 Zurich and London agreements that ended British colonial rule, the Greek military contingent of 950 men and the Turkish military contingent of 650 men who were also part of those agreements, and UNFICYP, the United Nations multinational peacekeeping force which has been in Cyprus since 1964 to monitor peace between warring Greek Cypriots and Turkish Cypriots. Today, this force consists of 1,500 soldiers from several countries who patrol the buffer zone separating the occupied part from the rest of the island. Across this dividing line, there are buried 17,000 land mines, which the Canadian government offered to help remove if and when both parties agree.

It is noteworthy to point out that the small island of Cyprus has seven airports, which are controlled by four different governments and international institutions: two by the Republic of Cyprus, two by Turkey, two by the British, and the Nicosia international airport (the only airport on the island at the time of the establishment of the republic in 1960) controlled by the United Nations peacekeeping forces since 1974. No wonder Cyprus has been called "a place of arms."[3]

By far the biggest threat for the longterm survival of Greek Cypriots is the presence of the Turkish troops. These troops are backed by 400 tanks and the Turkish fleet and air force. Cyprus, a small state, has neither a naval fleet nor an air force. Its only defense is the lightly armed National Guard and the support from Greece, which lies hundreds of miles away. The weakness of Greece in regard to Turkey was exposed during the 1974 invasion. Greek fighting planes, for example, could not stay for more than five minutes over Cyprus, or they would run out of fuel. Turkish planes, on the other hand, having their base only minutes away, controlled the skies and inflicted heavy damage on the Cypriot National Guard. Therefore, in the event of further hostilities, Turkey, a country of 65 million people, could easily overrun the southern part of the island, which is controlled by the Republic of Cyprus. Right or wrong, the dominant belief among Greek Cypriots is that Turkey covets the rest of the island and plans to conquer it, if and when the opportunity arises. At a minimum, Turkey's design all along, Greeks believe, has been to partition the island and make the northern part a province of Turkey. The memories of the invasion, with its thousands of casualties, are still vivid in the traumatized collective memory of Greek Cypriots. Such "wounds" are not helpful for compromised solutions.

Demographic Trends

Certain Turkish policies provide ammunition for these fears. The most controversial and alarming development is the colonization of the occupied part of Cyprus by thousands of settlers from the Turkish mainland, which has radically altered the population ratio of Greeks to Turks on one hand and Turkish Cypriots to Turks from Turkey on the other. Although accurate statistics are difficult to gather, various estimates for 1999 place the number of settlers from Turkey in the Turkish-controlled part of Cyprus as ranging from 100,000 to 120,000. At the same time, based on Turkish Cypriot sources, about 50,000 Turkish Cypriots have emigrated during the period between 1974 and 1999. The Turkish Cypriot community in 1999 was estimated to be about 90,000. That means that the indigenous Turkish Cypriot population, which prior to the "troubles" lived together with the Greek Cypriots, is now about equal to the number of settlers from Turkey.

Another alarming development for Greek Cypriots came with the declaration of independence of the Turkish-occupied part. No country except Turkey recognizes this Turkish Republic of Northern Cyprus, which Greeks refer to as the "pseudo-state."

A cultural threat also emerged with the invasion. The Turkish authorities systematically tried to wipe out any trace of Greek culture in the occupied part. Names of towns and villages have been changed from Greek to Turkish. Priceless icons in the many churches and monasteries have been looted or turned into museum items. Most important, of course, the north has been cleansed of ethnic Greeks, with the exception of about 500 elderly persons who remained primarily in the village of Rizokarpasso, the northeastern-most village of the island near the monastery of Apostle Andreas.

Another ominous policy of the Turkish forces of occupation, as far as Greek Cypriots are concerned, is the fact that the Turkish army systematically prevented any contacts between Greek Cypriots and Turkish Cypriots after the separation in 1974. Occasional attempts to reestablish sustained and ongoing informal contacts through international mediators and institutions, such as the United Nations, were routinely terminated for one reason or another. Therefore, since 1974, there has been no free movement or contact between the two sides that would have allowed the creation of any meaningful ties and mutual understanding. The separation has been absolute and total. A whole generation of Cypriots, Greeks and Turks, have grown up on the same island without ever meeting a member of the other group. They have learned about each other only through hostile stereotypes perpetrated in their respective schools and popular culture.

One would have expected that Turkish Cypriots would be content with the current arrangement, but that does not seem to be the case. They may feel physically safer within their zone and with the presence of the Turkish army; however, their cultural survival in the long run seems to be just as, if not more, precarious than that of the Greeks.

The Turkish Cypriots welcomed the 1974 invasion as a form of liberation, and to this day, they celebrate July 20 as a national holiday. For the Greek Cypriots, of course, it is a day of mourning, of bitter memories and frustration. Prior to the invasion, the Greek Cypriots were in control of most of the island and could perhaps have reached an accommodation with the Turkish Cypriots. But because of intra-Greek rivalries and deep suspicions that the Turkish Cypriots' aim was to bring Turkey to Cyprus, the few opportunities that may have been presented were missed. The charismatic leader of the Greek Cypriots, the late Archbishop Makarios, either did not wish or did not have the foresight to preempt the events that brought catastrophe to the island. With the invasion, the power dynamics dramatically changed. It is now the Turkish side that has the military upper hand. The Greeks, in a matter of days, became the military underdogs, suddenly discovering that in reality they are a threatened minority within the geopolitical sphere of influence of a powerful and populous hostile neighbor.

The Turkish Cypriots also paid a heavy price for coming under the military umbrella of their motherland. The biggest problem for them has been the influx of the settlers that has changed the population structure and the political dynamics within the Turkish Cypriot community. Friction with the settlers and lack of economic opportunities in the occupied north have led to an exodus of thousands of Turkish Cypriots. Voices of discontent have been heard periodically from local opposition parties and politicians. For example, the leader of the Turkish Republican Party, Ozker Ozgur, complained, "In the place of our people who flee abroad to earn their living, people come from Turkey under the name of 'labor force.' This labor force is turned into a vote force for conservative, chauvinist directed politicians. . . . We are faced with the danger of becoming a minority in northern Cyprus . . . foreigners in our own homeland."[4] The newcomers are culturally different from the Turkish Cypriots who, as a result of 400 years of coexistence with Greek Cypriots, including eighty-two years under common British rule, developed, like the Greek Cypriots, certain "Cypriot" cultural characteristics not shared by the mainland settlers—such as common food, common temperament related to hospitality, family centeredness, similar taste for popular music, common familiarity with England and the English language, and no differences in style of dress and physical appearance. Rauf Denktash, the Turkish Cypriot leader who has been ruling the Turkish Cypriots for several decades, and who has benefited politically from the presence of the settlers, dismissed the criticism stating that "Turks leave and Turks come," and that there are no "Cypriots." If trends like these continue, then indeed either through assimilation or emigration, there may not be any Turkish Cypriots but only Turks, making an accommodation with the Greek Cypriots even more remote than it is at present.

Environmental Crisis

The immediate impact of the Turkish invasion on the environment was the influx of the Greek Cypriot refugees who had to be accommodated in the southern part of the island, controlled by the government of the Republic of Cyprus. The negative longterm effects of the Cyprus crisis on the ecosystem can be considered severe for reasons that will become clear.

The economy of Cyprus suffered a major disruption in the aftermath of the invasion. Most of the tourist areas of the island and a large portion of its agricultural land came under Turkish military control. However, after that initial shock, the economy on the Greek Cypriot side of the divide began to recover so quickly that some called it "miraculous."[5] This economic miracle was brought about by a combination of factors, such as the efficient use of foreign aid, Cyprus's central location with good communication and transportation systems, the crisis in neighboring Lebanon that shifted the headquarters of offshore companies to Cyprus, and governmental policies that encouraged economic development and recovery. Most important, Cyprus enjoyed a well-trained, literate labor force. Greek Cypriots pride themselves on their business acumen, their work ethic, and their high levels of educational attainment. It is worth noting that the number of high school graduates attending colleges and universities is comparable to that in the United States and Canada.

The single-minded push toward economic recovery and prosperity was a matter for immediate survival for Greek Cypriots as it prevented a mass exodus from the island. A small population like that of Cyprus could easily be absorbed by Canada, Australia, Greece, and the United States where Greek Cypriots have strong ethnic connections. Prosperity kept Greek Cypriots at home while the poverty and lack of economic opportunity that plagued the occupied north sent thousands of Turkish Cypriots overseas.

The rapid economic development came at a high environmental price. For example, hotels to accommodate the ever-increasing number of tourists were built one after another along the few remaining beaches without much concern about the longterm impact of such construction on the ecosystem. The most dramatic example of such an unregulated, free-for-all development is the case of Ayia Napa, once a picturesque fishing village at the southeastern part of the island. In a matter of a few years, it lost all traces of its local identity with congested streets and "sardined" apartments, luxury hotels next to its sandy beaches, and noisy discotheques and bars at every street corner. Hardly anything of the local culture remained. Ayia Napa is an extreme case of what the rest of Cyprus might become if sustainable environmental and cultural policies are not immediately implemented to save a beautiful Mediterranean island for the benefit of present and future generations.

The automobile is another environmental hazard on a small island. Ownership of private automobiles in 1997 reached a high of 260,000. During the same year, the total number of all motorized vehicles in a population of 650,000 reached 472,000! With so many vehicles on congested roads, there were pressures for expanded highways which cut through agricultural and scenic parts of the island and polluted the atmosphere with leaded gasoline and diesel fumes. The local ecological movement has been too weak to offer any meaningful resistance against this onslaught on the environment. It required the intervention of Greenpeace, the international environmental organization, to ring the alarm as it tries to rescue the Akamas peninsula, for example, at the western corner of the island, a pristine nature refuge. Unregulated and rampant economic development has been causing irreversible damage to the island's ecology.

As threatening as the unchecked development may be, it pales by comparison to the potentially devastating impact on the future of Cyprus posed by the depletion of its underwater resources owing to a chronic problem with rainfall and inadequate snowfall on the Troodos mountains. The Greenhouse effect could be catastrophic for a warm island like Cyprus. For example, at the end of 1998, in the middle of the rainy season, the many dams constructed as a solution to the water problem held only 5 percent of capacity, leading the government to impose draconian impromptu ad hoc measures such as having the water pipes open only three times a week and only for a few hours. "The government," wrote a local English language paper, sounding the alarm of the water problem, "should halt all arms purchases and use the money to wage an environmentally sound war against the *real* enemy. Otherwise, the dreams for this island's bright future threaten to blow away in the dust of drought."[6]

What is the gist of the environmental crisis? The ongoing Cyprus problem with the military threats posed by the presence of the Turkish army has kept the society from pursuing a more carefully monitored economic development. The all-consuming attention of the president of the republic, the government, the political parties, the legislators, and the press to the "Cyprus problem" has left other sectors of society undeveloped. Attention was given exclusively to immediate survival in the face of overwhelming military threats. In doing so the social and cultural infrastructure atrophied, exposing the society to unfettered global economic forces that proved detrimental to an unprotected environment, perhaps undermining the quality of life on the island for future generations of Cypriots. The question that every Cypriot must ask is what kind of poetry, literature, art, popular culture, and lifestyle can emerge, nurtured and sustained within a devastated natural environment?

RESPONSE: STRUGGLES TO SURVIVE CULTURALLY

A Greek Cypriot View

Regardless of party divisions, disagreements, and conflicts, there has been a consensus among Greek Cypriots of what constitutes, under the circumstances, an acceptable solution to the Cyprus problem that could guarantee their longterm survival. They have remained committed to this position since the Turkish invasion in 1974. Its key elements are outlined below.

Return of Refugees to Their Homes

It is a fundamental demand of Greek Cypriots that returning to their homes is an inalienable human right. In the words of Cypriot ambassador to the United States Mrs. Erato Marcoullis, "How can we speak of democracy and building democratic institutions when a country is forcibly divided, and a foreign occupying army is preventing citizens from exercising their most fundamental human rights?"[7] For Greek Cypriots no permanent solution to the Cyprus problem is possible without accommodating the demand to return home. For a small face-to-face society like Cyprus, a village or a town is not simply a place of residence but a home that provides a sense of community, a sense of who one is, and continuity with the past. The town or the village is the reference point that informs a person of his or her primary identity. A whole generation of Greek Cypriots whose parents are refugees and who were born after the invasion still consider home their parents' village or town without ever having been there. This identification, taught by the refugee parents themselves, is systematically cultivated in the schools lest the new generation forget.

Return of Settlers to Turkey

Greek Cypriots fear that the settlers are displacing the Turkish Cypriots with whom they share common experiences from their long centuries of living next to each other. Furthermore, the settlers are viewed as totally foreign, a ploy of Turkey to manipulate the population dynamics on the island for its expansionist policies. With such a policy, Greek Cypriots believe, Turkey indicates that it seeks no solution to the problem but prefers the continuation of the division. Ammunition for such a belief is given by the political leadership of Turkey who miss no chance to state that the Cyprus problem has been solved with Turkey's "peace operation" in 1974.

Withdrawal of the Turkish Troops

Since the 1974 invasion, the Cyprus conflict is no longer between Greek Cypriots and Turkish Cypriots but between two neighboring states. From the point of view of Greek Cypriots, the issue is not the inability of two ethnic groups to live in peace but the violation of Cyprus' sovereignty by

Turkey through an invasion and occupation of their country. A solution then must include the withdrawal of the occupation forces.

The Cypriot government has repeatedly proposed the replacement of all foreign troops with an international force that both sides could trust. This force would have a mandate to keep order internally and protect the society externally. In addition, they proposed the total demilitarization of the island including the dismantling of all local militia including the Greek Cypriot National Guard. All moneys spent on the National Guard would then be diverted for use by the international military force and for further economic development.

Establishment of a Bizonal Federal Republic

After the Turkish invasion, it became clear to Greek Cypriots that *Enosis* was an unrealizable dream, a dead issue. Therefore, in 1977, the late Archbishop Makarios, as president of Cyprus, and Rauf Denktash, the Turkish Cypriot leader, reached a tentative agreement on principle to work for the establishment of a federal, bizonal, bicommunal republic. This agreement was doomed from the moment it was signed. Each side interpreted the meaning of "federation" in radically different and contradictory ways. The Greeks understood "federation" to mean that each ethnic group would have control of its zone, the size of which should be close to the population ratio. This "bizonality" must function within the context of one sovereign state with a strong central government. Each citizen should be guaranteed the three freedoms; the right to move freely anywhere on the island, the right to settle anywhere, and the right to own property anywhere within the federal state.

A Turkish Cypriot View

The Turkish Cypriot leadership, backed by the Turkish military, has rejected all of the above positions of the Greek Cypriots and has pursued its own goals and objectives, which can be summarized as follows.

No Return of Refugees

Whereas Greek Cypriots fear Turkey next door and the possible takeover of the rest of the island by the Turkish army, the Turkish Cypriots fear domination by the Greek Cypriots and their potential reduction to the position of second-class citizens. Turkish Cypriot leader Rauf Denktash routinely claims that the ultimate aim of Greek Cypriots is to unite the island with Greece. "The essence of the problem," he has repeatedly stated, "was Greek Cypriot usurpation of Turkish Cypriot rights by claiming sole ownership of the whole island."[8]

As in other similar conflicts, the contestants selectively remember only the hurts that the other side has inflicted upon them, never the hurts committed against the other side. The fact of the matter is that, during the last two years of British rule and again during the violent years of ethnic strife in the 1960s, extremist elements from both communities poisoned relations by committing atrocities against members of the other group. Turkish Cypriots focus on the atrocities committed against them at that time, and Greek Cypriots focus on atrocities committed against them by the invading Turkish army in 1974. For these reasons the Turkish Cypriot leadership has refused any return of the refugees regardless of guarantees of safety and security offered by the international community.

Permanent Presence of the Turkish Army

When Turkey invaded Cyprus, the U.S. Congress imposed an arms embargo on Turkey and demanded that the troops be removed and constitutional order be reestablished. The embargo was eventually lifted, but the troops are still there. Turkish Cypriots view the presence of the Turkish army on Cyprus as vital to their security; the Greeks consider it the source of their insecurity and their possible elimination as a community. Having overwhelming military superiority, Turkey refuses to remove its army in spite of repeated calls by the United Nations and other international organizations to do so. Turkey claims that the island is of paramount strategic importance.

Lifting of the Economic Embargo

After the invasion, the Republic of Cyprus, as the internationally recognized government, imposed an economic embargo on the occupied north to prevent the illegal exploitation of Greek Cypriot property by Turkey and the Turkish Cypriots. It is one of the few leverages that the militarily weak republic has at its disposal. This embargo, however, worked like a double-edged knife cutting on both sides. On one hand, it was an understandable reaction on the part of a government having to face one-third of its population being displaced by the Turkish army. On the other hand, it prevented any economic exchanges between the two sides. Such exchanges might have created conditions that could have prevented the rigid separation of the two ethnic groups that developed into a key policy of Turkey and the Turkish Cypriot leadership.

Recognition of the Turkish Republic of Northern Cyprus

In 1983 the Turkish Cypriot leadership declared independence and the establishment of a new state as a way of forcing Turkish plans on confederation. This move was based on the belief, strongly adhered to by the Turkish Cypriot leadership, that Greeks and Turks cannot live together within the same state. Therefore, Turkish Cypriots must have their own state, which will be guaranteed permanently by the presence of the Turkish troops. The declaration of independence, recognized by no state of the world except Turkey, is considered by foreign diplomats and United Nations mediators as a major blow to finding a peaceful solution to the Cyprus problem. In fact it is seen as another step in the absorption of the north by Turkey. "For the first time, a NATO member with a large United States subsidy would actually be digesting the physical territory of a small neighbor."[9]

Two Different Strategies

To pursue their contradictory objectives, the Greek Cypriots and the Turkish Cypriots (in reality, Turkish at this point) have followed various strategies. Militarily the underdog, the Greek Cypriots have focused on strengthening the international status of the Republic of Cyprus, which is recognized as the only legitimate state on the island. Therefore, they have made this political advantage the cornerstone of their "defence" policy. As a result, Cyprus, although a small country, has thirty-five embassies all over the world. (Malta, another Mediterranean island republic, has three.) Such costly investment for the "internationalization" of the Cyprus problem has borne fruit as it keeps Cyprus an active, viable member of the United Nations, which has monitored the peace on Cyprus since 1964. In the words of one Western diplomat, "Cyprus should be in the *Guinness Book of Records*. No place on this planet has so many emissaries, envoys and Excellencies per capita as Cyprus has."[10] At the same time, one has to ask, for how long can a small island republic, numerically the size of a New York neighborhood, be able to sustain such high-profile, international participation and presence before it becomes economically and politically overextended and overexhausted?

A central part of this policy of internationalization is the effort to become a full member of the European Union. It is believed that with such membership Cyprus will have a better chance of longterm survival. It would be more problematic for Turkey to attack a member state of the European Union. It is important to note that Turkey too is a candidate country for accession to the European Union, although it faces problems because of its poor economic and human rights record. Turkey, however, has shown no willingness to make a compromise on Cyprus, which will be included in the next enlargement of the European Union. It should also be noted that, as of January 2000, the Turkish Cypriots are not participating in any accession negotiations with the European Union and threaten to integrate fully the occupied north with Turkey.

In addition to the policy of uniting with Europe, the Cyprus Republic has placed its fragile military security in the hands of "mother" Greece. For example, the head of the Cypriot National Guard is a mainland Greek general. Furthermore, Cyprus and Greece follow a policy of "integrated defense dogma," meaning that an attack on Cyprus would mean automatic war with Greece. Of course, the very fact that Greece is so far away makes this integrated defense dogma questionable in terms of its practical effectiveness. Greek Cypriots, however, feel that only Greece can be relied on in case of a military emergency, and Greece's resolve to protect Cyprus is seen as a deterrence to Turkey. Furthermore, the Cyprus government has embarked on a program to fortify this integrated defense dogma by a desperate and expensive, multimillion dollar program of military buildup as a counterbalance to the heavily armed powerful Turkish army.

Nevertheless, in spite of the political tensions, so far Greece and Turkey have avoided a war over Cyprus because, in an odd way, even though they are traditional enemies, they are allies within the North Atlantic Treaty Organization (NATO) which was set up by the United States for the defense of Europe against the former Soviet Union. Both the United States and Europe have vested interests in preventing a war between two members of NATO. In fact, prior to the invasion of 1974, the United States intervened diplomatically twice to prevent a Greek-Turkish war from breaking out. In July 1974, however, as Kissinger pointed out in his memoirs, the Nixon White House was too preoccupied with Watergate to pay attention to the crisis that was brewing in Cyprus.

While Greek Cypriots have relied on Greece for military support, the Turkish Cypriots have relied exclusively on Turkey on all fronts: economic, military, political, and diplomatic. Furthermore, they have tried to forge close ties with Islamic countries with the aim of attaining recognition as a separate sovereign state. This move, however, has not borne fruit so far because these countries face problems with minorities of their own. Supporting secession in Cyprus would create a bad precedent for themselves.

Converging Interests

Certain preconditions appear to be clear if Greek Cypriots and Turkish Cypriots are to live in peace and survive as social and cultural entities on the same island. There is a paramount need for both Greek Cypriots and Turkish Cypriots to feel secure in their own homes. This is the most fundamental precondition for a lasting peace. So far, what was seen as security for one side generated insecurity for the other side. The Greek Cypriots feel insecure with Turkish troops on Cyprus while the Turkish Cypriots feel insecure without the military presence of Turkey. A mutual sense of security can be established only with the presence on the island of a third force, a neutral power that could guarantee the safety of all citizens. The two communities lived in peace and maintained close ties with each other when they did not fear that one side had a chance to dominate the other. For example, under British rule, before the outbreak of the anticolonial guerrilla movement in 1955, Greeks and Turks lived next to each other amicably for generations. Obviously one cannot advocate the reestablishment of British rule that many Greek Cypriots and few Turkish Cypriots blame for creating the divisions for its own colonial interests. But Greek Cypriots and Turkish Cypriots can join the European Union as one country and together agree on security arrangements that would involve European states both ethnic groups can trust. That would involve the dismantling of all local militia. To make such an arrangement possible, Europe must at some point admit Turkey itself to the European Union so that it has a motive to be more conciliatory over Cyprus.

Second, Greece and Turkey as traditional enemies, yet also as NATO allies, have long-standing disputes over the Aegean Sea. Cyprus in a very real sense became hostage to the dynamics of Greek-Turkish antagonism. Solving the Aegean problems and normalizing relations between Greece and Turkey will have a beneficial effect on the Cyprus problem. Here the United States (in cooperation with its European allies), as the only superpower and major arms supplier to both Greece and Turkey, can play a constructive mediation role in bringing about reconciliation.

Third, parallel to the above international preconditions for a possible solution, certain domestic preconditions are also called for. If Greeks and Turks are to live as members of the same society, a radically different political culture must emerge. So far, what has developed in Cyprus are two antagonistic nationalisms, one Greek and the other Turkish, which are perpetrated in schools, churches, popular culture, and nationalist rituals. For example, every July 20, the date of the invasion, Turkish Cypriots celebrate with parades and festivals. On the Greek side, there is mourning, anger, and sadness. April 1, the date of the launching in 1955 of the guerrilla war against the British for *Enosis* or union with Greece (a notion that Turks vehemently reject), is celebrated as a national holiday on the Greek side. The celebrations of one group are defeats of the other group. These mutually exclusive nationalist identities are systematically cultivated by extremists on both sides, a type of socialization that is not conducive to peace, cooperation, and ultimate survival. Therefore, radical educational reforms are needed on both sides to teach the younger generation those cultural elements of mutual understanding and respect that are essential for peaceful coexistence in a multicultural society. There is a need for both sides to admit publicly to atrocities committed by criminal, extremist elements of both groups during various crisis periods of the last forty years. This will have a cathartic, healing effect for both Greek Cypriots and Turkish Cypriots. Learning each other's language and culture is also an important ingredient for a progressive educational system that would serve the interests of all Cypriots rather than their respective nationalisms, as the case is today.

This can be done without threatening people's fundamental identities as Greeks and Turks.

Fourth, while diplomatic efforts are pursued for an overall solution, certain interim confidence-building measures are needed to overcome the wall of suspicion and separation. For example, Turkey, as a start, could allow the refugees of Famagusta, presently a ghost town, to return to their homes under United Nations control. In a reciprocal move, the Cyprus government could lift the economic embargo and allow trade between the two sides. This might create new economic bonds between the two sides that could displace the vested interests that have emerged and thrived because of the separation. The two communities could also cooperate in tackling the massive environmental problems, foremost of which is the water problem, the chronic drought that year by year threatens desertification of their common homeland.

Fifth, within the context of an effective solution, the influx of settlers from Turkey, which threatens both Greek Cypriots and Turkish Cypriots, must be stopped. Economic incentives must be implemented to repatriate most of them to Turkey. At the same time the standard of living of the Turkish Cypriots, which is far below that of the Greek Cypriots, must be brought up to the level of their compatriots in the south. The convergence of ethnicity with class inequities can undermine any solution no matter how fair and workable.

FOOD FOR THOUGHT

The conflict over Cyprus has been an intractable problem that has preoccupied the international community for several decades. It has repeatedly threatened the peace and stability of the Eastern Mediterranean by bringing Greece and Turkey to the brink of war and depriving generations of Cypriots of a peaceful, normal life.

Given the complexity of the problem, it is difficult to be optimistic that a comprehensive solution will be achieved soon, satisfying fully the demands and expectations of both sides. However, as Cyprus is preparing to join the European Union, more and more views are converging that the time has come for a long overdue settlement. The two communities are faced with a unique challenge and opportunity to resolve their differences, reunite their island, and become part of the European integration process, which can offer them the security and stability they have been longing for.

Given the realities of Cyprus—geography, economy, size, distribution of natural resources, demography, and the political failures of the past—a federal Cyprus with two ethnic zones seems to be a pragmatic way out of the stalemate. For a settlement to be lasting and viable, it should be sought through pacific means, evolutionary peaceful change, political and administrative adjustments, renovation of political thinking, and the cultivation of conciliatory attitudes. The entire population will be better off if the island ceases to be a place of arms and confrontation and the present status quo is replaced by a meaningful political order.

Questions

1. What are the threats faced by the Greek and Turkish Cypriots in their respective struggles for physical and cultural survival?
2. What do you think are the major obstacles, both domestic and international, that have prevented a solution to the Cyprus problem for so many decades?
3. Suppose you are a rational thinking Greek Cypriot. What policies would you want your government to implement (and why) in regard to Turkish Cypriots and Turkey and as relates to the environment? What if you are a Turkish Cypriot?
4. In what way has the location and size of Cyprus been a cause of its problems?
5. What should the role of the United States be in finding a solution to the Cyprus problem? In your answer consider that the United States is the only remaining superpower and it is an ally of and the major arms supplier to both Greece and Turkey.

NOTES

1. *The New York Times Almanac*, 1999, pp. 549, 554.
2. Henry Kissinger, *Years of Renewal* (New York: Simon & Schuster, 1999), 192.
3. Robert Stephens, *Cyprus: A Place of Arms* (New York: Praeger, 1966).
4. *Gunavdin*, January 14, 1986.
5. Demetrios Christodoulou, *Inside the Cyprus Miracle* (Minneapolis: University of Minnesota, Minnesota Mediterranean and East European Monographs, no. 2, 1992).
6. *Cyprus Mail*, February 2, 1999.
7. "Cyprus," Washington, D.C., embassy newsletter, April 1999.
8. *Kibris*, Northern Cyprus Monthly, January 1999.
9. Christopher Hitchens, "Block Aggression on a Divided Isle," *Los Angeles Times*, August 17, 1997.
10. *Cyprus Mail*, May 10, 1998.

RESOURCE GUIDE

Published Literature

Attalides, Michael. *Cyprus: Nationalism and International Politics*. New York: St. Martin's Press, 1979.

Durrell, Lawrence. *Bitter Lemons*. New York: Marlowe, 1996.

Hitchens, Christopher. *Hostage to History: Cyprus from the Ottomans to Kissinger*. New York: Verso, 1997.

Ioannides, Christos P. *In Turkey's Image: The Transformation of Occupied Cyprus into a Turkish Province*. New Rochelle, N.Y.: A. D. Caratzas, 1991.

Joseph, Joseph S. *Cyprus: Ethnic Conflict and International Politics*. New York: St. Martin's Press, 1997.

Kyriakides, Stanley. *Cyprus: Constitutionalism and Crisis Government*. Philadelphia: University of Pennsylvania Press, 1968.

Loizos, Peter. *The Heart Grown Bitter: A Chronicle of Cypriot War Refugees*. Cambridge, England: Cambridge University Press, 1981.

Markides, Kyriacos C. *The Rise and Fall of the Cyprus Republic*. New Haven, Conn.: Yale University Press, 1977.

Scherer, John. *Blocking the Sun: The Cyprus Conflict*. Minneapolis: University of Minnesota, Minnesota Mediterranean and East European Monographs, 1997.

Volkan, Vamik. *Cyprus: War and Adaptation*. Charlottesville: University Press of Virginia, 1979.

Films and Videos

Cyprus: History and Culture (1998). CD produced by the Cultural Division of the Ministry of Foreign Affairs of the Republic of Cyprus.

Our Love for Cyprus—Our Wall (1993). Film produced by ZDS (German Television, Channel 2) with Panikos Chrysanthou and Niyazi Kizilyurek.

WWW Sites

A comprehensive resource on the culture, politics, and economy of Cyprus.
http://windowoncyprus.com

A general overview of the history and culture of Cyprus and provides web indexes for the island and the republic.
http://www.ucy.cy/information/cyprus.html

The Web site of the Permanent Mission of the Republic of Cyprus at the United Nations.
http://www.undp.org./missions/cyprus

Covers relations of Cyprus with the European Union with emphasis on the accession negotiations.
http://www.Cyprus-eu.org.cy

A good source of news from the major news agency in Cyprus.
http://www.cyna.org.com

Organizations

Embassy of the Republic of Cyprus in the United States
2211 R Street, NW
Washington, D.C. 20008

Permanent Mission of the Republic of Cyprus to the United Nations
13 East 40th Street
New York, NY 10016

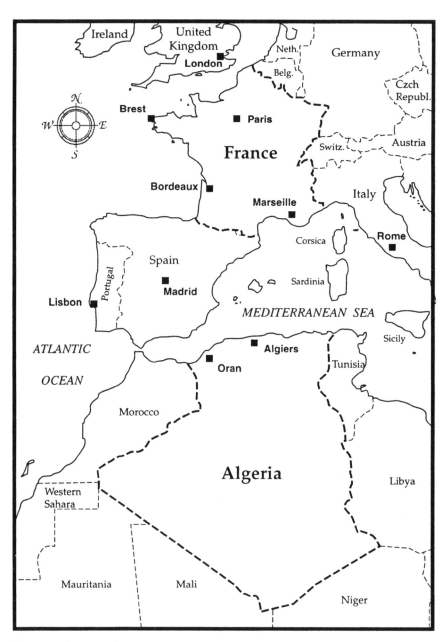

Courtesy of Mapcraft.

Chapter 5

The French Algerians
David Bloomberg

CULTURAL OVERVIEW

The People

The Algerian immigrants to France came from an arid environment to a wetter, more temperate climate with many industrial urban sites. France, a developed economic power, had colonized the North African nation from 1834 to 1962.

The history of Algerian immigration to France goes back to the beginning of the twentieth century, when Algeria was still a French colony. At that time, movement between Algeria and France was limited, despite a 1905 law ending the need for a special permit in order to travel between the two regions. Occasionally, North Africans were recruited to replace striking workers in France (who were often immigrants themselves), but the Algerian immigrant population in France still totaled only 5,000 in 1912. With the outbreak of World War I in 1914, this small group was gathered in the Bois de Boulogne (a forest on the outskirts of Paris) and forcibly repatriated. However, the European conflict, which lasted longer than anyone had expected, quickly resulted in a lack of workers for the French economy. As a result, the French government made an about-face and began actively recruiting colonial workers in 1915. When very few people accepted the offer to come to work in France, the government began drafting them into the workforce. Thus, in 1916 and 1917, 78,000 Algerians were forced to work in French factories, along with large numbers of workers from Morocco, Tunisia, Madagascar, and Indochina. Many others were drafted into the army. This large group of Algerians did not remain in France for long;

after the war, they were repatriated since their services were no longer needed by the mother country.

The number of Algerians in France soon began to rise again, however. French factory owners had come to realize during the war that Algerian workers provided a number of advantages over immigrants from Europe, most important, the ability to circulate freely between their homeland and France. For their part, the Algerian peasants had discovered that they could earn much more money working in French factories than they could toiling in the fields back home. Thus, the Algerian immigrant population quickly increased, from 45,000 in 1922 to over 100,000 in 1930. Nevertheless, in 1931, with only 3.2 percent of the immigrant population, it ranked a mere sixth on the list of the largest ethnic minorities in France. Even if Algerians formed only a small percentage of the total French immigrant population, the amount of mistrust and disdain they generated among French natives was certainly much greater. The words used to describe them during this period would hardly seem out of place today: primitive, violent, lazy, and lacking the necessary discipline to perform industrial work successfully. Even worse, it was claimed, there was no hope of ever integrating them into modern French society, because Islam, with its comprehensive regulations covering all aspects of daily life, prevented them from adopting a secular lifestyle. Considering this widespread attitude, it is hardly surprising that Algerian immigrants were the first in France to feel the effects of the Great Depression. As soon as economic times became hard, they were laid off and repatriated; their numbers were reduced by over 50 percent between 1932 and 1936. With the outbreak of World War II, all travel between Algeria and France came under strict government control and eventually was prohibited when the Allies began their invasion of the colony. When the fighting finally came to an end, only 22,000 Algerians remained in France.

After the war, France once again found herself with a severe manpower shortage and, as had been the case in 1918, she turned to her colonies to fill her hiring needs. Between 1947 and 1953, 740,000 Algerians arrived in France, according to immigration statistics, while 561,000 returned home—a net gain of 179,000 workers. There were some important differences between this new generation of Algerian immigrants and the ones that had preceded it. This new generation was, on the average, younger and better skilled. Its members tended to bring their families with them to France, implying that their departures from Algeria were permanent (or at least of long duration). A study made by the French Ministry of the Interior in August 1953 counted 5,000 families and 11,000 children among the country's Muslim population.

The Algerian War of Independence and Its Aftermath

On November 1, 1954, the Algerian War of Independence began. Contrary to what might have been expected, the outbreak of hostilities actually caused more Algerians to leave for France. According to census figures, the number of Algerians in France increased from 211,000 to 350,000 between 1954 and 1962, the year the Algerian war ended. This surge was largely due to the effects of the war on Algerian society in the rural areas where the fighting had destroyed agricultural lands and the peasant lifestyle. The war also was responsible for a great deal of violence in France. Two Algerian pro-independence groups were active in France—the Front de Libération Nationale and the Mouvement Nationaliste Algérien—and their intense rivalry resulted in 4,000 deaths and 12,000 injuries between 1956 and the war's end in 1962. Nor did the violence occur only between the immigrants themselves. On October 17, 1961, between 30,000 and 50,000 Algerian protesters were marching through the streets of Paris when the police confronted them. According to some sources, 200 died and an equal number were "missing"—their bodies were later found floating in the Seine.

After more than seven years of fighting, the French government and the Algerian revolutionaries agreed to the Evian peace accords in March 1962. The assurance of rights for nationals of the two countries was a primary concern of the document. Article 7 grants Algerian immigrants the same rights as those of French citizens, with the exception of political rights. Article 11 assures Algerian immigrants freedom of circulation between France and their native country. However, the Evian accords previewed little with regard to the control of Algerian immigration toward France. Such a measure would soon be proven necessary, as the economic devastation of Algeria (as a result of the war) caused a net increase of 46,000 within France's Algerian population during a two-month period at the end of 1962. In response to the continued migration, France and Algeria signed another agreement in early 1964, which previews the establishment of quarterly immigration quotas based on the available workforce in Algeria and job availability in France. When this failed to stop the influx, a third accord was signed at the end of 1968, which limits the freedom of circulation that had been guaranteed at Evian. Finally, in September 1973, Algeria suspended all immigration toward France. Ten months later, France stopped welcoming new immigrants (from anywhere, not just North Africa), including those who were reuniting with family, although this category was reapproved a year later. These measures were unable to completely stop Algerian immigration, but they did succeed in slowing it down.

Algerians looking toward France. Photo by Nadia Bendrallal.

Muslim Immigrants in France Today

In 1995 it was estimated that there were 1,953,000 immigrants living in France—3.38 percent of the country's population—including 619,900 from Algeria, 584,700 from Morocco, 207,500 from Tunisia, and 201,500 from Turkey. The total immigrant population from North Africa, legal and illegal immigrants and immigrants who are now naturalized French citizens, is approximately 2,453,000. (Morocco and Tunisia are former French protectorates that gained their independence in the 1950s.) In addition to the approximately two million Muslim noncitizens residing in France, there are more than 200,000 naturalized French citizens of North African origin. Like their noncitizen counterparts, this latter group consists mostly of Sunni Muslims, adherents of the majority branch of Islam. As for their geographical dispersal, the majority of Muslim immigrants can be found in the poorer suburbs of most major French cities, including Paris, Lyon, and Marseilles.

THREATS TO SURVIVAL

Religious Trends

Suppression of the religious aspect in their lives is no longer difficult for the North African population, many of whom have become, since immigrating to France, "Ramadan Muslims" (minimal practitioners of Islam who observe only the major commandments, such as fasting during the month of Ramadan).[1] This is particularly the case for Algerians, of all ages and of both sexes, who tend to be the least religious of all Muslim immigrant groups—a serious challenge to the claim that Islam prevents Algerian immigrants from fully integrating into French society. In a 1979 study, only 11 percent of Algerians reported going to a mosque or other religious place (such as a small permanent prayer room, common in Muslim immigrant communities) on a regular basis, compared to 34 percent of Mandés, an ethnic group from sub-Saharan Africa that was the most devout in this respect.[2] Similarly, 48 percent of Algerians claimed to either not have or not practice a religion, a figure higher than that reported for immigrants from Morocco, Turkey, and several sub-Saharan African tribes. The one area in which the study found that Algerians were continuing to observe the dictates of Islam was that of dietary proscriptions: 74 percent fasted during Ramadan, the same percentage abstained from eating pork, and 63 percent refused to drink alcohol. Even this high level of observance was lower than that of all other Muslim immigrant groups surveyed, with the exception of the Turks. Furthermore, among the second generation, observance of dietary proscriptions has served more as a form of cultural connection than as a means of pleasing Allah. Finally, the fact that most of the Algerian immigrants surveyed, even of the first generation, admitted to having eaten non-*hallal* meat (does not conform to Muslim dietary restrictions) at least once in their lives is a clear indication that even dietary proscriptions have given way to convenience and the dictates of modern French society.

Current Events and Conditions

Economic Difficulties

In the economic sphere, Algerians have tended to be less successfully integrated, unless one considers their sharing in France's high level of unemployment to be an example of successful integration. Between 1973 and 1982, due to the combined effects of reduced economic growth and the modernization of production methods, France lost a total of 654,000 jobs for nonskilled and semiskilled workers. Almost half of those left unemployed were immigrants (of all nationalities), even though this group accounted for only between 9 percent and 11 percent of the total salaried workforce. For Algerians, the situation was even worse; although they represented only 22 percent of the active immigrant population in 1982, they made up 32 percent of its unemployed members.[3] Several reasons contributed to this discrepancy. In part, Algerian workers generally occupied the least-skilled jobs in the industries that were most susceptible to economic downturns. It was also a result of the high percentage of youth, often poorly educated, among Algerian immigrants; in 1987, 41 percent of the population was under the age of twenty. Yet, without a doubt, French prejudices have also played a part in creating such a high level of unemployment among Algerians.

The Front National

These various factors—higher-than-average crime rate, competition for scarce jobs (even if Algerians are overrepresented among the ranks of the unemployed), and adherence to certain Islamic codes of behavior, such as dietary proscriptions—have been fervently seized upon over the last fifteen years by the anti-immigrant political party known as the Front National (FN). Voter surveys have shown that immigration and insecurity motivate 59 percent and 55 percent, respectively, of FN supporters nationwide, while a 1985 study in Grenoble recorded the values of 67 percent and 77 percent for these two motivating factors.[4] Other data collected in Grenoble are equally revealing of the views of FN supporters with regard to immigrants, particularly Algerians. Ninety percent of FN voters believed that there were too many North Africans in France, an opinion held by only 55 percent of the overall electorate. With regard to the integration of Algerians into French society, a 1988 national study found that 55 percent of the population considered Algerians to be the most difficult ethnic minority to assimilate. In the Grenoble study, FN voters were 22 percent more likely than the average voter to feel that the process of integrating Algerians had been unsuccessful, a greater discrepancy than for any other ethnic group. Finally, FN sympathizers were much more supportive than the average Grenoble voter of radical solutions to the perceived immigrant problem: 53 percent of the former wanted large numbers of immigrant workers to be forcibly repatriated, and 73 percent felt that "in order for France to remain French it was necessary to make a distinction between the true French and the others" (positions that garnered only 14 percent and 20 percent, respectively, of overall support).[5]

The Front National is led by the intelligent and charismatic Jean-Marie Le Pen. His political manifesto, *Pour la France* (For France), is filled with complaints about the effects already produced by immigration, the dire consequences of allowing the size of the immigrant population to continue to grow (through natural reproduction), and extreme solutions for preventing this impending doom. The problems, Le Pen contends, posed by a large immigrant population are many. Africans are responsible for almost 20 percent of all serious crimes, and their presence worsens the French unemployment situation. In addition, the presence of immigrants threatens the future of the French nation, since their growing numbers will affect France's foreign policy and force changes in the school curriculum. The acquisition of French nationality simply to ease relations with the police or given automatically to second-generation Algerians who do not want it causes a diminution in the honor attached to this important right. Finally, and most alarming, the French risk becoming a minority in their own country. The solution, according to Le Pen, is for the French government to adopt a number of restrictive measures that he groups under the banner of "National Preference," including revision of the nationality code, abandonment of multicultural education, reservation of social services to French nationals, expulsion of illegal immigrants and those with a criminal record, and government-financed repatriation of unemployed immigrants. By means of inflammatory rhetoric, Le Pen and the Front National have attempted to thwart the process of integrating Algerian immigrants into French society.

The Headscarf Affair

It is in this context that the headscarf has been thrust into the limelight of French politics in recent years. A significant number of young Muslim women, though by no means the majority of them, have chosen to wear traditional Islamic headscarves on a regular basis as a way of asserting their independence vis-à-vis both their families and French society, which tends to stereotype them into the category of the gentile *beurette*. As many of these young women are high school or university students, this means wearing headscarves during classes. This action is regarded by many in French society, including a significant proportion of educators, as a direct challenge to the sacred French principle of secular public schools. The fact that French law forbids the display of religious symbols only by teachers, while permitting it for students (as long as they do not use such insignia as a means of proselytism), has been largely ignored. The problem has been compounded by the fact that teachers in suburban schools with a large proportion of North African students already feel disheartened by the lack of respect they receive from students, the poor educational performance of their students compared to those from schools with many French natives, and the need to spend much of their time transmitting French culture to students—a task seen as the responsibility of parents—rather than teaching traditional subjects. The wearing of headscarves by young Muslim women is thus regarded as another blow to their identity as educators. Furthermore, since headscarves are associated with the repression of women in traditional Islamic societies, many teachers feel an obligation to liberate their veiled students, freeing them from the oppression under which they are imagined to be living. Thus, misunderstanding as to the significance of the headscarf in the eyes of the girls who wear it, combined with insufficient knowledge of the French laws on secularism, has created widespread political debate centering on the place of Muslim immigrants within French society.

The Citizenship Debate

Muslim, and particularly Algerian, immigrants have been at the center of the political debate concerning changes to French citizenship law. This discussion began in the early 1980s, when Algerian immigrants began complaining about the French citizenship that had been automatically bestowed upon those of the second generation. French citizenship law is based on the principle of double *jus soli* (a person born on French soil to parents also born on French soil is automatically French from birth), a notion contained in articles 23 and 44 of the French nationality code. Article 23 unconditionally ascribes citizenship at birth to third-generation immigrants, while article 44 attributes it to second-generation immigrants at the age of eighteen, unless, during the preceding year, they have chosen not to receive it. However, due to the fact that many first-generation Algerian immigrants were born in Algeria during the period of French colonization, their French-born children were considered, for citizenship purposes, as third-generation immigrants. Considering the long and bloody war they had fought for independence, it is hardly surprising that this automatic bestowal of French citizenship angered many Algerian parents, who did not want their children to belong to the former colonial power. In 1981 the Socialist-led French government began conducting negotiations with the Algerian government and, in 1984, an agreement was reached on military service for dual nationals, but the citizenship question remained unresolved.

Concurrent with these negotiations, the parties of the French political right—the moderate Rassemblement pour la Republique (RPR) and Union pour la Democratie Francaise (UDF) and the extreme Front National (FN)—began clamoring for a change in French citizenship law, arguing that its bestowal on second-generation Algerians should be voluntary and conducted in a manner that would restore honor to the process. In campaigns for the legislative elections of March 1986, these parties made reform of articles 23 and 44—and hence of *jus soli*—an important part of their platforms. However, when, after being returned to power, they began looking into possible modifications, the parties of the right encountered certain difficulties. Article 23 could not be modified because it would remove the easiest way for French natives to prove their status as citizens and would amount to a denial of French colonization of Algeria. The government did, however, propose to modify article 44 by making French citizenship contingent on a declaration of will made between the ages of sixteen and twenty and the reciprocal acceptance of that declaration by the French state. Unfortunately, this proposal was spurned by the French public, which considered it a veiled attempt to restrict access to citizenship, and the government was forced to withdraw the idea. Instead, it created a special commission, chaired by Marceau Long, which, in January 1988, submitted a list of proposed changes. These recommendations served as the basis for

the 1993 law that, indeed, made citizenship contingent on a formal declaration. With regard to Algerians, the law declared that a child born in
France to parents born in Algeria prior to 1962 would be French only if
the parents had resided in France for at least five years before the time of
the birth. While this modification did not help all Algerian immigrants, it
was beneficial for many, so that some good did indeed come out of the
long and heated debates on French citizenship law.

RESPONSE: STRUGGLES TO SURVIVE CULTURALLY

Adoption of the French Lifestyle

A look at the lifestyles of young French Algerians offers hope for the
government policy of successfully integrating all immigrants into French
society. Second-generation Algerians in France today lead lives very similar
to their native French counterparts (the same can be said for other second-
generation Muslim immigrants, as well). In large part, this is due to the
fact that, unlike their parents, who continue to entertain the hope of one
day returning to Algeria, young Algerians consider France to be their home,
since it is there that they were born and raised. The fact that Algeria has
been besieged by political chaos for several years only reinforces this con-
viction. A certain proof of the connection to France felt by young Algerians
can be seen in their growing acceptance of French citizenship, which now-
adays has less association with a rejection of faith and of ancestry. There
has also been a noticeable increase in the number of mixed marriages involving Algerians. In the numerous cases in which the partner is a native
French person, there is double evidence of successful integration, since the
decision to marry a non-Muslim, in violation of precepts of the Quran,
signifies the suppression of a person's Islamic identity to its secular French
counterpart.

Job Diversification

Algerian responses to economic difficulties have varied tremendously.
Some workers, who either have lost their jobs or are expecting to lose them
soon, have chosen to open up their own businesses. In 1987 North Africans
owned over 10 percent of the retail stores in Paris and 12 percent of the
businesses falling within the café-restaurant-hotel category. As such, they
comprised an astounding 80 percent of Parisian immigrant retailers. Another vocation that has become popular is that of the artisan, although
Southern Europeans still vastly outnumber Algerians in most areas of craft
production. Taxi driving, a traditional haven of immigrants, has also at-
tracted large numbers of unemployed Algerians. This profession offers a
number of advantages, including tremendous flexibility, reasonable finan-

cial rewards, and a very minimal skills requirement. It thus provides an attractive alternative to the manual labor that second-generation Algerians tend to detest with a vengeance. Yet another option has been to accept one of the new jobs created by numerous youth associations with the assistance of the government. These positions, which tend to be of a temporary nature only, include custodial work, vehicle repair, and cultural performance. Finally, some Algerians, frustrated with their economic and social situations, have turned to crime. As a whole, immigrants represented 27 percent of French inmates in 1983, up 7 percent from three years before; as was the case with unemployment, North Africans were once again overrepresented within the immigrant subgroup.

Re-Islamization

The ranting of Le Pen and the Front National, although so far unsuccessful in attempting to thwart the process of integrating Algerian immigrants into French society, has provoked a certain amount of re-Islamization. Before examining this phenomenon, however, it is necessary to note that the young Algerians (and other North Africans) who are part of this movement tend to be students or workers who are well integrated into French society, which shows that the two identities—French and Muslim—are not mutually exclusive. This caveat having been made, several explanations can be advanced for the reason for the emergence of this trend toward re-Islamization (other than FN provocation). It concerns, to a large extent, a search for identity and the attempt to reconcile Algerian ancestry with everyday life in France. This often includes a wish by young Algerians to satisfy the concerns of their parents regarding their identity. In addition, there is the desire to distance oneself from the Algerian government, which tries to control the lives of its nationals abroad, by reappropriating Islam. Dissatisfaction with the Beur movement as a path to full integration into French society is also an important cause. (The Beur movement was founded in the early 1980s to combat the inequality faced daily by Arab immigrants, but it soon turned to violence as a means of expressing the anger of its members.) Finally, the performance of important social functions, such as educational tutoring and drug prevention, by Islamic youth associations is crucial to the support they receive.

Because of the constraints placed on them by their family and by their ethnic community, the trend toward re-Islamization has been particularly important for young Muslim women in France. In traditional Muslim societies, the place of women is in the home; the public space is the domain of men. Since the late 1970s, this idea has been challenged in France by the growing number of young Muslim women who are receiving an education and accepting jobs outside the home, a process that is often easier for Muslim women than for the men due to French society's better perception of the women. Yet integration does not come without a cost, which, in the case of Muslim women, is an increase in repression on the part of their families. Women, and particularly daughters, are seen as representing the honor of the family, and extended stays outside the home risk calling that honor into question. When family honor is deemed to have been tarnished, the consequences can be brutal, as demonstrated by the decision of a young Turk to murder his sister, with parental approval, on the night of August 13, 1994, after she had dishonored the family by dating young men. Although such murders are unusual, lesser forms of punishment are common and can be found among the Algerian population, as well. As one observer has noted, "The more the men [in an immigrant group] find themselves belittled and subjected to humiliating measures within society, the more they have a tendency to discharge their aggression on the weakest members of their own family, the women."[6] Considering that Algerians are the most despised foreign population in France, their reaction to family dishonor is likely to be severe. For those Algerian women who are determined to free themselves from familial control and lead a life outside the home, two options are possible. The first of these is to reject their Algerian heritage completely by fully assimilating French norms, working in the public sphere, and moving in with a young Frenchman. Although this option was quite popular during the 1970s and 1980s, it is no longer feasible because the tight job market makes most young Algerian women dependent on their families for financial support. The other option, which has gained in popularity in recent years, is to adopt a strict Islamic lifestyle that allows a young woman to assert her independence through such statements as "I obey Allah and not my father" and "I am pure, thus I can stay outside the home and work there without anyone being able to suspect me of lacking modesty."[7]

FOOD FOR THOUGHT

Large numbers of North African immigrants have been present in France since the beginning of the twentieth century, yet despite the time elapsed they still face many problems in their adopted homeland. They have been partially assimilated, so that they have lost much of their cultural and religious identity, yet they still face persistent racism from a large part of the native French population. The primary victims of this incomplete integration have been North African youth, who genuinely want to be considered French but cannot because of the color of their skin. As a result, many have returned to their Islamic roots, but even this strategy has presented problems because the French public is not yet willing to tolerate public demonstrations of Islamic belief. Until the majority of French are truly willing to accept the presence of North African immigrants in their midst, the latter will unfortunately continue to suffer the economic, political, and social disadvantages that have plagued minorities throughout history.

Questions

1. Why are Algerian immigrants less accepted than those from other former French colonies, such as sub-Saharan Africa or Indochina?

2. Is the "headscarf affair" really about secular schools or discrimination against Muslims? Does the fact that French students are allowed to wear crosses and skullcaps change your opinion?

3. In 1984 France and Algeria signed an agreement removing the need for dual nationals to perform military service in both countries, following public opposition to the burden this placed on French males of Algerian descent. In 1993, following more opposition, French citizenship law was changed, but not to the benefit of all Algerian immigrants. Is the French government truly interested in helping Algerian immigrants or does it simply follow public opinion?

4. What cultural and historical factors might account for the differing degrees of religious observance to be found among Algerian and Turkish immigrants, on the one hand, and Muslim immigrants from sub-Saharan Africa, on the other? Can a similar distinction be made between the levels of religious observance of these groups in their native lands?

5. Algerian emigrants to France following World War II were better skilled than their predecessors, yet their children are often poorly educated and possess low-skilled jobs (many of which were lost during the recession of the 1970s and 1980s). Did post–World War II immigrants possess only a relative advantage over their predecessors while occupying low-skilled jobs themselves, or are young Algerian immigrants today less skilled than their parents? If the latter is the case, what accounts for this loss of skills? Finally, are the poor educational levels and low skills of young Algerian immigrants responsible for their high crime rate?

NOTES

1. Elisabeth Lévy, "L'Islam est-il soluble dans la République?," *Marianne*, March 9–15, 1998, p. 52.

2. David Assouline and Mehdi Lallaoui, "Troisième période: 1945 à nos jours," in *Un siècle d'immigrations en France* (Paris: Syros, 1997).

3. Ibid.

4. Nonna Mayer and Pascal Perrineau, eds., *Le Front national à découvert* (Paris: Presses de Sciences Po, 1996), 229–33.

5. Ibid.

6. Farhad Khosrokhavar, *L'islam des jeunes* (Paris: Flammarion, 1997), 118–21.

7. Ibid., 124–25.

RESOURCE GUIDE

Published Literature

History of North African Immigration

Amar, Marianne, and Pierre Milza. *L'immigration en France au XXe siècle*. Paris: Armand Colin, 1990.

Assouline, David, and Mehdi Lallaoui. "Troisième période: 1945 à nos jours." In *Un siècle d'immigrations en France*. Paris: Syros, 1997.

Social Conditions of North African Immigrants

Al Djazaïri, Selim. "Les Maghrebins en France." *Sou'al*, September 1987.

Khosrokhavar, Farhad. *L'islam des jeunes*. Paris: Flammarion, 1997.

Lévy, Elisabeth. "L'Islam est-il soluble dans la République?" *Marianne*, March 9–15, 1998.

Tribalat, Michèle. *Faire France: Une grande enquête sur les immigrés et leurs enfants*. Paris: Editions la Découverte, 1995.

The Front National (FN)

Le Pen, Jean-Marie. *Pour La France: Programme du Front national*. Paris, Albatross, c1985.

Mayer, Nonna, and Pascal Perrineau, eds. *Le Front national à découvert*. Paris: Presses de Sciences Po, 1996.

The Citizenship Debate

Brubaker, Rogers. *Citizenship and Nationhood in France and Germany*. London: Harvard University Press, 1992.

Weil, Patrick. *Mission d'étude des législations de la nationalité et de l'immigration*. Paris: La Documentation Française, 1997.

Films and Videos

Battaglia di Algieri (The Battle of Algiers), directed by Gillo Pontecorvo (1965).

Salut Cousin! (Hi Cousin!), directed by Merzak Allouache (1996).

WWW Sites

ArabNet
www.arab.net/algeria

Minorities at Risk Project at the University of Maryland
www.bsos.umd.edu/cidcm/mar/frmuslim.htm

Organizations

L'Institut du Monde Arabe (Institute of the Arab World, Paris)
1 rue de fosses-saint-bernard
75236 Paris Cedex 05
France
Web site: www.imarabe.org

Middle East Research & Information Project
1500 Massachusetts Ave. NW, Suite 119
Washington, D.C. 20005
E-mail: merip@igc.apc.org

SOS-Racisme
Web site: www.sosraccisme.org

Chapter 6

The Macedonian Minority in Northern Greece
Loring M. Danforth

CULTURAL OVERVIEW

The People

Among the two million inhabitants of Greek Macedonia in north-central Greece live somewhere between 20,000 and 50,000 people known as "local Macedonians" who are concentrated in the regions of Kastoria and Florina near the borders of Albania and the Republic of Macedonia. These local Macedonians are Orthodox Christians, like the vast majority of Greeks, but in addition to speaking Greek, most of them speak a regional dialect of the Macedonian language, a South Slavic language similar to both Serbo-Croatian and Bulgarian, but completely unrelated to Modern Greek. Many local Macedonians in Greece are farmers living in small villages; many are unskilled laborers, shopkeepers, and small businessmen; some are professionals working as architects, doctors, and teachers in cities and towns in the area. Almost all have at least one relative who has emigrated to Australia, Canada, or the United States in search of a new and more prosperous life for himself and his family.

These local Macedonians constitute a minority ethnic group with their own "local" language, folklore, traditional music, dances, dress, and other customs that are distinct from those of other ethnic groups in the area. The majority of local Macedonians, who call themselves "Greek-Macedonians," have been assimilated into modern Greek society and have developed a Greek national identity. In other words, they are Greeks from Macedonia; they are Macedonians *and* they are Greeks.

Perhaps as many as 10,000 of these local Macedonians, however, have

SERBIA

BULGARIA

Sofia

Skopje

FORMER YUGOSLAVIA

BLAGOEVGRAD

Blagoevgrad

Vardar

Struma

Mesta

Drim

MACEDONIA

Ohrid

Lake
Ohrid

Bitola

Sérra

M A C E D O N I A

Florina

G R E E C E

Kastoria

Salonika

ALBANIA

Vistritsa
(Aliákmon)

Mt. Olympus

AEGEAN
SEA

Macedonian-speaking areas

75   Km.   Miles

Courtesy of Nighthawk Design.

Village festival in the area of Florina in northern Greece. These festivals have become political events in which traditional "local" folk dances are claimed as part of Macedonian national culture by those identifying themselves as Macedonians and a part of Greek national culture by those who identify themselves as Greeks. Courtesy of Loring M. Danforth.

not developed a Greek national identity; they have developed a Macedonian national identity. That is, they define themselves as Macedonians and *not* as Greeks. The public everyday lives of most of these local Macedonians who have a Macedonian national identity are virtually indistinguishable from the lives of their neighbors who have a Greek national identity. It is only in private contexts (where the Macedonian language is more freely spoken) and on special ritual occasions such as village festivals or weddings (where Macedonian songs are sung) that this Macedonian national identity is expressed. In fact, there are no observable cultural criteria that reliably distinguish local Macedonians with a Macedonian national identity from local Macedonians with a Greek national identity. There are cases where members of the same family—two cousins or even two brothers—have different national identities, one Greek, the other Macedonian.

Since the mid-1980s a small group of people with a Macedonian national identity have been politically active and have begun to demand human rights for the Macedonian minority in northern Greece.

87

The Setting

To most people Greece is either an ancient land, the home of Zeus and Socrates, or a tourist destination, a place of sunny islands and sandy beaches. Greek Macedonia—especially the area near the borders of Albania and the Republic of Macedonia—is a very different place. Poor villages stand partly abandoned in high, rugged mountains; hard-working farmers grow wheat and herd cows in the dusty plains below; and in small cities shopkeepers and construction workers struggle to provide a better life for their children.

In antiquity Greek Macedonia was the home of Alexander the Great and his famous empire. Today it is an economically and politically important region in northern Greece whose capital, Thessaloniki, is a major port and leading industrial center. Greek Macedonia contains some of the richest agricultural lands in Greece, producing valuable crops such as wheat, tobacco, and sugar beets. Away from the coast of the Aegean Sea the climate of Greek Macedonia is continental, more similar to that of Central Europe than to the Mediterranean climate of southern Greece. One of the most impressive geographical features of Greek Macedonia is the series of river valleys flowing from north to south through the mountain ranges that separate Greece from its northern neighbors. Along the Vardar (or Axios) River run the major highways and railroad lines that link Greece to the rest of Eastern and Central Europe.

THREATS TO SURVIVAL

Of all the factors that have affected the fate of the people of northern Greece, the most important has been their painful history: throughout the first half of the twentieth century, their lives were repeatedly shattered by the tragic violence of ethnic conflict, foreign occupation, and civil war. When Macedonia was part of the Ottoman Empire, its population consisted of such incredible ethnic, linguistic, and religious diversity that it inspired the French expression *Macédoine*, meaning a salad of mixed fruits and vegetables. During the Balkan Wars of 1912–1913, the new states of Serbia (later Yugoslavia), Bulgaria, and Greece fought to acquire territory in Macedonia that previously had been under Ottoman rule. Each state justified its claims to this new land with the nationalist argument that the people living there were all Serbs, Bulgarians, or Greeks. As one observer at the time noted though, the problem with these arguments was that they left "so many corpses to testify to the contrary."[1]

At the end of the Balkan Wars the region of Macedonia was divided among Serbia, Bulgaria, and Greece. After World War I the southern half of Macedonia, which had come under Greek control, was subjected to a policy of forced assimilation, or Hellenization, a policy whose goal was to transform the diverse population of the area into an ethnically pure and homogeneous population consisting exclusively of Greeks. Through exchanges of populations, Bulgarians and Turks living in Greek Macedonia were sent to Bulgaria and Turkey, while Greeks living in Bulgaria and Turkey were settled in Greece. All Slavic (Macedonian or Bulgarian) personal and place names in Greek Macedonia were replaced with Greek names; for example, the city of Lerin became Florina and Mr. Jovan Filipov became Mr. Yannis Filippidis. In addition, all evidence of Slavic literacy (primarily inscriptions in the Cyrillic alphabet on gravestones and in churches) was destroyed.

Under the Metaxas dictatorship of 1936–1939, people who were not ethnically Greek and who were beginning to identify themselves as Macedonians experienced severe repression. They were beaten, fined, and imprisoned simply for speaking the Macedonian language. During World War II Greek Macedonia was occupied by the German and the Bulgarian armies. In the Greek Civil War which followed (1946–1949), Greek Communists, supported by many Macedonians living in northern Greece and by the Communist party of Yugoslavia, fought against the Greek government (which had the support of Great Britain and the United States) in what was one of the first battlegrounds of the Cold War. Among the primary goals of the Communist forces was the creation of an autonomous Macedonia.

When the Communists were defeated, some 35,000 Macedonians fled to Yugoslavia and other countries in Eastern Europe under extremely difficult circumstances. In the decades that followed, conservative Greek governments continued a policy of persecution and assimilation toward the Macedonians of Greece, perhaps the most blatant examples of which were the "language oaths" administered in several Macedonian villages, which required Macedonians to swear that they would renounce their "Slavic dialect" and from then on speak only Greek.

After the death of Marshal Tito in 1980 and the breakup of Yugoslavia, the Republic of Macedonia (which until then had been one of the six republics of the federal Yugoslavia) declared its independence in 1991. In response, Greece mounted a fierce campaign to prevent the international recognition of the Republic of Macedonia on the grounds that "Macedonia is, was, and always will be Greek." According to the Greek nationalist position (which is rejected by the vast majority of scholars and diplomats around the world), because Alexander the Great and the ancient Macedonians were Greeks, and because ancient and modern Greeks are bound in an unbroken line of racial and cultural continuity, it is, therefore, only Greeks who have the right to identify themselves as Macedonians, not the Slavs of southern Yugoslavia. Therefore, many Greeks deny the existence of a Macedonian language, a Macedonian nation, and a Macedonian minority in northern Greece. Macedonians, on the other hand, are committed to affirming their existence as a unique people with a unique history, culture, and identity and to gaining recognition of this fact internationally.

Because of this "global cultural war"[2] over the name Macedonia, the Republic of Macedonia has not been able to gain international recognition under its constitutional name (the Republic of Macedonia). It is still officially referred to in most contexts as the former Yugoslav Republic of Macedonia" or FYROM. In addition, the existence of a Macedonian minority in northern Greece has become an extremely sensitive issue for the Greek government, both domestically and internationally.

The most significant threat to the cultural survival of the Macedonian minority of northern Greece is the ideology of ethnic nationalism that is so prevalent in Greek public opinion, in the Greek mass media, and in Greek governmental policies. Nationalism is the principle according to which states (the major political subdivisions of the globe, usually referred to in everyday English as "countries") and nations (groups of people who share a common history, a common culture, and a common national identity) should correspond completely. Ethnic nationalism of this kind is often characterized by racism and xenophobia. The goal of nationalists is to create a territorially bounded political unit, a state, all of whose citizens are members of a single homogeneous cultural community, a nation. Nationalist politicians often start wars in an attempt to expand the boundaries of their state so that it will include all the areas inhabited by members of their nation. They also engage in campaigns of ethnic cleansing whose goal is to eliminate all people who are not members of their nation from within the borders of their state. In its literal form ethnic cleansing involves killing or driving out of the state everyone who is not a member of the dominant nation.

For the past fifty years, the Macedonian minority of northern Greece has been the victim of what could be called "symbolic ethnic cleansing," a policy by which the Greek government simply denies the existence of the Macedonian minority in Greece and attempts to assimilate it into mainstream Greek society. In this way, the Greek government seeks to maintain the fiction that Greece is an ethnically pure and homogeneous state inhabited exclusively by Greeks. Very few countries in the world, however—not even Greece—are ethnically "pure" in this sense. Virtually all countries, including Greece, contain some degree of linguistic, religious, or cultural diversity; virtually all have some minority populations who differ from the dominant group in some way.

In early 1992, in cities throughout Europe, North America, and Australia, hundreds of thousands of Greeks demonstrated against the recognition of the Republic of Macedonia by the European Union. The signs they carried clearly capture the essence of the dominant Greek position on the nonexistence of a Macedonian minority in Greece: "No 'Macedonia' for the Slavs! Macedonia is Greek," "Real Macedonians are Greeks," and "The Only Slavs in Greece Are Tourists!" In official contexts the Greek government refers to members of the Macedonian minority as "bilingual Greeks" or "Slavic-speaking Greeks" (just as it refers to members of the Turkish minority in Greece as "Moslem Greeks"). In this way the government attempts to maintain the fiction that all the inhabitants of Greece are really Greek, even if some of them speak another language or practice a different religion. In informal contexts, however, Macedonians are often referred to derogatorily as "Bulgarians" or "Skopians" (after Skopje, the capital city of the Republic of Macedonia).

The official Greek claim that no Macedonian minority exists in northern Greece is contradicted by clear and forceful assertions by members of this minority that they do exist and that they are Macedonians and not Greeks. From both an anthropological perspective and an international human rights perspective, these assertions in and of themselves demonstrate the existence of such a minority. Anthropologists generally define ethnic groups as "categories of ascription and identification" that people use to classify themselves and others.[3] Similarly, the final document of the 1990 Copenhagen meeting of the Conference on the Human Dimension of the Conference on Security and Cooperation in Europe stated that belonging to a national minority "is a matter of a person's individual choice" and concluded that "persons belonging to national minorities have the right freely to express, preserve, and develop their ethnic, cultural, linguistic or religious identity and to maintain and develop their culture in all its aspects free of any attempts at assimilation against their will."[4]

Greek government policies denying the existence of a Macedonian minority and pressuring its members to assimilate fully into modern Greek society have taken many forms. While there are no official restrictions on the use of the Macedonian language in private or in informal public situations, a climate of fear and intimidation still exists which inhibits many people from speaking Macedonian openly, especially in formal situations. Many middle-aged Macedonians remember being beaten with a switch on the palms of their hands by Greek elementary schoolteachers for speaking Macedonian on the playground. Some Macedonians object to the fact that Greek Orthodox priests will not allow their children to be baptized with Macedonian names or allow the Macedonian names of their dead relatives to be read at memorial services. Until recently local officials discouraged the singing of Macedonian folk songs at village festivals.

Macedonian human rights activists have been subjected to various forms of harassment and persecution. They are often the target of threatening articles published in *Stohos*, an extreme right-wing newspaper. One activist was forced to close one of his two bakeries after he found "No bread from the Skopian!" scrawled on the front window of his shop. Other Macedonian human rights activists have been subjected to criminal prosecution as a result of provisions of the Greek Penal Code, such as Article 191, which "prohibits spreading false information and rumors liable to create concern and fear among citizens and . . . incite citizens to rivalry and division leading to disturbance of the peace."

In 1993 Christos Sidiropoulos and Anastasios Boulis, both from the Florina area, were charged with criminal offenses as a result of statements they had made in a weekly magazine published in Athens. Sidiropoulos had said that, while he was a Greek citizen, he had a "Macedonian national consciousness." Boulis simply said, "I am not a Greek; I am a Macedonian."[5] During the trial members of neo-Nazi organizations demonstrated outside the courthouse shouting, "We will wash our hands with the blood of the Skopians!" Both men were found guilty, fined, and sentenced to five months in prison. After the human rights group Amnesty International expressed its concern over the case to Greek authorities and before either Sidiropoulos or Boulis had served any time in prison, the charges were dropped.[6]

Father Nikodimos Tsarknias, a priest who travels abroad to publicize the situation of the Macedonian minority in Greece, has been defrocked and excommunicated by the Greek Orthodox Church. In 1994 a Greek court sentenced him to prison for three months for impersonating a priest because he continued to wear his clerical robes. In his defense Father Tsarknias stated that he still had the right to wear his robes because he had become a monk at a monastery of the Macedonian Orthodox Church near Skopje. According to the court, as a Greek citizen, Tsarknias did not have the right to join a non-Greek church. At the conclusion of his trial, Father Tsarknias refused to promise that he would never wear his robes again. Therefore, he was immediately convicted a second time on the same charges and sentenced to another three months in prison. On appeal all Tsarknias' convictions were later overturned.

On September 8, 1995, officials of the Rainbow party, the political organization of the Macedonian minority in Greece, opened an office in Florina and placed a bilingual sign in Greek and Macedonian above the entrance reading "Rainbow, Florina Committee." On September 13, the public prosecutor of Florina ordered that the sign be removed. When the police removed it, members of the Rainbow party replaced it with another one. Later that night an angry crowd singing the Greek national anthem attacked the office, set it on fire and destroyed it completely. No one involved in the attack on the office was ever arrested, but leaders of the Rainbow party were taken to court on charges of "disturbing the peace" and "insulting the national consciousness of the citizens of Florina" by "calling into question the Greekness of Florina" and "supporting the territorial claims of Skopje."[7] The trial, originally scheduled for October 1997, was postponed until September 1998. Such delays are a common government tactic in cases like this because they avoid the negative publicity generated when international human rights organizations report on the trials, yet they still effectively maintain a climate of fear and intimidation that discourages additional activity in support of Macedonian human rights by other members of the Macedonian minority in northern Greece. When the case was finally heard in court on September 15, 1998, all of the leaders of the Rainbow party were acquitted.

Finally, in March 1998, Traikos Passois, another Macedonian human rights activist, was scheduled to be tried on charges of "spreading false information" for having entered Greece from the Republic of Macedonia with two wall calendars written in Macedonian which had photographs of villages and towns in northern Greece that were identified by their Macedonian (not their Greek) names. Passois' trial was postponed until November 1998.

In addition to prosecuting Macedonian human rights activists on criminal charges like these, the Greek government has used Article 20 of the Greek Citizenship Code to deprive Macedonians from northern Greece who are living abroad of their Greek citizenship. This article, which allows the Greek government to strip the citizenship of anyone living abroad who "commits acts for the benefit of a foreign state . . . and contrary to the interests of Greece," has been applied primarily in cases involving members of the Macedonian minority living in Canada and Australia who are active in Macedonian organizations such as the Macedonian Orthodox Church and Macedonian human rights committees. When the Greek Ministry of the Interior deprives someone of his citizenship, his name is removed from the citizenship register in the village of his birth; he is declared persona non grata; and the next time he attempts to visit Greece, he is refused permission to enter the country. In this way Greek officials are able to intimidate Macedonians from northern Greece who are living abroad, as well as their relatives in Greece, from asserting a Macedonian identity.

Another violation of the human rights of the Macedonian minority of northern Greece is the explicit exclusion of Macedonians from the general amnesty announced by the Greek government in 1982 according to which political refugees who left Greece at the time of the civil war were permitted to return to Greece. Only political refugees who were "Greeks by birth" were allowed to return to Greece. In 1985 a law was passed allowing for the return of property that had been confiscated by the Greek government from political refugees who left Greece after the civil war. This law, however, also applied only to political refugees who were Greeks by birth.

RESPONSE: STRUGGLES TO SURVIVE CULTURALLY

We want recognition and respect as human beings. We want to be free to express who we are—Macedonians, Slav-Macedonians. We want to be free to enjoy the songs and dances of our grandparents without being accused of being Bulgarians or Communists or agents of Skopje. We have the same language and traditions as the Macedonians of Yugoslavia but that doesn't mean we want to create a state with them. We don't want autonomy; we don't want to change borders. We want to eliminate borders, not build new ones. (A Macedonian human rights activist, Florina, 1990)

Leaders of the Macedonian minority in northern Greece realize that they are the last generation that can act to preserve their language and their traditions. They see that many of the younger generation are less interested in learning the Macedonian language than they are in assimilating fully into mainstream Greek society in the hope that they will become more upwardly mobile and professionally successful. As a result, leaders of the Macedonian minority have adopted a two-part strategy in response to the Greek government's policies of denying their existence, assimilating them into mainstream Greek society, and violating their human rights. They have formed a variety of cultural and political organizations in an attempt to assert their existence as an ethnic minority in Greece; to preserve their identity, language, and culture; and to protect their human rights as members of a minority. They would like to be able to attend Orthodox Church services conducted in Macedonian, listen to radio and television broadcasts in Macedonian, give their children Macedonian names, and send them to schools where they could learn Macedonian as well as Greek.

When leaders of the Macedonian minority have encountered opposition from the Greek government, they have appealed for support from organizations, groups, and institutions outside the Greek state. These include international organizations such as the United Nations, the European Union, and Amnesty International; communities of Macedonian emigrants living abroad in Canada and Australia; and the government of the Republic of Macedonia and various Macedonian emigrant and refugee organizations based there. In this way the conflict between the Macedonian minority in Greece and the Greek government, like other similar ethnic conflicts throughout the world, has become a global cultural war fought not only in Greece, but in Geneva, New York, Toronto, and Melbourne.

In 1984 Macedonian human rights activists issued a manifesto calling for the recognition of the human rights of the Macedonian minority in Greece, and they sent copies of it to officials of the Greek government, to all foreign embassies in Athens, to all European governments, and to the United Nations and a variety of other international organizations as well. In order to publicize their views and enlist support for their cause, they began publishing a newsletter written in Greek, which has since evolved into a larger and more sophisticated magazine, *Nova Zora* (Macedonian for "New Dawn"), which is written half in Greek and half in Macedonian. Articles focus on the Macedonian struggle for human rights in northern Greece, but they also deal with other local political issues, the struggles of other minority groups around the world (such as the Kurds and the Palestinians), and various aspects of local Macedonian folklore, such as Macedonian folk songs and the traditional Macedonian names for villages and towns in the area.

During the 1989 parliamentary elections in Greece, some Macedonians in northern Greece cast invalid protest ballots on which the following text was written:

I am a Greek citizen and a Macedonian by birth, and that is what I want to remain. I fulfill all my obligations to the state without enjoying the same rights as other citizens. My human rights are rudely violated and my nationality and my ethnic origin are not recognized. That is why I take part in these elections with a protest vote—in order to prove my existence, on the one hand, and to denounce the chauvinistic positions of the political parties on the other.

In the early 1990s leaders of the Macedonian human rights movement began to develop a more ambitious political program. They formed the Macedonian Movement for Balkan Prosperity, whose goals were to oppose racism, nationalism, and militarism in Greece and to work for peaceful coexistence and cooperation among peoples of the Balkans. Several years later they formed a political party, Rainbow, which was committed to respecting the inviolability of existing international borders; to developing Macedonian language, folklore, and culture in Greece; to ending the practice of revoking the citizenship of Macedonians living abroad, as well as the practice of preventing Macedonian political refugees from returning to Greece; and to striving for civic equality and social justice for all Macedonians in Greece.

The best example to illustrate the course of the struggle for Macedonian human rights in Greece is the case of the House of Macedonian Culture. In 1989 a group of Macedonians in the Florina area attempted to establish a nonprofit organization called the House of Macedonian Culture. Their application was rejected by a local court on the grounds that the main goal of the association was "the cultivation of the idea of the existence of a Macedonian minority in Greece, which is contrary to the national interest [of Greece] and therefore the law."[8] An appeals court in Thessaloniki upheld this decision in 1991 arguing that the House of Macedonian Culture was part of an attempt by "Skopje" (i.e., the Republic of Macedonia) to gain control of Greek territory and that the use of the word "Macedonian" in the name of the association was intended to falsify or misrepresent the Greek identity of Macedonia and therefore destroy the territorial integrity of Greece. In 1994 this decision was again upheld by the Arios Paghos, the Supreme Court of Greece in Athens.

Having exhausted all their options within the Greek legal system, the founders of the House of Macedonian Culture took advantage of the fact that Greece was a member of the European Union and a signatory of the European Convention for the Protection of Human Rights and Fundamental Freedoms, and they appealed their case to the European Court of Human Rights in Strasbourg, France. On July 10, 1998, nine years after the initial attempt to establish the association, the European Court of Human Rights ruled unanimously in favor of the founders of the House of Macedonian Culture. The court held that the Greek government had violated their human rights by infringing on their right "to freedom of peaceful assembly and freedom of association" guaranteed by Article 11 of the European Convention of Human Rights and Fundamental Freedoms. More specifically, the court ruled that the stated aims of the founders of the House of Macedonian Culture (to preserve and develop the traditions and folk culture of the Florina region) were "perfectly clear and legitimate" and that the opinion of the Greek courts (that the association represented a danger to Greece's territorial integrity) was based on "a mere suspicion" as to the true intentions of the association's founders. Finally, the court concluded that all the arguments put forward by the Greek courts against the association's founders were "baseless, vague and unproved," that "mention of the consciousness of belonging to a minority and the preservation and development of a minority's culture could not be said to constitute a threat to democratic society," and that "the existence of minorities and different cultures in a country was a historical fact that a 'democratic society' had to tolerate and even protect and support according to the principles of international law."[9]

Macedonians from northern Greece living in diaspora communities in Canada and Australia have played a key role in the globalization of the campaign for Macedonian human rights. Recent improvements in the fields of transportation and communication—intercontinental air travel, video cameras, fax machines, and the Internet—have made it possible for emigrants from Greek Macedonia living in Toronto and Melbourne to remain closely involved in the political issues of their homeland. Since many Macedonians in Canada and Australia have experienced significant upward mobility, they have educational, occupational, and financial resources that enable them to contribute significantly to the struggle for Macedonian human rights. Macedonian-Australian lawyers and wealthy Macedonian-Canadian businessmen have lobbied the governments of Australia and Canada to apply pressure on Greece to recognize its Macedonian minority. They have also joined activists from northern Greece to form "international Macedonian delegations" to present their case before the European Parliament and the United Nations.

In addition, contacts between Macedonian human rights activists in northern Greece and the Republic of Macedonia have contributed to the struggle for Macedonian human rights in Greece. Activists from northern Greece have attended the International Seminar for Macedonian Language,

Literature, and Culture held every summer in the Republic of Macedonia. There, in addition to improving their knowledge of the Macedonian language, they have had the opportunity to meet representatives of the Macedonian government, officials of the Center for Macedonians Abroad, leaders of the Macedonian minorities in Albania and Bulgaria, and members of Macedonian communities in Canada and Australia.

FOOD FOR THOUGHT

In light of the tragic wars in Bosnia and Chechnya that accompanied the breakup of Yugoslavia and the Soviet Union, the dangers posed to sovereign states by the ethnic nationalism of minority groups with their demands for ever-increasing political autonomy are all too obvious. Yet the dangers posed to members of minorities by the ethnic nationalism of dominant groups with their campaigns of forced assimilation and ethnic cleansing are equally real. Clearly, it is necessary to avoid both these dangers—in the case of the Macedonians in Greece as well as in the cases of the Basques in Spain, the Kurds in Turkey, and the Quebecois in Canada. All solutions to this dilemma must surely involve respect for the human rights of members of ethnic and national minorities in countries throughout the world. The late Kostas Gotsis, a leader of the Macedonian human rights movement in northern Greece, was fond of saying, "A garden with only one kind of flowers in it can never be as beautiful as a garden with many kinds of flower in it."

Questions

1. Why do so many people around the world want to live in countries that are ethnically pure and homogeneous—countries, in other words, inhabited exclusively by people whose language, religion, and culture are the same as theirs?

2. Why are some people willing to risk persecution, discrimination, loss of employment, prison, and even death to assert their membership in an ethnic minority?

3. If a government grants members of a minority group a limited degree of cultural autonomy (their own schools, churches, and cultural associations, for example), will that reduce or increase the number of people who demand a separate, independent state for members of the minority?

4. How is it possible to balance the right of a people to national self-determination, on the one hand, and the right of a state to defend its sovereignty and territorial integrity, on the other?

5. If you met a Greek who told you that there was no Macedonian minority in Greece, how would you try to convince him that there was?

NOTES

1. H. N. Brailsford, *Macedonia: Its Races and Their Future* (1906; reprint, New York: Arno Press, 1991), 218.

2. Mike Featherstone, ed., *Global Culture: Nationalism, Globalization, and Modernity* (London: Sage, 1990), 10.

3. Frederik Barth, *Ethnic Groups and Ethnic Boundaries* (Boston: Little, Brown, 1969), 10.

4. United States Commission on Security and Cooperation in Europe (Washington, D.C.: 1960).

5. *Ena* (Athenian weekly publication), March 11, 1992.

6. Human Rights Watch/Helsinki, *Denying Ethnic Identity: The Macedonians of Greece* (New York: 1994), 22–25; United States Department of State, *Country Reports on Human Rights Practices for 1992* (Washington, D.C.: 1993), 791.

7. Web site of the Rainbow party: http://www.florina.org/

8. Court documents provided by Macedonian human rights activists.

9. European Court of Human Rights, *Case of Sidiropoulos and Others v. Greece*, accessed August 17, 1998. http://www.dhcour.coe.fr/eng/SIDIROPOU-LOS%20&%20OTHERS%20ENG.html

RESOURCE GUIDE

Published Literature

Danforth, Loring M. *The Macedonian Conflict: Ethnic Nationalism in a Transnational World*. Princeton, N.J.: Princeton University Press, 1995.

Human Rights Watch/Helsinki. *Denying Ethnic Identity: The Macedonians of Greece*. New York: 1994.

Karakasidou, Anastasia N. *Fields of Wheat, Hills of Blood: Passages to Nationhood in Greek Macedonia: 1870–1990*. Chicago: University of Chicago Press, 1997.

Mackridge, Peter, and Eleni Yannakakis. *Ourselves and Others: The Development of a Greek Macedonian Cultural Identity Since 1912*. Oxford: Berg, 1997.

United States Department of State. "Greece." In *Country Reports on Human Rights Practices for 1997*, 1102–14. Washington, D.C.: 1998.

WWW Sites

European Court of Human Rights. *Case of Sidiropoulos and Others v. Greece* http://www.dhcour.coe.fr/eng/SIDIROPOULOS%20&%20OTHERS%20ENG. html

The Balkan Human Rights Web Pages
http://www.greekhelsinki.gr

Macedonian Human Rights Movement of Canada
http:www.mhrmc.on.ca/

Rainbow party
http://www.florina.org/

Organizations

Greek Helsinki Monitor
P.O. Box 51393
GR-14510 Kifisia, Greece
E-mail: office@greekhelsinki.gr

Human Rights Watch/Helsinki
485 Fifth Avenue
New York, NY 10017
E-mail: hrwatchnyc@igc.apc.org

Macedonian Human Rights Movement of Canada
2376 Eglinton Avenue East
Toronto, Canada MIK 5K3
E-mail: mail@mhrmc.on.ca

Rainbow Party
Stephanou Dragoumi 11
P.O. Box 51
53100 Florina, Greece
E-mail: misirkov@compulink.gr

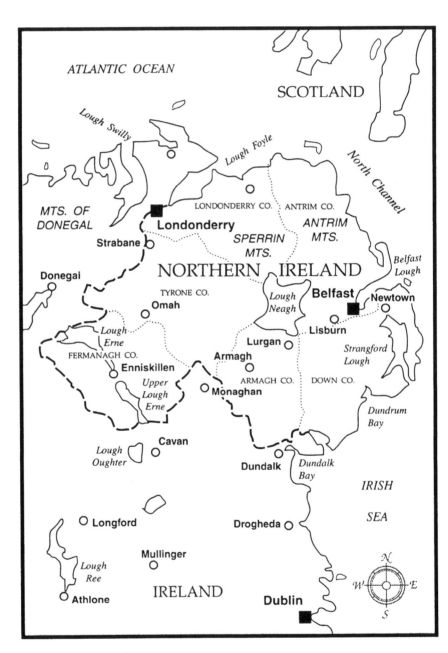

Courtesy of Mapcraft.

Chapter 7

The Northern Irish
Thomas Taaffe

CULTURAL OVERVIEW

> Just when you think you have the answer to the Irish question, the Irish change the question.[1]

The island of Ireland is home to 5 million people: 3.5 million in the Republic of Ireland and 1.5 million in Northern Ireland. While the Republic of Ireland has been independent since 1922 (and a republic since 1947), Northern Ireland is still a part of the United Kingdom. Most of the people in the Republic of Ireland are Roman Catholic (93 percent). In Northern Ireland, however, only 43 percent of the population is Catholic. The overwhelming majority of Protestants are the descendants of settlers imported from Scotland and England, starting in the 1600s. In the past thirty years, the historic tensions between the governments of Great Britain and the Republic of Ireland have greatly improved. In the north, however, relations between the two communities have only deteriorated.

Peoples and cultures can be endangered in many ways and on many levels. The volatile situation in Northern Ireland frequently leads to violence. In fact, the political structure in Northern Ireland could be described as institutionalized hatred and mistrust with confrontational events part of the overall structure of the communities. This chapter attempts to unravel this organization of antipathy, which threatens human existence in Northern Ireland. Battlefields are a threat to cultural survival.

For the past thirty years, a low-level ethnic conflict has engulfed Northern Ireland. The "Troubles" involve a struggle over national aspiration, conditioned by anti-Catholic, anti-Irish bigotry and violence. These hostilities have led to deep social divisions in the province. Unionist and Nationalist are terms used to define those national aspirations and the communities they represent. Nationalists want a united Ireland. Unionists want to remain a part of the United Kingdom, and historically they have controlled most of the province's resources and positions of power. Religion serves as a cultural marker for these communities. The overwhelmingly Protestant Unionists define themselves as "British," "British-Irish," or "Scots-Irish." Nationalists, usually Catholic, define themselves as "Irish." Republicans are activist Nationalists from primarily urban poor and working-class or rural backgrounds. Loyalists are activist Unionists primarily from urban poor or working-class, rural, or Christian fundamentalist backgrounds. Some Republicans and Loyalists support violence as a means to achieving or maintaining their national aspirations. The terms Loyalist and Republican are also used to describe neighborhoods, communities, and organizations where such ideologies predominate. The Troubles are a modern manifestation of a struggle to liberate Ireland from English colonialism that goes back 800 years.

History (and all its contested versions) is incredibly important to understanding the Troubles. To understand this conflict better, we need to examine the evolution of the Irish as a people, their colonization by Great Britain, and the evolution of this conflict.

The Setting

Ten thousand years ago, as the glaciers of the last ice age receded, the earliest settlers arrived in what is now Northern Ireland across the narrow strait from Scotland. They entered a plush forested world, a temperate rain forest. The island was once more than 90 percent forest, but now only 5 percent is forest. Most of the deforestation occurred during the 1600s, when England began to depopulate the island. Ireland is now trying to preserve the remaining forest and to repair the damage of the last 400 years. However, these efforts are small scale and sometimes threatened by modernization.

Ireland is bordered to the west and south by the Atlantic Ocean and to to the north and west by the North Sea and the Irish Sea. The warm currents of the Gulf Stream, which sweep past Ireland as it makes its way southward, protect the temperatures of Ireland, giving it a moderate climate. Temperatures range around 40°F in the winter to the 70s in the summer. Rainfall is common, though many days will see both sunny and cloudy moments. Rainfall varies from 32 inches in the lowlands to 79 inches in the mountainous highlands. The high rainfall creates a rich landscape, a land of low mountains and hills, forests, bogs, and verdant green valleys. Ireland truly deserves its moniker, the "Emerald Isle."

The People

Pre-Christian Eras

While Irish mythology recalls three successive waves of settlement, the archaeological record has not yet proved that history. The first settlers were primarily hunters and gatherers. Five thousand years ago, farming and raising domesticated cattle began to emerge as ways of life. Along with these subsistence strategies, the ancient Irish were excellent sailors, using curracks, which resemble canoes. Their trading routes took them from Scandinavia to Greece and along the North African coast. Their excellence in metallurgy made their jewelry, as well as other bronze and gold creations, prized possessions throughout the ancient European world.

Along with their craft work, the ancient Irish built huge megalithic earthworks, some of which predate the pyramids of Egypt. Some of these sites, which had important religious and cultural significance, can be found today at Knowth and Newgrange (County Meath).

Gaelic, the ancient language of Ireland, may have reached the shores of Ireland in the sixth century B.C. A Celtic language, Gaelic belongs to the Indo-European family of languages. While Gaelic has diminished in use, as a result of British efforts to stamp it out, it remains the official language of the Republic of Ireland. Thirty-two percent of the population speak Gaelic, although in varying levels of competence. Although Gaelic is an important part of Irish culture, English is usually the language of everyday life in most places. The Irish were among the first people of Europe to develop their own system of writing, Ogam. They later adapted the Latin alphabet to Gaelic and transcribed many of their oral traditions into beautiful manuscripts, which are themselves works of art.

Ancient Ireland was organized according to clans. In pre-Christian times, people named clans after animals, such as Osraige and Biraige ("deer people" and "beaver people," respectively), or after a product they produced, such as "basket makers." Clans were organized into several classes, and mobility from the lowest to the highest rungs was possible. The lowest of the classes were the "non-free" classes. The lowest (the *fuidhir*) were often war captives or criminals or they had debts they refused to pay. They were held in this state until they had fulfilled their sentence, the debt was paid, or their relatives had given tribute. They allowed the higher ranks of non-free persons to work as craftspeople, herdsmen, or household servants. While they could not vote in clan affairs, they could form guild associations and elect one of their number to vote at clan councils. They could hold land and, through their work, gain their rights as full citizens. Despite this low status, a *fuidhir* could become a full clan member and even rise to the highest levels of Irish society. Saint Patrick, captured from Wales as a boy, rose from the *fuidhir* class to become its most famous son. Debt did not pass from one generation to the next.

Above them was the freeman class. These itinerant workers, who hired themselves out as herders, took part in the clan's military activities and enjoyed the full rights of clan membership. However, because they were itinerant, they had little effective say in political matters.

The heart of the ancient Irish culture was the *ceile* class. Members of this freeman class were entitled to tracts of land, made up the military, paid taxes, and elected the clan council. Above them were the *flaith*, or the civil servant class, who were elected by the clan from the *ceile* class to handle administrative duties of the clan council. They received land in exchange for their duties.

Women played a powerful role in ancient Ireland. The religion of pre-Christian Ireland was polytheistic and matriarchal, as was the culture itself. Kinship was reckoned through the female line (descending from the mother). In some places, female kinship reckoning remained a part of the culture well into the Christian period. The creation legends place Danu (Dana), the mother-goddess, at the beginning of the creation. All gods and goddesses are reckoned by their descent from Danu. The spirit world itself, *Tuatha Dé Danaan*, means "Kingdom of Danu." Women were held in much higher regard in the years before Christianity, than in the centuries that followed. Eight forms of marriage and concubinage were recognized (and the legitimacy of children from those relationships). Divorce could be initiated by both women and men, and women could hold high office, including priesthood and kingship. Women sometimes led their people into battle, and they could also lead their families in the clan council.

Pre-Christian Ireland had a very complex political culture. The island was united by culture and language, but not politically. At the local level, the smallest political unit was the *fine*, or extended family. Several families organized themselves into a *tuath*, or kingdom. They called the leader *ri*, or king. While elected by a council made up of eligible freemen, the king, who could be male or female, usually came from a particular family line. The council, under certain circumstances, could remove a king. These "kingdoms" pledged allegiance to a more powerful king (who ruled a group of *tuatha*), upward to one of five provincial kings. Given the complexity of alliances, the political situation shifted constantly until the modern era of British colonization.

Kings shared their authority with priests and *brehon*, a professional class who served as mediators, judges, and lawyers. *Brehon* law, a complex oral tradition of laws (and their interpretations), provided for settling disputes and interpreting rights. Laws regarding inheritance (at least during the pre-Christian era) prevented any family from dominating a *tuath* for more than several generations. Ever-changing alliances and challenges, combined with a division of authority between *brehon*, kings, and priests, prevented any centralized nation-state from emerging, as it did in the rest of Europe.

Land was held in common by the clan and allotted according to one's status and service to the community. Sometimes parcels of land were apportioned by drawing lots. Wealth was determined in terms of cattle or other livestock (along with other material goods). Ireland was also the home of the first hospital in Europe, built in Armagh in 300 B.C., 700 years before the first hospitals of Rome. Irish physicians, renowned throughout Europe, evolved into a kind of "national health service," in which medical care was available to all regardless of status.

Change is part of life, and the politics of continental Europe affected Ireland before the Christian era. The arrival of the Roman Empire in Britain set changes in motion in Irish culture, even though the Romans never reached Ireland's shores. Elites of Ireland sometimes modeled their clothes after Roman elites. Changes in Irish culture gave rise to male ancestor clans (as opposed to the older animal or craft clans) such as the Uí Néill clan. Other disruptions also occurred before and throughout the periods before the arrival of the English, which sought to consolidate power in the hands of elites. Over time these efforts were successful in undermining the rights of common people and in consolidating power in a handful of kings. However, the complexities of Irish law and politics prevented more than a handful of provincial kings from successfully claiming the title of *Ard Rí* (high king of Ireland).

The Christian Era

While Saint Patrick is credited with bringing Christianity to Ireland in the fifth century, some Irish had already been converted before his arrival. The early Celtic Church was not fully allied with the Church in Rome. Early Celtic monks established many monasteries, not only in Ireland, but on continental Europe as well. Celtic Christianity provided a rival force to Roman Catholicism and led to the Roman Church's alliances with England in colonizing Ireland. During the so-called Dark Ages, Irish monks played an important role in building libraries and other centers of learning. They kept Christianity alive in Europe, where Germanic invasions had nearly extinguished its expansion.

In the ninth and tenth centuries, bands of Viking raiders and traders attacked Ireland. These Norse invaders established the first towns in Ireland, most notably Dublin, but also Cork, Waterford, and Limerick. The powerful Uí Néill clan (named after their ancestor, Naill of the Nine Hostages) held the Norse in check. While the Norse managed to establish trading towns, they did not gain much control over the island itself.

Brian Boru (founder of the O'Brien clan) defeated the Norse in 999 and 1012 and declared himself high king of Ireland. His victories ushered in two centuries of cultural renaissance in Ireland. Others tried to follow Brian Boru in claiming the throne of Tara (ancient "seat of the high kings"), but with limited success.

Social, Religious, and Political Organization

The English Arrive

If the King were as wise as Solomon the Sage, he shall never subdue the wild Irish to his obedience without dread of the sword . . . [even then he may fail, since] so long as they may resiste and live, they will never obey the King.[2]

The arrival of Norman-English invaders (led by Strongbow, in the late 1160s) interrupted any further political consolidation of Ireland into a centralized monarchy. In 1171 many clan leaders recognized Henry II (the Norman king of England) as lord of Ireland. This moment began England's involvement in Ireland which continues to this day in Northern Ireland.

While the English managed to establish themselves in the extended area around Dublin, known as the Pale, their authority beyond that small area was sketchy at best. The Roman Catholic Church supported their efforts and used the opportunity to try to bring the Celtic Church more in line with Roman authority. Welsh, Norman, and English warlords were given title to Irish lands, and they gave Irish nobles English titles. These invading groups (called Old English), quickly became "more Irish than the Irish themselves." By the thirteenth century, the English had set up an English-style administrative apparatus, including a parliament, and sought to replace the *brehon* legal system with an English one. Those outside the Pale turned to Edward Bruce, the brother of the Scottish king, Robert the Bruce, in 1315 but failed to expel the invaders. By the fifteenth century, the English crown was in decline. In Ireland, their influence to the Pale had lessened, and its elites paid tribute to Irish clan leaders who threatened it from time to time.

The Tudor dynasty, established at the turn of the sixteenth century in England, turned its attention to Ireland. In 1541 Henry VIII declared himself king of Ireland. England and Scotland were becoming Protestant (Anglican and Presbyterian, respectively), and tensions between Protestant and Catholic became important markers of distinction and allegiance. The English Crown launched a series of military campaigns against the Gaelic Irish and the Old English who had drifted from their allegiance to England. In 1601 the army of Queen Elizabeth I defeated the Irish in battle at Kinsale and marked the beginning of the modern era of English colonialism in Ireland. In 1607 the earls of Ulster (Red Hugh O'Neill) and Tyrconnell (Ruairi O'Donnell) set sail for Spain and took with them many of Ireland's most experienced warriors. This event is known as the Flight of the Earls.

The native Irish social, political, and legal system was smashed, and for the first time Ireland was under the direct domination of a strong alien power. Formal colonization began with the establishment of the Ulster plantation.

THREATS TO SURVIVAL

The Modern Era of Colonization

Colonization of Ireland has continually threatened the lives of the indigenous Irish. Throughout the first 400 years of English efforts to colonize Ireland, the powerful Uí Néill clan (O'Neill) and its allies were a major obstacle to English ambitions. Thus, conquest of the north was critical to the ability of the English to dominate Ireland. The methods they used would become the templates for English colonization in North America and elsewhere.

The main intentions of the colonization were to depopulate the land and resettle it with lowland Scots and English settlers loyal to the English Crown; to destroy all remaining vestiges of Irish culture, language, and identity; and to terminate the Catholic Church's presence on the island. From the sixteenth century onward, the imposition of Protestantism in Ireland was a central part of the colonial effort. This effort largely failed, however, due to the close association of Protestantism with colonialism. Most of the Protestants in Ireland were descended from Protestant settlers. This established social stratification, with the colonial Protestants as the elite.

The nearness of Ireland to Great Britain made it attractive to Britain's rivals, Spain and France. Ireland's elites had ties with these two countries, and both countries figured in Irish efforts to break free of England's grip over the next 200 years. Ireland became a pawn in the struggle of developing colonial empires. Aware of its potential vulnerability to attack from the Irish coast, England was committed to colonizing Ireland thoroughly and making Ireland "British." Ireland was about to enter the darkest centuries of its history.

In 1609 England commissioned the Ulster plantation, the first modern reservation system in the world. All "wild Irish" were ordered to move onto nine reservations, and they forfeited their lands to English nobles, who in turn brought Scottish peasants in to till the land. The next forty years proved to be a hostile time as the Irish peasants reorganized themselves and attacked settlements. In 1641 the Irish took advantage of the English civil war and rose up against their English overlords, this time with the support of Irish and Old English elites. England, now controlled by Oliver Cromwell and a radical Puritan Parliament, sent tens of thousands of troops to Ireland and laid waste to the countryside. Many of the ruined castles and churches seen on the Irish landscape were destroyed during Cromwell's campaign.

Cromwell ordered all "wild Irish" still living in the east and south into Connaught, a rocky and inhospitable place in the west of Ireland. Connaught was planned as a "great reservation" for all the indigenous inhabitants. Orders were given to put any Irish found outside the reservation to death. This order was never carried out, however, because the English soon realized that they needed Irish labor. They seized landholdings and continued the expansion apace. Irish and Old English nobles saw their lands confiscated, and many were put to death. The English reduced the native Irish peasantry to marginal tenancy on their own land, and the deforestation of Ireland began in earnest. By 1778 only 5 percent of all the land was still in Catholic hands. Most of that land was in the hands of its wealthiest and most compliant nobles. Within a few years, 600,000 Irish had perished through violence, famine, or disease. One to two hundred thousand Irish (more than 15 percent of the population) were taken from their homes or kidnapped off the streets and sold into slavery (mostly to the sugar cane plantations of the West Indies). The English reduced the population from approximately 1.5 million to 600,000. Another 40,000 left or were sold into foreign armies. Hunting rebel Irish, who hid in the mountains and forests of Ireland, became sport for the next hundred years. Monetary rewards were offered for killing a rebel. Many of the leading figures of early English colonization in America, including Captain John Smith, John Mason, and Miles Standish, learned their trade in the Irish conquest. Their tactics became a model for the conquest of North America.

Soon after the final conquest of Ireland, the English began to increase their oppression in the hopes of driving out the remaining Irish and destroying all vestiges of Irish culture. Once again, the Irish faced this threat to their survival and attempted to rid themselves of their oppressors. This time they allied themselves with the Catholic King James II of England, after William of Orange had deposed and replaced him. This alliance proved disastrous for the Irish, as James proved to be a less than competent general, and William of Orange, by contrast, a most effective one. The new king made a compact with Ireland's Protestant settlers to ensure the exclusion of Catholics in all forms of life and to preserve Protestant privilege over them. The Penal Laws were passed to prevent Irish from reclaiming their land. Land sales by Protestants to Catholics was forbidden, and no native Irish could own a horse worth more than five pounds. Educating Catholics either in Ireland or abroad was prohibited, and Catholics were not allowed to hold office or become lawyers. Any Catholic priest who came to Ireland could be hanged. Speaking or teaching Gaelic was forbidden, and marriage between Catholics and Protestants was prohibited. Catholics were denied the right to bear arms or be citizens. They were not allowed to travel more than five miles from their home. Rents consumed most of their crops, and landlords could remove them at a moment's notice. While the Irish constantly sought to rid themselves of their colonial masters, they were not seeking to establish an Irish nation. Their goal was simply to rid the island of its invaders. The concept of Irish nationalism was the brainchild of Protestant settlers. Non-Anglican Protestants (most Scots-Irish were Presbyterian), though privileged over the native populations, faced discrimination in terms of religious freedom and economic opportunity. Intermittently, they also rebelled against English rule, though not to the same degree as the indigenous population. In the 1790s they formed the United Irishmen movement. This movement sought to unite Protestant, Catholic, and Dissenter in armed struggle to liberate Ireland from England and to set up a democratic republic modeled after the United States. "Dissenter," in their terms, meant Presbyterian, and Protestant meant Anglican. While hundreds of thousands of Irish Catholics were involved in the uprising that followed, Protestant settlers primarily made up its leadership. This failed effort was the beginning of the republican movement. The mantle of the United Irishmen would be taken up again and again by the Irish. The ideas of republicanism would become the driving force of Irish history from this point on. In 1795 the Orange Order—a sectarian organization dedicated to uniting all non-Catholics—was formed. It has grown in strength and power over the past 200 years, and in the twentieth century it became the backbone of Protestant/Unionist power in the Northern Ireland. We will return to the Orange Order later in this chapter.

Following Cromwell's conquest, the extreme oppression of the Irish population continued for the next 200 years. Potatoes (introduced from the Americas) suffered repeated crop failures that led to seven major famines between 1745 and 1879 that devastated the population. These famines caused massive deaths and forced emigrations to the United States, England, and later Australia. While England provided some modest relief, it was usually in the form of soup lines. However, in order to receive that soup, the starving person had to convert to Protestantism. Needless to say, very few Irish ever converted. The English rejected larger relief programs because they violated the market principles of a free market economy.

The worst of these famines was the Great Hunger of 1845 to 1850. Before the modern age of English colonialism, the Irish had primarily been shepherds. Colonialism had turned them into tenant farmers. In the years leading up to the nineteenth century, the British increasingly demanded that Irish crops maintain the British war machine. This led to great dependence on the potato as a staple food. After the war of 1815, when the English demands changed from tillage to pasture, massive unemployment resulted. The population of Ireland, which had reached eight million by 1841, began to collapse under the weight of the famine. The potato proved to be vulnerable to disease and crops failed repeatedly. The remaining harvests were exported out of the country under armed guards, leading to mass starvation. Mass emigration to America and Great Britain followed. By 1851 two million had either died or fled to other places.

From the beginning of the nineteenth century, Great Britain had attempted to make some reforms to relax the worst of its oppression. Following the violent suppression of the United Irishmen rebellion, and the subsequent rise of other rebellions, Great Britain repealed the odious penal laws. The general conditions of the common Irish were not much better, but it gave more room for their elites. Daniel O'Connell, the Great Emancipator, sought change through peaceful political action and massive rallies to achieve a measure of Irish autonomy. He succeeded in removing restrictions against the Catholic Church and won some relief from the more punitive edge of English oppression. Catholics could now hold political office. Still, while his reforms succeeded in gaining greater religious freedom, it did not change the lot of most Irish peasants. It did, however, expand the rift between the Irish elites and the peasants. With the onset of the Great Hunger, the independence movement took on a proletarian character and a more violent tone.

For the rest of the century, successive movements emerged, were suppressed, and were regrouped into new movements to liberate Ireland from the clutches of English colonialism. Each rebellion begat the next, as the Young Irelanders (1848), followed by the Fenians (1865–1868) each took their turn trying to drive out the British. The Fenians, also known as the Irish Republican Brotherhood (IRB) (1860s to early 1900s), advanced dramatically in military capability and internal organization. Increasingly, socialist and Marxist ideas began to influence the leaders of these movements. The Catholic Church, having won government pay for its clerics in O'Connell's reforms, distanced itself from the aims of Irish independence, though individual priests were often ardent supporters.

While the late 1800s saw some land reform, the die had already been cast. Hundreds of years of oppression were not to be satisfied by modest reforms that did nothing to remove the hated English from Ireland. Continuing pressure came from unions and home rule organizations. Increasingly (thanks to O'Connell's reforms), they began to use the political landscape as one more terrain of struggle to liberate Ireland. It was a combination of political struggle and guerrilla war that finally liberated most of Ireland from the direct grasp of British colonialism. If the twentieth century was the era of national liberation movements, that era began in Ireland.

Liberating Ireland

Another component of Irish nationalism began to emerge at the turn of the twentieth century: the Irish culture movement, dedicated to the survival of Irish forms of self-expression. Language, games, history, sports, and even the older pre-Christian faith were explored. Reviving Gaelic and other cultural pursuits, such as Irish dance, were the main efforts of the Gaelic League, founded in 1893. Sinn Féin (meaning "Ourselves, Alone"), formed in 1907, was dedicated to creating a "united, Socialist Ireland." Sinn Féin had close links with the IRB. Many of the Nationalist political parties in both the Republic of Ireland (including the four largest parties) and in Northern Ireland are schisms of Sinn Féin and draw from its tradition.

In 1913 a Home Rule Bill was passed in the British House of Commons, but it was defeated in the House of Lords. In the north of Ireland, 400,000 Ulster Protestants signed a petition opposing it. The eruption of World War I sidelined further reforms. The following year, the Ulster Volunteer Force (UVF), a pro-British paramilitary, formed and received a large shipment of weapons from South Africa. In 1916 James Connolly and Padric Pearce declared Ireland an independent republic and led a failed uprising. Their executions enraged Ireland and led to widespread unrest. The IRB, the National Volunteers, and the socialist Irish Citizen's Army combined to form the Irish Republican Army (IRA).

In 1918 the election of British members of Parliament (MPs) in Ireland led to a massive victory for Irish nationalism. Sinn Féin took seventy-three seats; moderate nationalists, six seats; and Unionists, thirty-one. The next year, the Sinn Féin MPs met in Dublin and formed the first independent government of Ireland. The war of independence was now in full swing and, led by Michael Collins, the IRA waged war against the British presence in Ireland for the next two years. In 1920 Great Britain created two parliaments for Ireland, one in Belfast, the other in Dublin, both subordinate to the parliament of London. Sinn Féin (124) and other nationalist candidates (6) unanimously dominated the elections for the southern parliament. Unionists dominated the parliament of the north, with forty Unionists, six Nationalists, and six Sinn Féin candidates.

In 1921 Michael Collins and the British met in London to negotiate the end of the war. These negotiations produced a treaty that divided Ireland into two parts. Twenty-six counties would make up a "free state" (within the British Commonwealth), and six counties in the north would remain a part of the United Kingdom. The Irish Parliament (the Dáil) passed the treaty by a narrow margin. Widespread violence broke out in the north. Protestants took their revenge on the Catholic populations, burning neighborhoods and beginning a reign of terror that continues today. Éamon de Valera, the leader of Sinn Féin, walked out of the Dáil, and Ireland descended into civil war. Great Britain provided the free state government with arms to put down the rebellion. The IRA killed Michael Collins, the leader of the free state. While they negotiated a truce in 1923, the IRA and Sinn Féin remained committed to an independent Ireland. An intermittent guerrilla war continued for thirty years in the south. Sinn Féin leader de Valera formed a new party and reentered politics. He is considered by many the Father of Irish independence.

In 1947 Ireland declared itself a republic and left the British Commonwealth. Fortunes in Ireland remained dim for many years, and poverty was common. In the later part of the 1980s, however, things began to change dramatically for Ireland. Ireland's entry into the European Union led to new investment from the European Union. American technology companies made significant investments, and Ireland became the fastest growing economy in Europe. Combined with its already strong tourism industry, Ireland became known as the "Celtic Tiger." The former industrialized, economic stronghold of the north began to look south at the changing economic forces that were improving lives there, as the north sank deeper into economic depression.

Contemporary Events and Conditions

The Orange State

> I have always maintained that I am an Orangeman first and a politician and Member of Parliament afterwards. . . . All I boast of is that we are a Protestant parliament for a Protestant people.[3]

If fortunes for Irish Catholics changed dramatically for the better in the south, threats to their survival were heightened in the remaining six counties of Northern Ireland. Unionists quickly took advantage of their autonomy and began constructing an apartheid political structure. They denied the right of every adult to vote until the 1970s. The right to vote was restricted to "heads of households." Several generations of Catholics were crammed into one house, while the northern government readily gave single Protestants their own homes. Rich people got more votes in proportion to the size of their landholdings. The effect of this was to allow a majority of Protestants to vote, while denying the majority of Catholics the same right—a clear threat to their economic and political survival. The United Unionist party gerrymandered electoral districts (divided to ensure Protestant majorities) and enjoyed an unquestioned predominance until the 1970s. It remains the largest party in the north. The very creation of a Northern Ireland was the result of gerrymandering a small section of Ireland to extend Unionist control as far as they could. For the British, retaining the industrialized north was important. Ireland's shipping, military factories, and shipyards were all in the north. Along with its ports, keeping

Northern Ireland maintained British control over the North Sea. In exchange, Britain gave Unionists the power to abuse its newly created minority, in any manner that suited their desires.

Protestants refused to sell land to Catholics, refused to employ them, harassed them on the street and in their place of business, and burned them out of their homes. Unionists institutionalized themselves in all corners of Northern Ireland, taking over the policing, the civil service, and the media. Businesses regularly and openly discriminated against Irish Catholics, both as customers and workers. They marginalized and oppressed Catholics in ways they had not seen since the penal laws. Various forms of martial law (usually called emergency acts) have been in effect since 1922, suspending many civil liberties. These laws usually have only affected Catholic working-class neighborhoods and, to a lesser degree, Protestant working-class neighborhoods. Gaelic could not be spoken openly; it marks one as a "Republican" (a person who advocates a united Ireland), and the speaker may be open to harassment or even death. Daring to wave the Irish tricolor flag—which symbolically unites Green (Nationalists) and Orange (Unionists)—has sometimes led to police or Unionist violence. Many of these conditions continue to this day, though the economic condition and political power of Irish Catholics has improved.

This dominance is buttressed by a large paramilitary police force. At the center was the Royal Ulster Constabulary (RUC) formed out of the hated, preindependence British police force, the Royal Irish Constabulary. The RUC was reinforced by nearly 100,000 B Specials, an exclusively Protestant, part-time police force notorious for their brutality and violence. When the British disbanded the B Specials in the early 1970s, they allowed them to keep their guns. Also a part of the police state was the Ulster Defence Regiment (UDR). This British Army reserve corps was used primarily to put down Irish Catholic resistance to the Protestant order. In the 1970s the British reorganized the UDR into the RIR, or Royal Irish Regiment. The RIR remains predominantly Protestant and hostile to the Catholic population.

The RUC also remains overwhelmingly Protestant, even to this day; 93 percent of its force comes from the Protestant population. Most of the 144,000 people in Northern Ireland licensed to carry weapons are Unionist, including many who were once B Specials. The RUC forbids all members of Sinn Féin, on the other hand, from having gun licenses.

The key to Protestant domination has been the Orange Order. Along with the Apprentice Boys, the independent Orange Order, and the Royal Black Preceptory, these loyal orders form the cultural foundation of Protestant supremacy. The loyal orders exclude Catholics and require that its members be Protestants, born of Protestant parents. Intermarriage is forbidden, and it is violently opposed to any rapprochement with the Catholic minority. At least half of the members of the United Unionist party executive are members of the Orange Order. Most Unionist MPs to the British Parliament, including the first minister of Northern Ireland, David Trimble, are also members of the loyal orders. The Orange Order has many members and supporters in the institutions of Northern Ireland, in its police and civil service and among the landed elites and the urban Protestant working class. For fifty years (1922–1972) it held unchallenged authority in Northern Ireland, and membership was critical to any career. At least 15 percent of the Protestant male population are members of the Orange Order.

The Orange Order, founded in 1795, seeks to unite all Protestants in common purpose to promote the domination of Protestants over Catholics. By marching through Catholic neighborhoods (in what is known as the Marching Season), they declare the land for the British crown. From the Monday after Easter to the end of August, they organize more than 3,000 loyal order marches throughout Northern Ireland. Its parades have led to deadly violence since its founding. These parades usually include bands who are allied with Protestant paramilitary organizations. In many places, loyal order parades are a weekly occurrence. The RUC, for the most part, has violently suppressed Nationalist protests against these marches. In 1998, however, the British government took some measures to prevent the most contested parades from passing through Catholic neighborhoods. When the British government has tried to restrain the Orange Order, it has taken to the streets and paralyzed the countryside. Generally it has gotten its own way and has ensured that Protestant supremacy is preserved.

RESPONSE: STRUGGLES TO SURVIVE CULTURALLY

The Troubles

Following the division of Ireland, members of the IRA were hunted down in both the north and south. The IRA made several attempts to launch campaigns to liberate the north and to unseat the free state government, which the IRA refused to recognize until the 1970s. The IRA's last effort before the Troubles began was in the 1950s. It failed to win popular support and was swiftly crushed.

Following World War II, the industrial base of Northern Ireland began to erode. Until then, working-class Protestants could count on preferential treatment for jobs. Now they found themselves facing a declining job market. Protestant ghettos began to emerge. Even though job discrimination against Catholics continued unabated, Protestant hostility toward Catholics increased. A young Free Presbyterian minister, Ian Kyle Paisley, whipped up anti-Catholic resentment among the working class and, in 1966, along with his associates, formed a new Ulster Volunteer Force (UVF). Violence against Catholics increased.

In the late 1960s, a new generation of activists (including some Unionists) were inspired by the civil rights movement in the United States. Their goal was to model a similar movement in Northern Ireland. Their primary issues were "one person, one vote"; an end to housing discrimination, electoral gerrymandering, and religious discrimination; disbandment of the B Specials; and equality for all people. John Hume (cowinner of the Noble Peace Prize in 1998) and Bernadette Devlin (the youngest ever elected a British MP) were among the leaders of the civil rights movement. They organized peaceful protests and sit-ins. Opposition to their efforts quickly led to civil war.

As the civil rights movement gathered steam, Great Britain brought pressure to bear on the Unionist party to reform its discriminatory laws and practices. To the right, Paisley and his followers demanded a crackdown on the protests. The Unionist government brought in the RUC and the B Specials and savagely beat the protesters. As events gathered force, Protestant mobs, vigilante groups, and the police targeted Catholic homes and families. An ethnic cleansing campaign began, and Catholics living in Protestant neighborhoods were harassed, assassinated, and burned out of their homes. Towns all over the province divided into Catholic and Protestant neighborhoods. The violence and rioting was so great that the Irish government considered invading to protect the Irish populace against a rising pogrom of violence. The IRA (which had withered to the point that its acronym was jokingly said to mean "I Ran Away"), began to rearm with guns provided by the Irish Republic. The UVF exploded several bombs which were blamed on the IRA. Irish survival was threatened again.

The civil rights movement was shattered with the escalation of violence. Some, faced with the violent response of the Protestant majority, joined the IRA, or Sinn Féin. Others joined members of the Nationalist party (which elected a few members to the Northern Ireland Parliament, but had no voice) to form the Social Democratic Labour party (SDLP). The Unionist party was itself under stress as factions fought either to hold the line against the Catholic minority, or sought to make minor reforms. While the British increased pressure on the Unionist government to reform itself, opposition from within Unionism prevented any real reform from happening.

In 1969 the British government sent the army in, ostensibly to protect the Catholic population from the Protestant mobs. Some Catholic populations on their arrival even cheered them. Within a few days, however, that welcome turned sour as the British army began to turn its arsenal on the Catholic population as well. The IRA began to rearm, with guns provided by the Irish government. Hostilities between the IRA and the security forces (police and army) began to escalate as Loyalist crowds attacked Nationalist communities and homes. Police and the B Specials participated in these attacks.

The IRA, caught in tensions between an older socialist leadership centered in Dublin and a younger, more radical, but less ideological membership from Northern Ireland, split in 1969. The older group became known as the Official IRA, and a new group, the Provisional IRA, was born. Sinn Féin also split in 1970 into the same factions. Both groups targeted army personnel in a war of liberation. In 1972 the first British soldier died in an attack made by the IRA. At a peaceful protest march in Derry, the British army opened fire on the protestors, including women and children. Fourteen people were killed. This moment, known as Bloody Sunday, became the turning point. From then on, what was left of the civil rights movement ended, and the Troubles began. IRA attacks escalated. The British dissolved the Northern Ireland Parliament and instituted direct rule from London. The British government ordered internment and arrested 2,000 Republicans, but only 100 Loyalists. Those arrested were tried in secret courts (known as diplock courts). These actions were criticized internationally for their human rights violations.

In 1973 peace talks (which excluded the IRA and Sinn Féin) produced a coalition government of the SDLP and the Unionist party. This agreement was known as the Sunningdale Agreement. A very large Protestant paramilitary was formed called the Ulster Defence Association (UDA). The Unionist party split, and several new, anti-agreement factions emerged. The largest of them was the Vanguard party (David Trimble was then its deputy leader). Anti-agreement Unionists, led by Ian Paisley, the Vanguard party, the UDA, the UVF, and the Ulster Workers Council, organized a mass strike. Electrical power was cut off; transit was paralyzed; roads, seaports, and airports were blocked; and attacks were increased on the Catholic population. The UVF bombed Monaghan and Dublin (both in the Republic of Ireland), killing thirty-three people. The Provisionals (both IRAs had been on cease-fire), broke their cease-fire after attacks on their communities, and the coalition government collapsed. While the agreement was dead, many aspects of the agreement resurfaced, from both sides of the conflict, before it returned in the form of the 1998 Good Friday Agreement.

For the next thirty years the war dragged on and all struggled to survive. Loyalist death squads targeted random Catholics, their homes, bars, and churches. The Republican paramilitaries waged war against the British and retaliated against Loyalist attacks. In the mid 1970s, a cross-community women's group, known as the Peace People, led by two homemakers from both sides of the conflict, sought to broker an end to the fighting. While they enjoyed high visibility and the two women won the Noble Peace Prize in 1976, their efforts were short lived. The war raged on. Nonetheless, the ideas of the Sunningdale Agreement and the efforts of women and church groups became the foundation for beginning a peace process.

In 1976 paramilitary prisoners lost their prisoner-of-war status and were declared ordinary criminals. The "dirty protest" followed in the prisons, as both male and female IRA prisoners refused to wear the prison uniforms and instead wrapped themselves in blankets. They also engaged in hunger strikes. The most famous of these was the Hunger Strike of 1981, in which ten prisoners starved themselves to death in protest of the conditions of their incarceration. The most famous of these was Bobby Sands, who was elected to the British Parliament while on a hunger strike. The use of the hunger strike harkened back to a method of charging grievances under the code of ancient *brehon* law. According to *brehon* law, a person might starve himself at the door of someone he had a grievance with, until that person made amends. That person was Prime Minister Margaret Thatcher. Thatcher let them starve to death.

Their deaths galvanized the Nationalist population. Recruits flooded to the IRA, and Sinn Féin began to emerge as a viable political party. Two years after Bobby Sands had been elected and died, Gerry Adams was elected as MP from the hard-core Republican stronghold of West Belfast. Like all elected Sinn Féin officials, Adams refused to take his seat in Parliament and instead used his office to advocate for a United Ireland. The British began to use the RUC as the front line of defense, conducted intensive espionage, and backed the police with a ruthless military branch, known as the Security Advisory Services (SAS). Prisoners were regularly tortured during interrogation. The British also used spies inside the Loyalist paramilitaries to direct death squads, targeting known Republicans. British security's shoot-to-kill policy, combined with the Loyalist death squads, increased pressure on Republican communities. The IRA increasingly bombed nonmilitary and civilian targets, attempted assassinations of prominent British politicians (including Thatcher), and received large shipments of weapons from Libya.

Building the Peace Process

Secret negotiations between the Sinn Féin and the British and the Irish governments were initiated several times. The British and Irish governments set out a series of declarations and agreements in 1980, 1985, 1991, 1993, and 1995, inching toward the framework for ending the conflict and creating a peaceful Irish homeland.

In 1988 two Nationalist party leaders, John Hume (SDLP) and Gerry Adams (Sinn Féin), began discussions that became the framework for a possible peace agreement. Culminating in their joint declaration of 1993, they argued for the self-determination of all the people of Ireland and laid out a framework for ending the conflict. Political parties representing the Loyalist paramilitaries emerged, and their leaders held secret talks with Sinn Féin as well. In 1994 the IRA declared a cease-fire, and the Loyalist paramilitaries soon followed.

Though Prime Minister John Major (Conservative party) wanted negotiations, his slim majority in the House of Commons was dependent on Unionist MPs (the Ulster Unionist party [UUP] and Ian Paisley's Democratic Unionist party [DUP]). Both parties opposed any settlement. Major soon demanded that the IRA hand over its guns, a demand that was never made of any other paramilitary group in Irish history. The IRA refused. For two years an uneasy cease-fire was maintained. President Bill Clinton visited Northern Ireland, and Major appointed former Senator George Mitchell chair of the peace talks. Elections were held to pick representatives to the peace talks. Ten parties were elected to represent the people of Northern Ireland at the talks, including Sinn Féin, parties representing the Loyalist paramilitaries (the UVF and the UDA), the major parties, and the Women's Coalition (which included former members of the Peace People). The daily work of building bridges between communities flowered during the cease-fire of 1994–1996. Church and women's groups worked to advance understandings between the two communities.

However, in 1995, the Orange Order laid siege to the small Catholic Garvaghy Road community and tried to paralyze the countryside when its parade was rerouted away from this small Catholic ghetto. The siege of this community has become an annual celebration of bigotry and hatred since 1995. It is known as Drumcree (named after Drumcree Anglican Church where the Orange Order ostensibly marches to religious service). In 1995, between 20,000 and 30,000 people surrounded the Garvaghy community for nearly two weeks. Orange Order supporters attacked police and the army with rocks, bottles, firebombs, homemade hand grenades, and an occasional bullet. Meanwhile, over a dozen food venders fed the Orange Order supporters. Others sold T-shirts celebrating famous Loyalist assassins, in an atmosphere resembling a medieval festival. Provincewide, Orange Order supporters burned several hundred people out of their homes (including policemen's families). They also firebombed thirteen Catholic churches, destroyed dozens of Catholic businesses, and drove hundreds of families from their homes with harassment and threats. They blockaded roads, and Loyalist neighborhoods rioted.

Rioting over Drumcree paralyzed the province in 1996, as it had the previous year. Faced with continuing refusal by the British government to allow Sinn Féin into the peace talks, the IRA exploded several large bombs in London. The cease-fire was shattered.

The following year, the Labour party, led by Tony Blair, swept to power. Blair appointed Marjorie "Mo" Mowlam as the secretary for Northern Ireland. Unlike previous British representatives sent to Northern Ireland, Mo Mowlam took a far more inclusive approach to the process of building the consensus for the peace process. She violated the code of exclusion policed by middle-class Unionists, and met with prisoners from both sides, Sinn Féin and the Loyalist parties representing the paramilitaries. The IRA reinstated its cease-fire and the Loyalist paramilitaries did so as well.

Sinn Féin, following the cease-fire, was admitted into the peace talks. Two Unionist parties, led by Ian Paisley's DUP (third largest party in

Resistance march in Belfast, June 1998. Courtesy of Thomas Taaffe.

Northern Ireland) and the smaller UKUP (United Kingdom Unionist Party), withdrew from the talks and went into active opposition.

In April 1998, following intense negotiations, eight parties and two governments agreed upon a complex framework for building a shared government. Unfortunately, the DUP, the UKUP, the Orange Order, and sections of the UUP still refused to support the agreement. While 71 percent of the population supported the Good Friday Agreement (81 percent voting), its support varied considerably between communities. While as much as 99 percent of the Nationalist community supported the accords, only 55 percent of the Unionist community voted in favor of the deal. The agreement created the framework for the two communities to work out their disputes in a manner that did not (in theory) require violence (including the question of national aspiration). Unfortunately, the Marching Season was already under way, ensuring that political tensions and antagonisms would rise. The elections for the assembly produced unanimous support for the agreement among Nationalist and cross-community parties, but an almost even split among Unionist parties. The UUP offered qualified support for the agreement, but have met strong internal dissent for that support.

Emergent Peace or Continuing War?

In the months following the Good Friday Agreement, Northern Ireland experienced a roller-coaster of events. While the three major paramilitaries remained on cease-fire, factions within them split and continued the conflict. On the Loyalist side, dissidents from the UVF and the UDA formed the LVF (Loyalist Volunteer Force) in 1997. They continued their campaign of assassination and terror. When they went on a cease-fire themselves in May 1998, two new Loyalist paramilitaries emerged shortly afterwards, the Orange Volunteers and the Red Hand Defenders. On the Republican side, the INLA (Irish National Liberation Army), founded in the mid-1970s, continued its campaign, as did the Continuity Army Council (CIRA), founded in 1994. Dissidents from the Provisional IRA formed the "Real" IRA. The loyal orders paraded increasingly to try to reinforce their domination of the landscape in a rapidly shifting political moment. Meanwhile, international and cross-community efforts attempted to encourage a break with the past.

The sieges continued every year. On July 11, 1998, Loyalists burned three small Quinn boys to death (Richard [ten], Mark [nine], and Jason [seven]). Political sentiment began to turn against the Orange Order. After the deaths of those children, the numbers outside the Garvaghy community dwindled, but hundreds remained. The sieges of this community continue on an annual basis with nightly marches, frequent rioting, and hundreds of attacks on Catholic homes and businesses.

The killing of the three Quinn boys shocked the province and perhaps embarrassed the Protestant community into withdrawing much of its support for the Drumcree siege. Similarly, the bombing of Omagh by the Real IRA had a similar effect on the Republican community. The bomb, planted by the Real IRA, exploded in a largely Catholic town, on a high holy day (the Feast of the Assumption) and killed twenty-nine people, most of them Irish Catholics. It was the deadliest event in the thirty-year history of the Troubles. Many hoped that it would mark the end of the Troubles. Following that disaster, the INLA and the Real IRA declared a cease-fire. While the Continuity Army Council refused to declare a cease-fire, their guns have been silent.

Many realized that any resolution to the national question would not be possible as long as the animosity between the two communities remained at a violent level. Both sides had committed atrocities toward each other. Nearly 3,700 have been killed and almost 50,000 wounded since the start of the Troubles. Unionist support for a United Ireland, though never significant, declined. While the agreement did not resolve issues of equality and national aspiration, it created a framework to address those issues. While over 70 percent of the population voted for the agreement, skepticism about its success ran high. Although the Loyalist paramilitaries maintain their cease-fire, they have suffered from significant defections to newer groupings. The Unionist support for the agreement has not risen much above 50 percent. That all but two Unionist Assembly members come from parties that are either opposed to the agreement (28) or are nominally pro-agreement (28) speaks volumes about how the Unionist political leadership feels about change.

For nineteen months after the Assembly elections (June 1998), the UUP continued to refuse Sinn Féin admittance into the Assembly's executive, as mandated by the agreement, unless the IRA decommissioned its weapons. When Sinn Féin conveyed an IRA offer to begin decommissioning, provided that it was admitted into the executive first, Unionists turned that offer down and boycotted the Assembly. According to the agreement, voluntary decommissioning was intended to be carried out over a two-year period. The Assembly executive, however, was supposed to be set up after the Assembly elections (June 1998). In December 1999 the UUP finally agreed to allow the agreement to be implemented but added a new condition: the IRA had to begin decommissioning by January 31, 2000, a demand that was completely outside the agreement. To ensure that political pressure would be brought to bear on Sinn Féin and the IRA, David Trimble handed a postdated resignation letter to the president of his party, Josias Cunningham. Political pressure increased dramatically on Sinn Féin and the IRA, leading to increased defections by IRA members to the anti-agreement Real IRA. While the IRA did meet with the International Body on Decommissioning as stipulated by the agreement and agreed as well to consider how decommissioning might be effected, the British nonetheless suspended the agreement and its political bodies, and reinstituted direct rule in February 2000, when it appeared that the UUP would accept Trimble's resignation. Sinn Féin and the Irish government argued that this violated the agreement and the Irish constitution.

FOOD FOR THOUGHT

The peace process is in a terrible state. While no one expects the IRA to begin fighting again—in fact it had only two weeks earlier stated that it fully supported the agreement and "posed no threat to peace"—Unionists once again seized on the decommissioning issue to avoid staying in government with Irish Republicans. While the UUP were permitted for nineteen months to stall implementation of the Good Friday Agreement, neither the Unionists nor the British were willing to wait more than two months for the IRA to decommission, even though they were not required to decommission so quickly under the terms of the agreement. Neither could Sinn Féin or any other party be removed from office, so long as they remained committed to exclusively peaceful and democratic principles, which they repeatedly stated.

As a consequence, the agreement is in danger of being abandoned, and what hope there had been for a resolution to the conflict and an end to the threat to survival is quickly evaporating. Although significant prisoner releases have been made, proposals for reforming the police have been brought forth, and several committees mandated by the agreement have been formed, all of the power-sharing elements of the agreement have been blocked by 99 percent of the Unionist Assembly members. By suspending the agreement, the British government has undermined progressive elements in the IRA—as well as the pro-agreement parties—and has validated those who said the British could not be trusted.

While the British have made some minor efforts to dismantle their security apparatus, Northern Ireland remains—in many places—the most militarized landscape in Western Europe. The cost of that military presence is more than 2 billion dollars a year. The RUC continues to harass Nationalists; New Loyalist paramilitaries, the Red Hand Defenders, and the Orange Volunteers have attacked Catholics, though of late, that has subsided. The Orange Order remains at Drumcree (almost two years later) and its protests often turn violent. Speaking Gaelic outside Republican strongholds is still dangerous. In Portadowr, the LVF and UVF are engaged in a deadly feud. Seventy-five percent of the civil service in the Northern Ireland office and 93 percent of the police remain Protestant. In March 2000, the UUP passed new restrictions on entering a coalition government, requiring that the name of the police and its symbols (including a crown on top of a harp) be retained, while former Orange Order Grand Master, Martin Smyth, was narrowly defeated in a challenge to Trimble's leadership. The fourth largest party in Northern Ireland, Sinn Féin (only 6 percentage points behind the largest party, the UUP) is being blamed for a crisis created by escalating Unionists demands. While John Hume (SDLP) and David Trimble (UUP) have received the Noble Peace Prize for their efforts, the question remains—are we seeing the end of the Troubles, or simply entering a new phase? Is Irish cultural survival possible in a land continually caught between war and peace?

Questions

1. In what ways does Irish history resemble or differ from Native American history?

2. In what ways does the oppression of Irish Catholics resemble or differ from the oppression of African Americans?

3. How does the English oppression of the Irish compare to the Euro-American oppression of Native Americans and African Americans? Are there any connections?

4. In the nineteenth century, the English refused to intervene in the Irish famine of 1845–1850 because it violated the principles of free trade. Are there any recent examples of this ideology leading to disaster in other places?

5. In what ways is the history of the Irish struggle for independence similar to or different from other European efforts? Why?

NOTES

1. W. E. Gladstone, British prime minister 1868–1874, 1880–1886.
2. Report by the Royal Command to the King of England, 1515, quoted in Mary Francis Cusack, *An Illustrated History of Ireland: From AD 400 to 1800* (1868; reprint, London: Bracken Books, 1995), 389.
3. Sir James Craig, prime minister for Northern Ireland, 1934, quoted in Kevin Haddick-Flynn, *Orangism: The Making of a Tradition* (Dublin: Wolfhound Press, 1999), 331.

RESOURCE GUIDE

Published Literature

Curtis, Liz. *The Cause of Ireland: From the United Irishmen to Partition.* Belfast, Northern Ireland: Beyond the Pale Publications, 1994.
de Paor, Liam. *The Peoples of Ireland: From Prehistory to Modern Times.* Notre Dame, Ind.: University of Notre Dame Press, 1986.
Ellis, Peter Berresford. *A History of the Irish Working Class.* 1988. Reprint, Chicago: Pluto Press, 1996.
McGarry, John, and Brendan O'Leary. *Explaining Northern Ireland.* Cambridge, Mass.: Blackwell Publishers, 1995.
Ward, Margaret. *Unmanageable Revolutionaries: Women and Irish Nationalism.* 1989. Reprint, Chicago: Pluto Press, 1995.

Courtesy of Mapcraft.

Chapter 8

The Rusyn of the Carpathians

Richard Wallace

CULTURAL OVERVIEW

The People

The Rusyn are a Slavic people whose mountainous homeland straddles the northeastern part of Slovakia, the southeastern corner of Poland, and the westernmost part of Ukraine. They consider themselves distinct from their neighbors. Their religion is Graeco-Catholic or Orthodox Christian as opposed to their neighbors' Roman Catholicism, and their language is slightly different than their regional counterparts. Some argue that their speech is merely a dialectical variation; others, certainly most Rusyn, consider their speaking constitutive of a language separate from such institutionalized and internationally recognized languages as Slovak, Ukrainian, and Polish.

The name, Rusyn, connects the nationality to the East historically because of its association with the medieval state known as Rus', in what today is Ukraine. The name, Rusyn, however, is today significant and somewhat problematic. This chapter is obviously concerned with the Rusyn, but, depending on to whom you might talk, this nationality may also be labeled Rusin, Rusnak, Rusnyak, Руске, Rushin, Rusynian, Ruthenian, Ruthene, Ruten, Rus, Sub-Carpatho Rus, Carpatho-Russian, Carpatho-Ukranian, Carpatho-Ruthenian, Uhro-Rus', Uhro-Russ, Uherski-Rusin, Orosz, Lemko-Rusyn, Hutsul-Rusyn, Russian-Hungarian, or Little Russian, or perhaps even some other name. Different reasons exist for these different names; for example, the Ruthenian identifier comes from an old Greek pronunciation. The Greeks seem to have been one of the first people to recognize and write about the Ruthenian as distinct (Greek has a "th"

125

sound but, ironically, Rusyn does not). The Uhro- and Uher- tag comes from the Hungarian monarchy that ruled much of Transcarpathian land historically; the label describes the people as Hungarian first, Rusyn second. The Russian designation seems to come from a mistaken association of Rusyn with Russian because of the closeness of the words as well as cultural similarities between Rusyns and Russians. The Carpatho- label is clearly a way to tie these people to the geographical space known as the Carpathian mountain region.

The difficulty of locating a standardized name by which to call one's ethnic group presents problems, but is not altogether uncommon. Very often the name of a people is given by outsiders, and that can be the name that sticks however mistakenly it is applied. For example, the people that in English we call Hungarian call themselves Magyar and usually resent being associated with the Huns. The Native American Indians were labeled Indians because Christopher Columbus did not know where he was. In the case of the Rusyn, we can see the various historical derivations of their name, but in the present day it creates a problem because, with a population of only somewhere between 1.25 million and 1.5 million people worldwide, it makes it more difficult to organize as a people when so many do not know what to call the group. This chapter uses Rusyn because increasingly it appears, along with the appellation Carpatho-Rusyn, to be the standard designation used by most Rusyn people.

Another difficulty of standardization is a diversity within the Rusyn population itself. With the Rusyn people scattered through a half dozen different countries in Eastern Europe, and a North American population of Rusyn-identifying people, subgroups exist that consider themselves distinct. Within the generally contiguous Transcarpathian Rusyn region, historians have divided the area into four ethnolinguistically distinct settlements: the Lemko region is in Galicia, a part of southeastern Poland, and in northeastern Slovakia; the Bojko settlement is in the north-central part of the Rusyn Carpathian region; the Transcarpathian settlement is south central and within the nation-state of Ukraine; and the Hutsul are located in the southeastern stretch of the territory along the Ukraine-Romanian border. For example, in the Lemko region, some of the people "lumped" into the category of Rusyn for this chapter actually consider themselves as being of the Lemko ethnicity. They hold to cultural traditions and speak a particular dialect that makes them distinct from their Rusyn neighbors to the east. Likewise, the Hutsul have, to some extent, a sense of a Hutsul identity. Often these groups will be called Lemko-Rusyn or Hutsul-Rusyn, respectively, but that does not satisfy everyone.

Complicating the Rusyn identity further are Rusyn-identifying immigrant populations. The Rusyn people that have lived in the territory of today's Serbia and Croatia since the 1740s have developed their own traditions and will sometimes call themselves the Vojvodina Rusyn. Rusyn living in

North America often find this all most confusing and do their own part to mix it up further. On the one hand, some North American Rusyn, many of whom are third or fourth generation Americans or Canadians, look back at the homeland with a nostalgia that we might say is frozen in time; that is, if a Rusyn-identifying person's grandparents immigrated a century ago, she or he may know about their Rusyn identity only through stories passed down in the family, stories that probably reflect a place of 100 years ago, *not* the present day place. Some of these North American Rusyn may go back to their homeland and try to find that traditional place. Even though the Rusyn homeland does not really exist as it does in their mind's eye, they want to find this place so badly that they idealize the place and create somewhat warped perceptions of the Carpathian region. This creates differing "realities" that further tangle ideas of what it means to be Rusyn.

The Setting

The Rusyn live in or at least regard their homeland as the Carpathian region of Eastern Europe, which runs from Poland and Slovakia into Western Ukraine. A few Rusyn population centers can also be found in dispersed villages in northern Romania and northeastern Hungary.

Immigrant Rusyn populations live in other countries as well. Some live in neighboring areas, the most significant of which would be the Vojvodina Rusyn who live in northern Yugoslavia and along the Danube River in Croatia. Outside of Eastern Europe, North America is now the home for more Rusyn than anywhere else; 250,000 Rusyn immigrated to northeastern U.S. and Canadian industrial cities in the late nineteenth and early twentieth centuries.

Traditional Subsistence Strategies

Traditionally most Rusyn living in the Carpathian homeland were peasants. Their economy was largely agrarian, and they subsisted on the meager crops they could coax from mountain farmsteads, from their flocks of sheep in the hills, and from work connected to highland forests. Because the rugged landscape prevented any larger scale agriculture, the Rusyn were a poor people who often had to migrate to neighboring areas to find work or even emigrate permanently overseas.

Up until the latter half of the twentieth century, most Rusyn lived in small villages with usually fewer than a thousand people. Although, typically, Rusyn peasants formed the majority, other ethnicities inhabited the small villages often playing specific social roles. Jewish families were often the small merchants or innkeepers, and Gypsies came and went from settlements on the edge of the village. Also, depending on the region, typically a Slovak, Hungarian, or Polish schoolteacher and a government official lived in such rural Rusyn villages to carry out governmental administrative roles.

Rusyn usually did not make up much more than a small percentage of the population of the larger cities in or near the Transcarpathian territory. When Rusyn, usually a rural peasant people, migrated to the larger cities, they became assimilated into the dominant urban and state structures and typically into the wealthier population base in the city. They picked up the language and habits of the city-dwellers and lost their Rusyn identity in an effort to "fit in." Consequently, many Rusyn today claim that their numbers would be far greater if not for these assimilative practices.

Rusyn today do not have their own nation-state, nor have they had anything like a state or national structure except during fleeting historical moments. In some cases today, Rusyn are a recognized national minority within the nation-states in which they live, but for much of their history, the dominant populations have usually tried to count the Rusyns within their own and downplayed the idea that there was any ethno-linguistic difference between themselves and the Rusyn people. Nation-states very often have a tendency to favor a "homogenized" population, that is, a population wherein every citizen shares the same integral cultural traits, language, and values. Such a population, it is believed, is more unified behind the nation-state and more likely to go along with state policies.

Many Rusyn historically went along with this assimilative process because "fitting in" often meant greater economic and social acceptability. It is simply easier to go along with the more powerful, urbanized population. Imagine a poor Rusyn villager trying to get a city job at a workplace owned by Ukrainians. The person doing the hiring asks, "You speak a little oddly! You are Ukrainian, aren't you?" When one's number one priority is to get enough food on the table for one's children, it is unlikely a person would stand up and say, "No, I'm not! I'm proud to be Rusyn!" It is easier to hide one's accent and Rusyn ways. Furthermore, it makes sense to teach one's children to act like the dominant population so that they will have a greater chance of escaping the peasant life of mountain farming by succeeding in schools and workplaces where they need to speak Ukrainian. Perhaps the children and grandchildren grow up not knowing their ethnic identity or associating it with "backwards" country people and being ashamed of it. They might identify only with the dominant ethnicity and completely forget their Rusyn heritage.

Language

Just as language historically has been regarded as vital to the cultural survival of so many ethnicities and non-state nationalities, the question of language and linguistic differentiation has been paramount for Rusyn. Rusyn speak a language similar to most other languages spoken in the Transcarpathian area, but they claim that theirs is not a dialect of another language but is instead a distinct language unto itself. Like Slovak, Polish, Russian, and Ukrainian, Rusyn is a Slavic language, a branch of the Indo-European language group. Rusyn has the characteristics of East Slavic languages, particularly Ukrainian, and like most Eastern Slavic languages, the Rusyn language uses the Cyrillic alphabet, the letters that we associate with Russian, Ukrainian, and Serbian.

Because the Rusyn language tends to be a minority language in every region that it is spoken, however, it has heavy influences from languages of an immediate given region. Therefore, Rusyns living in non-Slavic Hungarian language areas, for example, incorporate a considerable amount of Hungarian vocabulary or pronunciations in their everyday speaking. The Rusyn language is also influenced by Church Slavonic historically because of the Rusyn's unique religious background, and this helps differentiate it from other regional languages.

Educated Rusyn used their vernacular language and the liturgical language of Church Slavonic to write books as early as the seventeenth century, and it was an important part of their form of Eastern Christianity. In the nineteenth and twentieth centuries, Rusyn writers were still using their vernacular, but Ukraine and Russian became more common in the region as literary languages and many Rusyn writers used them. Rusyn writers, no matter whether they were writing in Rusyn, Church Slavonic, Ukraine, or Russian, have almost always at least found as their base a lyrical expression of their love of their homeland and the beauty of the countryside, as well as a focus on rural life and the suffering of their peasant people under the yoke of other national states.

The language and its literary use have been the subject of debate in the Rusyn region and will probably remain so for some time to come. Very often in Ukraine, Ukrainian writers called Rusyn a regional dialect and attempted to bring Rusyn under a Ukrainian umbrella.

In the Vojvodina, in northern Yugoslavia, on the other hand, Rusyn were able to use their language in education and literature more or less without interruption for 250 years. In the former Yugoslavia, authorities recognized and respected the rights of the Rusyn as a national minority, and the Vojvodina Rusyn culture, albeit in a small pocket, was able to survive and flourish. However, in the 1990s, as Yugoslavia was breaking up, the Vojvodina Rusyn population found themselves in the cross fire between Serbs and Croats because they lived on or around the border of Serbia and Croatia. Some Rusyn were expected to fight for one side or the other in the conflict, and some were killed in the earliest fighting in the Yugoslav struggle. Many Rusyn were dislocated and their economies and lives severely altered. It remains to be seen if this already small population will be able to regroup and reestablish its national identity even as Croatian and Serbian national problems remain tense at this border area.

In the Prešov region of Slovakia and in the Lemko region of Galicia in Poland, where dominant populations very often downplayed a Rusyn existence, the current situation for Rusyn appears to have been improving of late. In the 1990s, with the relatively greater openness of current governments in the area, a Rusyn resurgence has led to greater efforts to use the Lemko Rusyn language in its written form. In Slovakia, Rusyn have codified their language; that is, they have created a literary standard so that they will have more agreement on how grammar and vocabulary will be taught. Prešov now hosts periodic conferences that have been focal points in the effort to assert a Rusyn identity, as well as a Rusyn theater and publishing facilities for Rusyn newspapers and journals. A Rusyn resurgence has not been without obstacles, however: the Slovak government, for example, has in recent years been slow and even preventative in the effort to institute Rusyn as a language of instruction in Slovakia's Prešov region.

Academic institutions within the region have played a major role in maintaining and reviving Rusyn literature and cultural life. Slovakia's Institute of Rusyn Language and Culture in Prešov and the Institute of Carpathian Studies at Ukraine's Uzhorod University, as well as the Department of Rusyn Language and Literature at Yugoslavia's University of Novi Sad and the Department of Ukrainian and Rusyn Philology at Hungary's Bessenyei Pedagogical Institute, have been important to Rusyn culture because, whether it focuses on folk traditions, on language, or on particular historical events, history is vitally important in shaping the present. Likewise, the Carpatho-Rusyn Research Center in the United States and the prolific work of University of Toronto professor Paul Robert Magocsi have been vitally important to keeping a Rusyn tradition alive. Rusyn, as a stateless people, outnumbered by other nationalities in the region, have needed to maintain their historical footing in the past in order to continue stepping into the future as a people.

As with many peoples of Eastern Europe, the folk culture spawned by rural living has been an important part of the Rusyn identity. Rusyn wear distinctively embroidered clothes and have their own folk singing and dancing traditions. A number of museums display Rusyn folk art and foster further Rusyn creativity in Poland, Ukraine, and Slovakia. *Skanzens* in the region, or ethnographic museum-like wooden villages, also preserve the look and feel of traditional Carpathian peasant settlements and Rusyn domestic living. Particularly distinctive are Rusyn churches which are distinguished by their characteristic wooden architecture sometimes with multiple "onion-shaped" cupolas topping a structure.

Religion

Folklore and language have been crucial components in the survival of Rusyn cultural traditions to the present day, but religion arguably may be one factor that has kept the Rusyns particularly distinct in the Carpathian region, and it remains an important factor in the Rusyn present. Rusyn churches reflect the milieu of the Eastern Orthodox and Western Christian cosmological traditions, incorporating elements of both services.

Rusyn, like most early Slavic populations, appear to have held an animistic spiritual world view, holding to pagan beliefs, until two brothers, Byzantine monks from Thessaloniki, Cyril and Method, brought Christianity to the Carpathian region sometime in the latter half of the ninth century. Pagan practices of the early Rusyn became syncretic elements of the Christianity. For example, the preexisting winter festival marking the winter solstice, *koljada*, became a celebration of the birth of Christ.

In the eleventh century great differences existed between Eastern and Western Christian power bases, and this led to a split between Rome and Byzantine Constantinople in 1054. The Rusyn remained, figuratively, on the Eastern side of the split, remaining Eastern Orthodox, which even to this day, helps them differentiate themselves from their largely Roman Catholic Slovak, Hungarian, and Polish neighbors. Unlike Roman Catholics, who have celibate priests celebrating mass in Latin, receive bread as the holy host, follow the (Western) Gregorian calendar, and look to the pope as God's representative on Earth, Rusyn worship with married priests speaking Church Slavonic in their liturgy, take both bread and wine at communion, use the Julian Calendar, and respond to the ecumenical patriarch in Constantinople as their spiritual leader. Rusyn people do use many of the Western church's rituals, however, which makes them different from their Eastern brethren; for example, Rusyn church music features more singing, which reflects their proximity to their Latin-rite neighbors.

In the sixteenth century, the Protestant Reformation and then the Catholic Counter-Reformation swept through Central Europe affecting the Rusyn too. The largely Roman Catholic elites in the Carpathian area, who were usually Hungarian or Polish, tried to shore up the strength of the Roman Church and bring Eastern Orthodox Rusyn into the fold. This resulted in the creation of an Eastern Christian Church in union with Rome in 1596. This was called the Uniate Church or what would be later known as the Greek Catholic Church. A large minority of Rusyn joined this church, which had to be in allegiance to Rome but was allowed to keep almost all of its traditions (including married priests). For this reason, many Rusyn villages still today have both a Greek Catholic and Orthodox church and, even though the liturgical services of each are quite similar, there has been friction between the two churches. Secular authorities have at times in the past persecuted either church, sometimes playing one group of adherents against the other, thus leading to a sometimes less unified Rusyn people at some points in their history.

Social and Political Organization

Slavic peoples appear to have first come to the Carpathian Mountains during the fifth and sixth centuries, and included in this migration would have been the ancestors of the Rusyn. These tribes settled on both the northern and southern slopes of the Carpathians where they built fortified settlements to protect their people. Slavs were organized into kingdoms for short times in the eighth and ninth centuries, and sometime in the middle of the ninth century, many Slavs were Christianized by early Byzantine missionaries. In the late 890s, however, the Magyars, a warrior people from Asia (today known as Hungarians by English speakers), invaded the area, defeated Prince Laborec', the founder of today's city of Uzhorod, and established their rule in the Carpathian Basin to the south. Initially, the Hungarians were not able to control the Carpathian Rus' region, and it stayed under the influence of the Kievan Rus' principality to the east. During this time Eastern people, who were distinguished by their adherence to Byzantine Christian rites, came to settle in the Carpathians and, although it is definitely subject to debate, it is these people who are traditionally thought to be the ancestors of the Rusyn.

In the eleventh century, the kingdom of Hungary controlled the Subcarpathian Rus' with a hold that lasted, in varying permutations and degrees of intensity, until 1918. In the early sixteenth century, the Ottoman Turks conquered much of southern and central Hungary, and although the kingdom of Poland controlled the Lemko region until the late eighteenth century, most of the Rusyn lands remained in nominal Hungarian control with rule divided between the Habsburg Empire and Hungarian Transylvania. In the eighteenth century, the Habsburg dynasty regained control of the Carpathian Basin, and the Subcarpathian Rus' remained firmly in what in the nineteenth century would become known as the Habsburg Austro-Hungarian Empire until its collapse during World War I.

In the earlier part of the millennium, the Carpathian Rusyn area was sparsely settled, but over time, the population grew. The Rusyn became serfs in a feudal system of rule under Hungarian landholders. During this time, the small and usually poor Rusyn made some efforts toward autonomy, but this did not meet with much success through the centuries. In the middle of the nineteenth century, when the peoples throughout Central and Eastern Europe were "awakening" to the idea of nationhood, Rusyn leaders, lead by Adolf Dobrianskyj, pressed the Habsburg rulers to create an autonomous Rusyn province that would unite the Rusyn within the Austro-Hungarian Empire. These appeals fell on deaf ears.

THREATS TO SURVIVAL

The Habsburg Austro-Hungarian Empire, which was on the losing side of World War I, had collapsed by 1918. A new Hungarian government, formed late that year, declared the Rusyn territory autonomous at year's end. At the same time, the Lemko Rusyn created a self-governing republic that lasted a little over a year until early 1920 when Poland took control of the area. These two attempts at Rusyn autonomy and independence were short lived. A voluntary unification of the Rusyn living south of the Carpathians with the newly established state of Czechoslovakia in spring 1919 had longer lasting effects. In the postwar Paris Peace Conference, the Treaty of Saint Germain, with an understanding that Rusyn would have autonomy, recognized this joining with Czechoslovakia. This province was created and called Subcarpathian Rus', and it had its own Rusyn governor and a limited degree of autonomy. Rusyn living in the more western Prešov region and in Polish Lemko, however, were not included in this province. Their efforts to join with Subcarpathian Rus' were thwarted by both the Czechoslovakian and Polish governments. The Subcarpathian Rus' province functioned until 1938 when the manipulations of Nazi Germany and Czechoslovakia's betrayal at the hands of its allies (notably, Britain, France, the Soviet Union, and the United States) altered the Czechoslovakian state structure. Subcarpathian Rus' became autonomous and self-governing for a short six months, until Nazi Germany completely dismantled Czechoslovakia by occupying the Czech Lands and imposing a puppet fascist government on Slovakia in March 1939. That same day, the people of the Subcarpathian Rus' region declared themselves an independent sovereign republic with the name Carpatho-Ukraine. Also, that same day, Nazi-allied Hungary invaded and began its occupation of the region which lasted until 1944. Carpatho-Ukraine is sometimes known as the "one-day republic."

When the war ended, the region experienced another short period of self-rule when the Soviet army pushed out the Hungarians. A national council governed the region, known as Transcarpathia, from autumn 1944 until the council, under pressure from the Soviet Union, decided to unify with the Soviet Union's Ukraine in 1945. Thus much of the Rusyn area became part of the Ukraine within the Soviet Union when the Soviets annexed the region that had before been part of Czechoslovakia. In Czechoslovakia's Prešov region, Rusyn set up a national council in order to maintain autonomy, but the Communist government did away with it in 1949. Thus by the 1950s, with only one significant exception, all European Rusyn people were living in the Soviet bloc whether they were in Poland, Czechoslovakia, Romania, Hungary, or the Soviet Union, and the Rusyn were largely ignored as a nationality, and the Graeco-Catholic church was outlawed. In Ukraine, the Soviet government pressed Rusyn to become Ukrainian by downplaying and even outlawing it as an ethnicity. Similarly, in Poland

and Czechoslovakia, Rusyn was not recognized as a nationality. When census takers asked Rusyn their ethnicity, they had no box to check off as Rusyn, so they were usually labeled Ukrainian. Many Rusyn people were displaced in the years following World War II and, removed from their homeland and with their nationality utterly unacknowledged, some Rusyn lost touch with their ethnic background. The Vojvodina Rusyn were the only population exempt from this treatment. They lived in Communist Yugoslavia, but Yugoslavia was not aligned with the Soviets, and perhaps for that reason their rights as a national minority group were respected.

RESPONSE: STRUGGLES TO SURVIVE CULTURALLY

Recent Activity

After the Eastern European revolutions of 1989 and the breakup of the Soviet Union, the Rusyn people revived their ideas of autonomy as they became citizens of several newly established nation-states. The Lemko Rusyn remained part of Poland, and small clusters of villages remained part of Romania and Hungary. The Rusyn in the Transcarpathian area became part of independent Ukraine in 1991. In the Prešov region, they became part of the newly independent Slovakia (1993). The Vojvodina Rusyn were separated between Serb territory (still called Yugoslavia) and the newly independent Croatia (1991).

In Ukraine's Transcarpathian region, Rusyn sought a return to their historical autonomy. In a referendum in December 1991 on Ukrainian independence, more than three-quarters of the region's populace voted for "self-governing status" within Ukraine. The Ukrainian government, however, did not implement the obligations of this referendum, and Rusyn leaders formed a provisional government for the Republic of Subcarpathian Rus' in May 1993. Since that time, Rusyn have struggled for autonomy by means of their Transcarpathian National Council, which is a form of a regional parliament, but they have made little headway. Some council members seek autonomy, some seek outright independence, but all wish to see the Ukrainian government address their regional concerns with the respect they feel is due the "historically autonomous" region.

Rusyn have also been active in the last decade in Poland, Slovakia, and Hungary. The Lemko Association in Poland, the Rusyn Renaissance Society in Slovakia, and the Organization of Rusyns in Hungary are cultural organizations that were established with the goal of having the Rusyn recognized as a distinct nationality within each country. In Slovakia and Poland, they also codified Lemko Rusyn as a literary language for educational purposes and for mass media and theatrical use. These organizations, along with the Ukraine-based Society of Carpatho-Rusyns, the former Yugoslavia's Rusyn Matka, the Czech Friends of Subcarpathian Rus', and the

United States' Carpatho-Rusyn Research Center, have created contacts and worked jointly in forming the World Congress of Rusyn. This body now meets regularly to work in common to preserve and promote the Rusyn people as a distinct nationality. Not only must Rusyn leaders fight with state governments for their cultural and linguistic rights in media, schools, and workplaces, they must also foster an awareness of Rusyn culture and traditions among their own people, many of whom are increasingly influenced by Western European and North American economics and popular culture and have been assimilated into the cultural practices and languages of the dominant nation-states within which they live.

FOOD FOR THOUGHT

Rusyn leaders must work hard to gain and maintain their cultural and linguistic rights in education, on the job, and within the broad scope of media influence. The various distinct groupings and their seemingly continued divergence pushes many Rusyn to work even harder to foster an awareness of Rusyn culture and traditions among their own people. Cultural survival is an ongoing challenge for every group of people in this rapidly modernizing world.

Questions

1. Had you ever heard of the Rusyn people? Why do you think that you had or had not heard of them?
2. How do national identities affect the way in which a people look at themselves and the way in which other people perceive them? Or *not* perceive them?
3. Have divisions within the Rusyn community contributed to an overall weakness in the Rusyn as a people asserting their rights as a nationality?
4. What is the difference between political rights and cultural rights?
5. If you were a Rusyn person living in the Carpathian homeland, would you be fighting for your national rights? If you were a person of Rusyn heritage living in North America, would you contribute to the Rusyn efforts back home?

RESOURCE GUIDE

Published Literature

Dyrud, Keith. *The Quest for the Rusyn Soul. The Politics of Religion and Culture in Eastern Europe and in America. 1890–World War I.* Philadelphia: Balch Institute Press, 1992.
Horak, Stephan. *Eastern European National Minorities. A Handbook.* Littleton, Colorado: Libraries Unlimited, 1985.
Magocsi, Paul R. *Our People: Carpatho-Rusyns and Their Descendants in North America.* 3rd ed. Toronto: Multicultural History Society of Ontario, 1994.

———. *The Rusyns of Slovakia. An Historical Survey.* New York: Eastern European Monographs, Columbia University Press, 1993.

———. *The Shaping of a National Identity. Subcarpathian Rus', 1848–1948.* Cambridge, Mass.: Harvard University Press, 1978.

Magosci, Paul R., ed. *The Persistence of Regional Cultures. Rusyns and Ukrainians in their Carpathian Homeland and Abroad.* New York: Eastern European Monographs, Columbia University Press, 1993.

Mayer, Maria. *The Rusyns of Hungary: Political and Social Developments, 1860–1910.* New York: Eastern European Monographs, Columbia University Press, 1997.

Němec, František, and Vladimír Moudry. *The Soviet Seizure of Subcarpathian Ruthenia.* Westport, Conn.: Hyperion Press, 1955.

Winch, Walter. *Republic for a Day: An Eyewitness Account of the Carpatho-Ukraine Incident.* London: Hale, 1939.

WWW Sites

Carpatho-Rusyn Genealogy Web Site
This site includes surname listing, immigrant listing, and other information for persons who are interested in Carpatho-Rusyn ancestry.
http://www.rusyn.com

The Carpatho-Rusyn Knowledge Base
This site is highly recommended. It is a rich assemblage of texts about the Rusyns, although the reader should be particularly wary of some strong biases in individual contributions to the Web site.
http://carpatho-rusyn.org

Researching the People from 'No Mans Land': The Carpatho-Rusyns of Austria-Hungary
http://feefhs.org/fij/peters1.html

Welcome to Transcarpathia
"Home of Ukrainians, Russians, Hungarians, Slovakians, Czechians, Romanians, Polonians" [*sic*], but there is no mention of Rusyns.
http://cr.karpaty.uzhgorod.ua:8101/Transcarpathia/index.html

Руске Дружтво Сиверней Америки
The Rusyn Association of North America (mostly written in Rusyn using Cyrillic text, but it is interesting to see whether you can read it).
http://members.tripod.com/~rdsa/index.html

Русин
This Slovak-based database is also written in Rusyn.
http://rusyn.vadium.sk/

Organizations

Carpatho-Rusyn Research Center
P.O. Box 131-B
Orwell, Vermont 05760

The Carpatho-Rusyn Society
125 Westland Drive
Pittsburgh, Pennsylvania 15217–2538

The Rusin Association of Minnesota
1115 Pineview Lane North
Plymouth, Minnesota 55441–4655

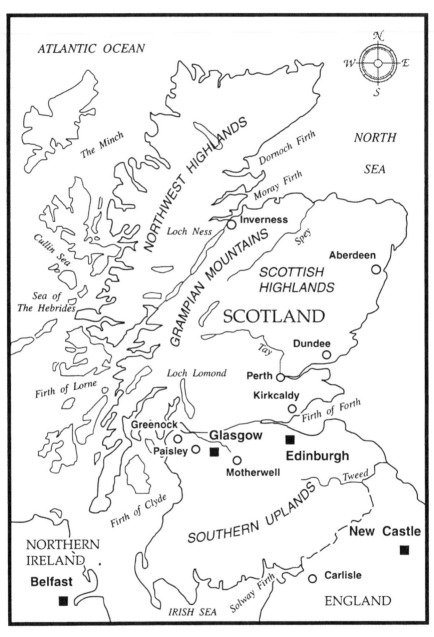

Courtesy of Mapcraft.

Chapter 9

The Scottish Highlanders

Kelli Ann Costa and Jean S. Forward

CULTURAL OVERVIEW

To clearly see the threats to cultural survival in the Highlands of Scotland, one must see the whole interactive system of Highland culture, the people, and their environment. The greatest resource has been and is the people and their very human adaptive abilities to interweave various other resources—limited agricultural land, ocean resources, sheep and cattle, and tourism—into a tapestry of subsistence activities that allow the people to survive and reproduce. These are cultural adaptations for survival in a very physical world.

The People

The Scottish Highlanders are self-identified, active members of a long-standing Highland cultural system. They were part of the Celtic linguistic fringe pushed to the marginal environments of northwestern Europe by the Roman colonization of the Gauls. Other Roman campaigns reached into the Midland Valley of Scotland itself where the Romans were harassed by the Picts, one of the resident groups of that area. In fact, Hadrian's Wall is a solid boundary that was meant to keep the Picts out of the southern half of the island.

The name, Scotland, comes from a word for the land of the Scotti, a Celtic tribe who invaded from Ireland sometime after A.D. 200 and settled on the western side of Scotland. The Scots, the Anglos, and the Picts competed for control of the resources and the territory. The Picts usually were dominant until the Vikings began to raid in the ninth century. The response to the increased Viking presence was the unification of the three kingdoms: the Scots kingdom of Dalriada, the Pict kingdom of Caledonia, and the Anglo kingdom of Strathclyde became Alban under Kenneth MacAlphin in 844. Malcolm II Mackenneth led the Alban invasion which conquered its southern neighbor, Northumbria, at the Battle of Carharn in 1018 and created the kingdom of Scotland.

The Setting

In Gaelic *Tuatha* means land and it means people.[1] Wholistically speaking, the Highlands of Scotland are the homeland for Scottish Highland Celtic culture. The land was carved by very slow moving glaciers combined with very fast running water into twisting small valleys, cool wooded glens, and a great many lochs (lakes) spread throughout the mountains. The Highlands refer to all of the northern mountainous portions of Scotland including all of the islands except the Orkney and Shetland islands. Since 1975 the Highlands and islands have also been established as local government districts and regions. This economic political structure is part of the ongoing process that helps to maintain and perpetuate an ethnic identity in today's world.

Social and Political Organization and Subsistence Strategies

The clan system—a group of people who recognize a common ancestor— organized the people in Scotland. The clans in Scotland could be mobilized for defense or offense or for group subsistence activities (raiding, fishing, and so on). They were integrated through trade, marriage, and political alliances. Clan lairds governed by example and with the approval of the people within the clan. The position of laird or chief was a permanent role, but the person who held the job usually had to prove his worth as well as have appropriate kin relationships. Inheritance could pass through either the mother's or father's line, contrary to the English system of primogeniture in which the oldest son in the father's line inherits everything.

The clan system was well entrenched before the Anglicization of the laws of town and court began to be institutionalized after William the Conqueror. Edgar the Ethelring, a Saxon, sought refuge from the Normans with the Scottish king, Malcolm Canmore, the great grandson of Malcolm II Mackenneth). Edgar's sister married the allegedly barbaric Scottish king and brought with her notions of English propriety and customs. Part of this reformation was establishing English laws whose authority would supercede that of the clan lairds, a process of centralizing power which spread throughout the Anglo-dominated globe. Initially, even with these laws, feudalism was unable to displace the clan system.[2] From the thirteenth century on, however, English domination increased; and Scottish self-determination, both as a kingdom and as clans, decreased.

The thirteenth century was the era of William Wallace and Robert the Bruce. Edward I of England was determined to bring Scotland, as well as Wales and Ireland, under English law. The identity of Highland Scots and clans was part of a sociopolitical network that became ever more tightly interwoven into the Anglo-dominated political and economic system. This system was hierarchical, with the English on top and everyone else somewhere below. Even within the Anglo homeland there was a clearly stated hierarchical order from the king down to the lowliest chimney sweep and beggar. Edward I claimed divine right to rule the entire island. Highlanders fought the authority and hierarchy of the English crown, and the clans resisted centralization. This resistance to a permanent central authority is a Celtic trait, traceable back to the days of the Roman invasion of the Celtic homeland, Gaul.

After Edward I invaded Scotland at the end of the 1200s, he installed feudal laws with himself and the English at the head of the government. He sought relentlessly to control the Scottish land and people. Resistance to Edward resulted in the destruction of farms, crops, castles, and people by Scottish nobility handpicked by Edward I to replace Highland lairds. When Edward's control diminished, the Highland lairds gained ascendancy, an ongoing, oft repeated pattern between crowns and clans, with Anglicized, industrial, political, and economic dominance gradually gaining. This is illustrated in the growth and decline of the strength of the Lordship of the Isles in the Hebrides from the twelfth century to the fifteenth century. In 1493 the Anglicized Scottish crown finally outlawed any independent (i.e., indigenous) Gaelic kingdom. (This was a significant year in the nation-state building of Europe—see chapter 3.) Many of the actions were the result of a push in Western Europe to create homogeneous nation-states. Edward's policies were to replace Highland nobility with Lowlanders and Englishmen and to force marriages between the two groups to breed out the "wild" Highlanders.

By the seventeenth century, when the right to the land became a lease, the clan system began to unravel. In 1609 the Statutes of Icolmkill outlawed the ancient Celtic system of fostering which had sustained and perpetuated the clan system. Every Highlander with sixty or more head of cattle was required to send his children to boarding schools where English was the only language allowed. This was just the beginning of a thorough, systematic effort to eliminate the Gaelic language and culture from the land. This effort included the suppression of bards who passed on clan history in Gaelic and the decree that heirs of Highland lairds must be able to read, write, and speak English to be legally acknowledged as heirs.

The English and other outsiders used leases to permeate the Highland system. To undermine kinship relationships, leases were available to the highest bidder, not just kith and kin. More and more land was controlled by the English and the Scottish Lowlanders through a thoroughly Anglicized, political economic legal system. Emigration increased as the people lost their land and were transported to the various British colonies, where they spread the Highland traditions and identity.

The emigrations from the Highlands dramatically increased after political and economic support for the Scottish crown resulted in its major military and political defeat at Culloden in 1746. Culloden was a slaughter by Hanoverian troops not only of the Scottish army and supporters, but also of many of the Scottish people. It was not stopped until George II's son, William Angustus, duke of Cumberland, and his troops deemed that the clans were no longer functional. Again, war had devastated people, land, crops, and castles in the Highlands. It became illegal for approximately forty years (two generations) to wear kilts and plaids, to prepare special Highland food items, to play the bagpipes (war weapons), and to speak Gaelic. Sometimes restrictions or attempts to eradicate symbols of ethnic identity can work to strengthen the very identity that the laws intend to crush. In this case, wearing plaids survived as a symbol of Scotland within the domain of lairds and the Highland regiments in the British army. Because boarding schools beat the captive sons of Scottish lairds for speaking Gaelic, the language was passed down through families as a badge of identity in spite of and because of the restrictions. Gaelic was the language of the home, and formal education in English was part of the identity of the oppressive English "other."

In terms of agriculture, the Scottish Highlands has always been marginal land, land that cannot sustain human populations without the supplement of other forms of production, including kelp, fish, cattle (raising and reiving or stealing), weaving, sheep, whiskey, Highland Regiments, and tourism, to name the most prominent.

The Scottish Highland identity of the people connected to this homeland has developed through and persisted over centuries. This identity is tied to the Highlands themselves and the necessary measures people must adapt to in order to sustain themselves and their descendants. The markers of this identity today still include crofting (a nineteenth-century system of agriculture), the Gaelic language, the clan system, kilts and plaids, and bagpipes and haggis (a special food) to name a few. The identity markers of the Highlands are identity markers recognized by the Lowlanders as well, but identity as a classification should not be seen as static, but as a process, complex and flexible with fluid boundaries.

Although it was never the language of all of Scotland, Gaelic is the language that identifies the Scottish Highlander. Historically, the peasants spoke Gaelic, and the Scottish nobility spoke both Gaelic and English. Language frequently acts as a boundary mark for ethnic identity, and the per-petuation of spoken Gaelic proclaims and reinforces Scottish Highland identity.

The perseverence and persistence of the Highland identity is also due, in part, to the contrast between the Highland and the Lowland/Sassenach (Saxon) way of life. The Highlander image is rural, slow moving, informal, immature, and "fiery and ferocious," as opposed to the Lowland image, which is urban, fast paced, formal, and sophisticated. The dichotomy is further encouraged today by the fact that Englishmen often own the leases to Scottish land and use the land only for visits to the "country." This reinforces the stereotype of the sophisticated, rich English/Lowlander who oversees the backward Highland peasant. Ethnic identities are often main-tained through opposition to the "other." Learning who "we" and "they" are is part of child rearing and the learning of one's own ethnic identity. Anthropologists call it enculturation; formal educational programs call it history. The Gaelic language was part of this "backward" Highland iden-tity for centuries. Modern revival policies are changing that to a certain extent. It is now becoming "posh" to speak Gaelic.

In 1777 the Gaelic Society of London was able to persuade the crown to repeal some of the repressive acts that were enacted after Culloden. In 1822 English king George IV visited Scotland. The pageantry included the wearing of Highland garb by George himself as well as by the rest of the court. The rotund George was much spoofed in the newspapers, but the re-sult was that kilts were fashionable again. Preceding this visit, specific plaid patterns had numbers. "Because of the huge demand that preceded the visit, patterns were assigned to different clans as they came off the looms."[3] Thus specific plaids became associated with specific clans.

By 1840 crofting symbolized the Celtic way of life in Highland Scotland. The Scottish Highlands is a difficult environment for sustaining human populations. What has worked there was a communally (clan) controlled land system which included individual crofts and was woven into the fabric of their identity. This system of the symbolic and real intertwinement of land and people was handed down perhaps for centuries as part of Celtic identity. By the late nineteenth century, it was known as crofting.

The Scottish crofter is the tenant of a croft, or small unit of agricultural land (less than fifty acres, and on the island of Lewis in the Outer Hebrides usually three to five acres). The croft (is a strip) of land that usually encompasses both well-drained and boggy land and adjoins a main road; the croft house (owned by the crofter) sits next to the road and usually has a small garden patch behind it. Possession of a croft includes a share of the common grazing land held by a crofting township, the members of which share the responsibility of maintaining the land and fencing, organizing communal sheep roundups, and in general acting to promote the agri-cultural viability of the township.[4]

This is the basis of a crofting community, a way of life indigenous to the Scottish Highlands.

A series of nineteenth-century disasters left the Scottish Highlands economically depressed. The market for kelp, which had long been an integral thread in Highland subsistence, was destroyed, fishing declined, and the government placed restrictive taxes on whiskey production. A potato blight and general overuse of the land caused farmers to sell cattle to pay rent. All of this hastened the conversion of more land to sheep farming. While crofting communities were considered the embodiment of a traditional, Scottish Highland, Celtic (agricultural) way of life, they needed a supplementary production system to be sustainable,[5] and this became more and more difficult from the eighteenth century on as sheep farming diminished the land's productive capabilities in other areas.

From the late eighteenth century through the middle of the nineteenth century, land was systematically cleared of people to make more room for sheep. This era is referred to as the "Clearances." The "Clearances" remain a symbol of injustice between crofter and landlord until this day. In fact, it was the 1886 Crofters Act that finally took a legal stand to save the crofting way of life. The Crofters Act is a body of law that seeks to perpetuate crofting townships, a crofting lifestyle, and the Highland identity. The act links both with agricultural activity in an environment that cannot sustain agricultural production except on a small scale. Therefore, other supplementary production activities are necessary, and this necessity is woven into the identity.

This identity is tied to the Highlands themselves and the necessary measures people must adapt to in order to sustain themselves and their descendants. Ownership of large tracts of land by the clan laird and the clan has been replaced by more Anglicized nobility with no kin relationship to the crofters/tenants. The 1886 Crofters Act created an aura of security around the perpetuation of crofting townships and access to grazing land, but the crofters still do not own and therefore totally control the production uses of the land that their homes, which they do own, sit on. The boundary between crofting communities and the economic elite is still wide indeed.

Crofting townships do persist and do support some agricultural production. Over time, supplemental activities have varied according to ecology, economics, and individual talents. Weaving plaids, Argyles, and other patterns is a large and profitable industry linked to raising sheep. With the decline of the fish and related production activities (kelp, fishing boats, and so on) other economic activities have developed. Lowlanders have long seen the Highlands as a place of retreat and relaxation (it is the birthplace of golf), and the development of tourism as a seasonal moneymaker is increasing. The Internet can supply the population of the globe with personalized Highland walking tours, clan kilts, bagpipes, haggis, and Gaelic language teaching tools. A Scottish Silicon Valley has also developed. The production activities within the Highlands may change over time, affecting the composition of Highland identity, but the recognition of a separate Highland identity does not change. In other words, the material culture may change, but the recognition of a Highland "us" persists.

The Highlands and islands are now constructed into political units with accompanying economic advantages. The reorganization in 1975 abolished counties and burghs and replaced them with nine regions and three island areas. The nine regions are further divided into fifty-three districts administered by councils with four-year elected terms. The British Conservative and Labour parties have dominated the seventy-two Scottish seats in the House of Commons and sixteen seats in the House of Lords. The Scottish Nationalist party ebbs and flows in its influence. Currently, strong Scottish nationalism has encouraged the populace to consider a bid for a separate Scottish parliament. On September 9, 1998, the Scottish people voted to recreate a Scottish parliament and on May 6, 1999, they elected their first active parliament in 300 years. Some are calling this the quiet revolution.

Religion

Scottish Presbyterianism is a strong element of Highlander identity. There are three Presbyterian churches: the Church of Scotland, the Free Presbyterian Church, and the Free Church. Although Presbyterianism in general is a marker of Highland identity, the persistence of Presbyterianism and its strict Calvinist doctrine fly in the face of the romantic vision of Highlanders held by many outsiders. Calvinists believe that the individual alone must assume responsibility for himself or herself and must shun personal vanities. This contradicts the romantic notion of the communal, cooperative crofting community. It can by understood, though, as part of the maintenance of the Highland identity versus the Lowland/English forms of Protestant churches. The churches also function as places to socialize and to speak Gaelic. The three distinct churches divide communities, yet they also weave threads of solidarity throughout the Highlands.

THREATS TO SURVIVAL

The Scottish Highlands has always been a marginal environment for agricultural production. Its true wealth has been its people and the social structures that they have created to sustain their lives in a poor, mountainous region. As the English nation-state developed, especially legally, in the sixteenth and seventeenth centuries, it attacked the social fabric of the Highlands and imposed an Anglo patriarchal system.

An economic decline in the late seventeenth century led to a resurgence of Scottish self-determination in the early eighteenth century, which unfortunately ended at Culloden in 1746. Highland identity had a resurgence later in the eighteenth century only to meet with the late eighteenth-century Clearances, an attempt to improve the economic profitability in the Highlands for the benefit of the landowners, usually Lowland/English "others." Peasants (i.e., crofters) were displaced; many emigrated to areas of previous and current British colonies where earlier Scottish colonists had established themselves.

The nineteenth-century onward continued to see ebbs and flows to the sustainability of the Scottish Highland identity. In the late nineteenth-century, a national formal educational system was established by the English—in English. It was a continuation of the policy of cultural dominance, a strategy of linguistic dominance. We now see policies within Scotland focusing on the revival of Gaelic language and culture. The identity of the Scottish Highlander is a commodity that is bought and sold on the global market.

Current Events and Conditions

Globally, tourism is a major moneymaker. The selling of Scottish Highland identity is demonstrated in such media events as the movie *Braveheart*, the *Highlander* movies and television series, Celtic fairs, Highland gatherings in many former British colonies, and even a Loch Ness theme park with a plastic Nessie. Interactions with descendants of those who emigrated help keep the tapestry tightly woven. Clan gatherings take place all over the globe. Yet, while pockets of Highland emigrés perpetuate that identity, does it encourage perpetuation in Scotland itself?

Obviously, Scotland is still an arena where the forces of globalization continue to battle with a regional identity and independence movement. This battle is being played out all over Europe with more or less violence. The political-economic domination of the world capitalist system often portrays the local peasant/working class as victims, unable to control the forces of capitalist intervention, overwhelmed and destined to disappear, but this is a view which many of the oppressed would contest. Can Highland identity and the accompanying crofting communities survive? Are they sustainable to begin with? Most crofting communities are small and on the fringe; how do they interact with the larger communities? With the European Union? With the world market system? How does Scottish nationalism aid or hinder the Highland identity and way of life?

Changes in income activities other than crofting have changed the land. Changes from producing barley and potatoes for humans to the production of oats for livestock and the change in livestock from predominantly cattle to predominantly sheep has helped to deplete a mediocre soil. Cattle fertilize a field better than sheep, but wool and weaving are important industries, too.

The increase of tourism, while bringing in needed revenues for local folk,

The Scottish Highlands. Courtesy of Greg Mulkern.

also opens the Highlands to global access by hundreds, even thousands, of tourists who penetrate the Highlands on walking tours and buses. Erosion and pollution, especially litter, often follow. Access to historical sites and the growth of museums also attract tourists. Effective organization is required to preserve the sites while efficaciously using this resource. Large groups of people change an environment with their use of that environment, and then humans must, yet again, adapt to those changes.

Probably the greatest threat from human use of the earth's resources is the development of oil deposits along the coast, especially in the Highland and Grampian regions. The effects of oil development may vary according to the size of the oil industry site and the regional differences in size, population numbers, and resources. However, clearly the introduction of the oil industry is not like the introduction of cattle, potatoes, or even sheep.

Each of these industries acted as a supplement to crofting and each was woven into the Highland identity and economic system, on thin or thick threads. The profits of the local laird had a greater impact on the local economy than the profits of multinational petroleum companies. Today's local lairds are at the top of the social hierarchy in a very linear system: they consume more resources than the average crofter and are expected to do so. Crofters are expected to produce the goods and services that support the lords and the linear hierarchy.

The oil industry consumes local natural resources but returns little to the local Highland economy. Industrialization, in general, and the development of oil sites, in particular, tend toward urban concentrations of people because centralized populations are cheaper to feed and house. However, little of the Highlands constitutes suitable space for the growth of cities. Also, generally but certainly not always, urban groupings tend to break down close kin systems. Some oil sites attract larger population groups than have usually been sustained in that area. The overall effects on the Scottish Highland identity, culture, and environment have yet to be evaluated thoroughly.

The potential environmental threat from oil development is significant. Oil spills, leftover or discarded oil equipment, and increased human presence pose significant problems to an environment that marginally supports human occupation. A similar disaster to the Exxon Valdez spill in Alaska could deteriorate the coast of the Highlands past the point of supplementing a crofting subsistence system or any other human settlement site.

The most recently perceived threat to the health of the population comes from working at computer-related industrial plants in Silicon Glen, Scotland's answer to Silicon Valley in California. Reports of the ill effects of such industrial production are heartily debated.

NATO's practice bombing raids constitute another threat to the Highlands. The results are a lot like those of bombing raids anywhere. Land is blown up and razed. Flora and Fauna are annihilated within the live bomb range. The larger area (inactive bombs used) and the active bomb area all suffer from intense amounts of waste from planes and the effects on wildlife of breaking the sound barrier two hundred feet above the ground.

RESPONSE: STRUGGLES TO SURVIVE CULTURALLY

Scottish Highland/Celtic identity is tied to place through kin and social structures. Some supplemental activities have come and gone (kelp); others have persisted (weaving). Oil development has had a greater impact and poses a greater environmental threat.

Highland peoples have responded through actions such as the formation of various political, social, and economic groups. The Crofters Holdings (Scotland) Act of 1886 legalized the melding of crofter, Celt, Highlands, and Scottish identity. Since the 1886 act, rent is fixed at fair prices (a few pounds per year), and crofters have a security of tenure and hereditary succession. "Fairness" is monitored by many agencies.

The Highlands and Islands Development Board was established by the Highland and Islands Development (Scotland) Act of 1965. The act monitors and encourages various uses of the land. In general, the board's goal is to raise the productivity of land and labor in the region. Activities of the board include livestock breeding programs, marketing (especially distribution) schemes, special projects such as bulb growing, shrub farms, a blueberry pilot project, and red deer farming. Many of these supplementary production activities provide employment, full and part time, for female labor in remote locations.[6] The board is often regarded by Highlanders as an institution belonging to the elite others and their activities as enforced by the outside powers that be, but the result has been an increased cash flow into the Highlands.

In 1976 the Crofting Reform (Scotland) Act was passed, giving the crofter the statutory right to own the land that their croft sits on and to buy the land from the landlord at fifteen times the annual rent, or at a price negotiated between the landlord and the tenant. The 1976 act sounds like a boon to crofters. Public discussion included the view of the Highlander as tightly woven with the land. However, the act of 1976 is seen as more of the same injustices perpetrated against the Highlanders by outsiders. The major result of the 1976 act was that landlords went to Land Court to gain a fixed rent that reflected the *landlord's* estimate of the ultimate purchase price of the land. The questions of who actively participates in a crofting community and who self-identifies as a Highlander were ignored.

Gaelic Culture

Another response to the threat to identity was the reintroduction of Gaelic into public life. In 1973 the Gaelic College, Sabhal Mor Ostaig, was founded on the Isle of Skye. Official local government business in the Western Isles became bilingual. Gaelic is slowly being reintroduced into some public school systems, but the policy of reintroducing Gaelic is sometimes seen as imposed by others, or outsiders.

Even though crofting communities have fewer crofters and more and more are regarded as quaint preservation pieces and retirement homes, the Gaelic-Celtic-Scottish Highland identity persists. Emigrés contribute to the preservation through interaction with the core culture through the arts and language. For example, Gaelic language, dance, and song are taught at the Gaelic College in Saint Ann's, Nova Scotia, Canada. Emigration is part of the expectation of parents and children in the Highlands. Emigration spreads the Scottish Highland identity and reinforces it both at home and in colonial pockets. The tourism which results from the return of emigrés to the Scottish Highlands perpetuates the culture economically and socially. One Internet provider sets up walking tours in Scotland. These tours, which employ friends and relatives, are labor intensive in a rural area where jobs are sorely needed. The tours require local people to meet and escort tourists from plane to hotel, to bus, to train, to boat, to walking areas.

As such labor-intensive tourism develops, a multiplier effect occurs. Development is encouraged not only of tourism shops and bed and breakfast inns, but also of such support industries as salmon farms, historic museums, and cleaning and management industries. Scottish history, loaded with the symbolic images of William Wallace, Culloden, and the Clearances, is woven into the attraction for tourists. Many are returning emigrés who financially, as well as ideologically, support Scottish Highland identity and its cultural system.

FOOD FOR THOUGHT

The Scottish Highland identity is tied to place, kin, and a linear social structure that supplements agriculture through fishing, weaving, and other activities. The perpetuation of these kin and social relationships on all levels could be the determining factors in the future of Scottish Highland culture. Highlanders have survived English policies, military, social, and legal "ethnic cleansing." One hundred and fifty years after Culloden, they seem to be gaining political economic power. The threats have changed; now it is globalization with its environmental and assimilative social impacts that must be confronted and survived.

Questions

1. How has the ongoing colonization of Scotland by England affected the social organization in the Highlands of Scotland?
2. Is crofting a sustainable lifestyle?
3. Can tourism be woven into the Highland subsistence activities as a long-range supplemental activity? Can Silicon Glen? NATO bombing practices? Oil development?
4. Can a Scottish parliament make a difference in the preservation of the Scottish Highland culture?
5. Can ethnic identity survive globalization?

NOTES

1. Sharon MacDonald, *Reimaging Culture: Histories, Identities and the Gaelic Renaissance* (Oxford, England: Berg, 1997).

2. Susan Parman, *Scottish Crofters: A Historical Ethnography of a Celtic Village* (London: Holt, Rinehart & Winston, 1990).
3. Ibid., 76.
4. Ibid., 1.
5. Ibid.
6. John Bryden and George Houston, *Agrarian Change in the Scottish Highlands* (Inverness, Scotland: John G. Eccles Printers Ltd., 1976), 123.

RESOURCE GUIDE

Published Literature

Bryden, John, and George Houston. *Agrarian Change in the Scottish Highlands.* Inverness, Scotland: John G. Eccles Printers Ltd., 1976.
Byron, Reginald. *Sea Change: A Shetland Society, 1970–1979.* St. John's, Newfoundland: ISER, 1986.
Goodlad, John D. "Fisheries and Oil: An Update of the Shetland Experience." In *Fish vs. Oil: Resources and Rural Development in No. Atlantic Societies,* edited by J. D. House. St. John's, Newfoundland: ISER, 1986.
MacDonald, Sharon. *Reimaging Culture: Histories, Identities and the Gaelic Renaissance.* Oxford, England: Berg, 1997.
Nadel-Klein, Jane. "A Fisher Laddie Needs a Fisher Lassie: Endogamy and Work in a Scottish Fishing Village." In *To Work and To Weep: Women in Fishing Economics,* edited by Jane Nadel-Klein and Dona Lee Davis. St. John's, Newfoundland: ISER, 1988.
Parman, Susan. *Scottish Crofters: A Historical Ethnography of a Celtic Village.* New York: Holt, Rinehart & Winston, 1990.

Film

Battle of Culloden. BBCTV (1972).

WWW Sites

YWAM Scotland
http://www.ywamscotland.org

Walking in Scotland
www.b-mercer.demon.co.uk

The definitive source of information about Scotland on the Internet.
http://www.geo.ed.ac.uk/home/scotland/scotland.html

Information on Scotland's present day government and political system.
http://www.scotlands.com/elected/

International Campaign for Responsible Technology
http://www.svtc.org/icrt.htm

Organization

Scottish National Party
SNP Press Office
Telephone: 0131 226 3661
Web site: http://www.snp.org.uk

Chapter 10

The Slovaks

Richard Wallace

CULTURAL OVERVIEW

One of the newest nation-states in the world, Slovakia became independent from Czechoslovakia at the stroke of midnight with the New Year of 1993. As they now constitute a sovereign nation-state, it might seem that the Slovak people "have arrived," Slovakia is now recognized by the world community. Foreign embassies are open in the capitol, Bratislava. The Slovak flag flies above dozens of new Slovak embassies in major world capitals and in front of the United Nations in New York City.

Still, the underlying uncertainty of Slovakians make them an interesting case study to consider a people as a nation and as a nation-state. Many Slovak people regard their nation and their nationality as things that almost were not. Their people have been marginalized by dominating neighbors for much of their history, and Slovaks have vivid memories of various times when they feared for their continued existence as a people. Those fears persist today, despite sovereignty.

As Slovaks confront the issues of today—transformations in the Slovak economy as a Western "free" market is implemented to replace state-owned enterprises, and the cradle-to-grave security of socialism is dismantled; as a brain drain takes away many of the country's best and brightest for dollars or deutsche marks abroad; as countries to the west and north try to form a single European Union, while countries to the east and south split apart—Slovakia has become a nation-state at a historical moment when some political and cultural theorists are saying that the nation-state is an outmoded concept. As globalization occurs and business and cultural communications cross borders with fewer hindrances of time, space, and

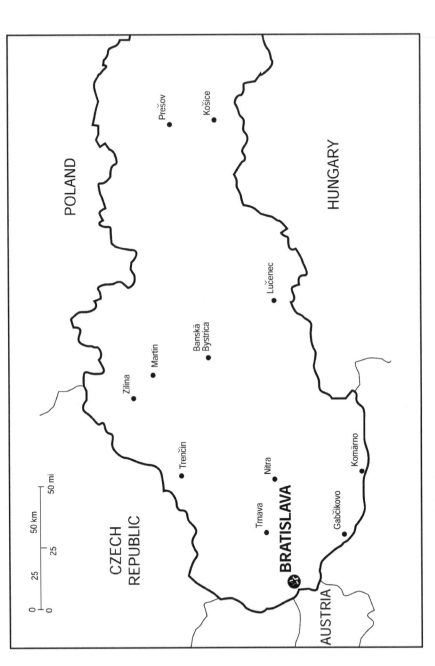

Slovakia. Courtesy of Nighthawk Design.

Four generations of a Slovak family, August 1999, Setechov, Slovakia. Left to right: Martin Slesar, Veronika Slesarová, Martin Slesár, and Daniela Biddiscombe (née Slesárová). Courtesy of Martin Biddiscombe.

tariff, Slovaks and their culture may indeed "have arrived" but how and where exactly?

The People

Once primarily a rural people, Slovaks have been increasingly located in urbanized settings; more than 57 percent now live in cities. Of the citizens of the Slovak Republic, 86 percent identify themselves as Slovak, 11 percent as Hungarians, 1.5 percent as Romany (or Gypsy), 1 percent as Czech, and 0.6 percent as Ukrainian or Rusyn.[1] Saying that a certain percentage of people *identify themselves* as some ethnicity is important. Some people with varying backgrounds may claim Slovak ethnicity when talking to the Slovak census taker, but in other situations in their town or village they may be proud to identify themselves as something else. For example, social pressure may influence Rusyn people to want to present themselves as integrated with the dominant Slovak nationality. Another example would be the Romany people, who frequently face serious discrimination and may wish to identify themselves as Slovak. For this reason, many people estimate that the Romany and Rusyn peoples make up a larger percentage of the Slovak nation-state's population.

Language

Slovak is the language spoken by most citizens in the Slovak Republic. A western variant in the Slavic family of languages, its vocabulary and grammar are similar to Russian and Serbian, but a Slovak speaker generally finds it difficult to understand these languages. Slovaks, however, have a much easier time understanding more geographically proximate languages such as Czech and Polish. Indeed, the difference between Czech and Slovak is even less, for example, than the difference between the relatively mutually intelligible Spanish and Italian languages.

Hungarian, the second most common language spoken in Slovakia, is used primarily by the Hungarian population in the southern lowland part of the country. In some villages in this area it is not uncommon to hear nothing but Hungarian, and some Slovak nationalists have found this reality offensive. They have attempted to pass restrictive language laws to promote Slovak and restrict the use of Hungarian. This kind of friction between Slovaks and Hungarians is not a recent manifestation of Slovak independence; indeed, according to Slovaks, the root of this conflict dates back centuries.

The Setting

Slovakia makes a good claim to be at the center of Europe—almost geographically equidistant between Portugal and the Ural Mountains, equally as far from Dublin as from Moscow, or as far from Stockholm as from Istanbul. If you look at a map of all of Europe, landlocked Slovakia will be the little space, smack dab in the middle. The Danube, the grand river of Europe, makes up Slovakia's southeastern border, shared with Austria and Hungary in the fertile floodplain of the Danubian Basin. Most of the country, however, is mountainous—the White Carpathian Mountains run along the border with the Czech Republic to the northeast; the high peaks of the Tatra Mountains mark the Polish border to the north; and the northern part of the Greater Carpathian range make up the eastern border with Ukraine.

Slovakia runs about twice as long east to west (264 m) as north to south (121 m). With approximately 30,000 square miles of land area, Slovakia is a little bigger than the states of New Hampshire and Vermont put together. Sixty percent of the territory is situated at an altitude over 900 feet above sea level and, with mountains and deciduous forest covering most of this land area, agriculture has been relatively difficult throughout much of the country, except in the limited floodplain region to the south. Nonetheless, the Slovaks were primarily an agrarian and pastoral peasant people through most of their existence until the last fifty years.

The territory of Slovakia belongs in a moderate climate zone and has regular alterations of the seasons. The land is best suited for growing grains like wheat, barley, and corn, as well as root crops like potatoes and sugar beets. Orchards and vineyards are common in the low hills. A very traditional and romantic image of Slovak pastoralism is of highland shepherds with their small flocks of sheep, but today cattle and pigs are the most common livestock.

Bear, deer, chamois, and wild boar live wild in the forests and uplands of Slovakia but no longer in great numbers. The hunting of such animals is a restricted sport and contributes little to overall subsistence. Wood is harvested in the forests, but pollution and acid rain from industry and brown-coal burning heating systems have severely decelerated forest growth.

Bratislava, a city of about 450,000 people in the southwestern corner of the country, is Slovakia's capital and largest city. Slovakia's second largest city, Košice, is the major city in the eastern part of the country with a population of close to a quarter million people. Other major cities include centrally located Banska Bystrica, Nitra in the west central region, Žilina in the northwest, and Prešov in the east, each with populations of just under 100,000 people.

Social, Political, and Religious Organization: A Historical Overview

Most historians believe that the Slovak forebears first settled in the territory in the fifth or sixth century A.D. when large migrations of Slavs came from the east. Some Slovaks, however, have argued that wandering tribes of Slavic people were in the region hundreds of years before this, but because they were not a settled population archaeologists have had difficulty tracing their material remains. Recent Slovak historians have therefore tried to claim that Slavic peoples (or "proto-Slovaks") were in the Danubian Basin from the first millennium B.C. While this may not seem significant to many outsiders, some Slovak historians consider it important to be able to trace Slovak precedents back to the most *primordial* origins. This bolsters the Slovak national identity and their claims to legitimacy as an independent state. Especially with regard to Slovak perceptions of their interloping neighbors, many find great pride in being able to say, essentially, "We were here first."

Most historians, however, will agree that there was a Slavic presence in the region as early as the sixth century A.D. This presence, however, is most significantly seen around the turn of the eighth and ninth centuries with the first supra-tribal Slavic formation, which was known as the Great Moravian Empire. The Christian missionary work of two brothers from Macedonia, Cyril and Metod (known as Constantine and Methodius in English) and the reign of Svätopluk in the latter half of the ninth century marked the high point of the empire. Cyril, besides converting the Slavs to Christianity with his brother, invented *glagolitics*, a system for writing Slavic sounds that he used to translate the Gospel of Saint John. This was the first Slavic writing, from which the Slovak language is derived. King Svätopluk united the largest territory of Slavs in the Great Moravian Empire, which Slovaks today perceive to be the earliest form of their people organized in a state. Cyril, Metod, and Svätopluk are considered by Slovaks to be their most important national figures prior to the nineteenth century.

Germans, Czechs, Turks, and Magyars

By the tenth century, the Great Moravian Empire had disintegrated. Slovaks usually attribute this fact to pressure from Magyar (Hungarian) tribes coming into the region. Indeed, as viewed by most Slovaks, the next millennium was one of Magyar domination in the territory of Slovakia, although other peoples and empires held sway at various times. For example, Ottoman Turks conquered much of southeastern Europe and even made it into Slovak territory at their apex. Germans and Czech Hussites also made cultural and economic beachheads at various times, particularly in larger towns and mining centers, the influence of which can still be seen today. Important figures resided in, ruled from, ruled over, and fought over Slovak territory, but these people usually spoke German or Latin, or later Czech or Hungarian. The illiterate peasants spoke Slovak, and almost anyone in a position of power would not have understood themselves as being Slovak. Some people have argued, in fact, that no one would have seen themselves as "Slovak" per se because a "Slovak identity" as such had not yet been invented.

Slovaks were largely Catholicized by Cyril and Metod over a thousand years ago, and Slovaks remain largely Roman Catholic today. Over the centuries, however, religious waves came and went largely with the political tides. Many in Slovak territory converted to Lutheranism during the Protestant Reformation of the sixteenth century. Many converted back to Roman Catholicism, however, during the Counter-Reformation when the Habsburgs and Hungarians held sway. Slovaks therefore entered the eighteenth century with the majority of the people Catholic as part of the Habsburg Empire, but there existed also an upper class of Czech and German Protestants.

Magyarization and Resistance

After the late eighteenth century, after the Ottoman Turks had been driven back in southeastern Europe, Hungarians became the dominant ethnic group in the Carpathian Basin (although they were still part of the Habsburg Austro-Hungarian Empire). This was the time when Magyarization began to occur in Slovak territory. Magyarization was the organized process by which the Magyars (Hungarians) attempted to assimilate culturally and linguistically the non-Magyar peoples under their political control. Subscribing to the idea of "one state—one nation—one language," the Magyar assembly passed laws making Magyar the official language of their whole territory. The Magyar language, for example, was the only language of instruction allowed in schools, even elementary schools. These measures met with varying degrees of resistance in Slovak territory, but they were most firmly implemented in the latter half of the nineteenth century when the most forceful form of Magyarization took place. During this time, the Slovak people "awakened" and begin to intensify their national struggle.

In resisting Magyarization, Slovaks had a close Slavic ally in the Czechs. However, the Slavic intelligentsia debated how close Czechs and Slovaks were all during this time. Were they one "tribe" (*kmen*), the "Czechoslovak tribe" of the Slavic "nation" (*slovanský národ*), or two distinct "tribes" speaking two distinct languages? The issue of language had become very important. While the Czech language had been codified (i.e., written and standardized) centuries before and the Czechs could claim a rich literary history, Slovak had not been codified and its legitimacy as a language was questioned. Literate Slovaks (besides using Magyar, Latin, or German) used *bibličtina*, or "Bible-language," because it was based on a form of Czech used to write the Bible. Slovaks had begun introducing parts of their dialect into their use of *bibličtina* (perhaps unconsciously), but *bibličtina* reinforced the idea that the Czech and Slovaks were one people.

A Catholic priest, Father Anton Bernolák, introduced a written form of Slovak in the late eighteenth century based on a West Slovak dialect. Known as *bernoláčina*, the language influenced Czech and Slovak linguistic separatist ideas in some strata, but it never received wide acceptance.

Lúdovit Štúr is today considered to have been the most important patriot in Slovak history largely because his codification of Slovak stuck. Born in Central Slovakia in 1815, Štúr was influenced by European liberalism, the romantic movement, and the conception of an ethnic nation. Štúr's seminal work began in the 1840s when he and his followers determined that they would write only in Slovak. His new codification of Slovak, based on the Central Slovak dialect, is what essentially constitutes modern Slovak. Štúr used it in his newspaper, *Slovenskje národnje novini*, which many Slovaks consider to be the first Slovak political newspaper. Initially, Štúr demanded only Slovak autonomy, but in the 1850s he began to demand separation from Hungary, with Slovakia subordinate only to the Habsburgs. He was accused of rebellion and arrested, and the lived under police observation until his death in 1856.

Despite an early death, Štúr's legacy merged pan-Slavic ideals with a strengthened idea for an independent Slovakia. The Slovak cultural organization *Matica slovenská*, founded in 1863, developed these goals. Many Slovaks can tell the history of *Matica slovenská* and cite it, or at least the idea of it. It is considered essential to preserving the Slovak nation through what are remembered as the darkest days of Magyarization despite the Hungarian government's ban on the organization in 1875. Slovaks renewed *Matica slovenská* after World War I, and it still exists today as an important cultural organization. It has also, however, been increasingly aligned to certain political parties, and for this it has drawn both kudos and criticism.

Forming Czechoslovakia

With the pressure of Magyarization, the Slovak intelligentsia worked under difficult conditions to prevent their total denationalization and often turned to the Czechs and the idea of the unity of the Czech and Slovak people (or, of course, the Czechoslovak people). During World War I, exiled Czechs, including T. G. Masaryk and Edvard Beneš, and Slovaks, such as Milan R. Štefánik, led the Czechoslovak Foreign Committee (based in London) and Slovak and Czech organizations based in Allied countries in calling for the establishment of a Czecho-Slovak state because the Austro-Hungarian Empire was a Central power. This was formally declared in the Pittsburgh Agreement in 1918. Simultaneously, Slovak groups in the Czech city of Prague made the Declaration of the Slovak Nation wherein they expressed the will to join with the Czechs in a common state. Notably, however, not all Slovak groups supported the Czechoslovak idea. In fact, some Slovaks today claim that Slovak leaders at that time had insisted on a clause promising autonomy for Slovakia in their talks with Masaryk. Nonetheless, the idea of "Czechoslovakia" emerged and became a political reality when the Austro-Hungarian Empire was dismantled by the victorious Allies. The Czechoslovak Republic, with the Czech T. G. Masaryk as its leader, was declared independent on October 28, 1918.

Differing Slovak and Czech Views on the First Czechoslovak Republic

Czechs and most Western historians usually talk about the First Czechoslovak Republic (1918–1938) with unequivocably positive statements. As most postwar Central and Eastern European governments remained unstable for years before sliding into fascism (or, in the case of the Soviet Union, Stalinism), the liberal constitutional democracy of the Czechoslovak Republic had multiple political parties that managed to maintain a surprising degree of social stability in the young republic. Today Czechs tend to remember Masaryk as a "father figure" who fostered the nation into a shining example of democracy and economic prosperity.

The Slovak view of Masaryk and the First Czechoslovak Republic is decidedly more ambiguous. Some Slovaks point out that the gap between the industrialized Czechs and the still largely agrarian Slovaks actually widened during this time. They believe that Masaryk's centralizing of power in Prague deliberately excluded Slovaks and their national aspirations. The Pittsburgh Agreement was meant to give Slovaks their autonomy, they claim; it was meant to be only a temporary arrangement, a step toward ultimate Slovak independence. The interwar period was a time of mixed blessings for Slovaks. On the one hand, they were no longer pressured to discontinue being Slovaks as they had been under Hungarian rule; on the other, however, Slovaks regard this period as a continuation in their struggle for national identity and political sovereignty, this time under Czech domination.

Hlinka and Wartime Slovak Autonomy

Andrej Hlinka's political career and legacy reflect the ambiguity with which Slovaks today consider the First Czechoslovak Republic and Slovakia's role in World War II. Born in Central Slovakia in 1864, Hlinka was a priest and a politician who fought for Slovak rights during the most intense periods of Magyarization before World War I. In the First Czechoslovak Republic he led the Slovak People's party (later renamed Hlinka's Slovak People's Party, or HSPP) as a major Slovak political organization in parliament. Some people think he believed in the Czechoslovak idea of working for Slovak causes within the federal structure. Others remember him as a leader who battled Prague centralism and advocated Slovak independence.

Hlinka died in 1938 shortly before pressure from Nazi Germany broke up Czechoslovakia. The Nazis manipulated a proclamation of Slovak autonomy from the Czechs, and Slovakia became an ally (or puppet state) of Nazi Germany. Another Catholic priest, Father Jozef Tiso, actually led the HSPP in declaring Slovak autonomy in 1938. This followed the Munich Agreement wherein Germany took over part of the Czech Lands and Hungary occupied southern Slovakia. The HSPP governed wartime Slovakia, taking cues, if not direct orders, from Adolf Hitler.

Today's view of wartime Slovakia is a source of contention among Slovaks. A small, sometimes anti-Semitic, minority are outspokenly in praise of Father Tiso and speak warmly of "independent" Slovakia as being a prosperous time for Slovaks. This minority is countered, however, by those who scorn this view and regard Tiso as one of Hitler's minions because of the willingness with which his clerical-fascist government shipped two-thirds of Slovakia's Jewish population to concentration camps at Treblinka and Auschwitz. Often overlooked by outsiders is the view of many Slovaks who are not really sure about Tiso: they are not entirely certain that Tiso knew about the nature of the Jewish deportations and wonder if perhaps Tiso had simply been doing the best he could for the Slovak people during a difficult time. Tiso and the HSPP were Hlinka's inauspicious legacy, with fascist distortions promoting his career (e.g., the fascist youth group was called the Hlinka Guard), and it has resulted in mixed understandings of

Hlinka's role. Nonetheless, in 1995, the Slovak government approved a new monetary note bearing Hlinka's image, which, while "raising some eyebrows," failed to ignite any major protest in Slovakia.

Despite its government's being allied with Nazi Germany, Slovakia was credited with having been on the winning side of World War II by virtue of the Slovak National Uprising. Central Slovak partisans began this anti-Nazi rebellion in the late summer of 1944. Most Slovaks look to the Uprising with pride, but degrees of historicism have caused distortions. The Communist party subsequently claimed to have led the resistance to the exclusion of many other true heroes. For this reason, Slovaks even today sometimes view information regarding the Slovak National Uprising with skepticism.

Postwar Czechoslovakia

After World War II ended and the Cold War began the West conceded Czechoslovakia to Joseph Stalin's sphere of influence. Leaders of the First Czechoslovak Republic, who had been in exile in London, initially led a restored Czechoslovak government, but Klement Gottwald, a Czech Communist leader, became prime minister, and several Communist party members held key government positions. In 1946, in what were considered free and fair elections, more Czechoslovaks voted for the Communists. Some Slovaks will point out, however, that the Czechs voted for the Communists; in the Slovak part of the country, another party, the Democratic party won. This is a way of blaming communism on the Czechs, because, in 1948, the Communist party, exploiting non-Communist parties' weaknesses, took complete control of the government.

The Communist party followed the Soviet Stalinist model of government and changed Czechoslovak political, economic, and social life. In establishing the "dictatorship of the proletariat" and Marxism-Leninism as the governing ideology, private business and agriculture was nationalized in a "command economy," and state security forces persecuted any opponents as being enemies of the working class. The government followed the Soviet example in instilling changes in people's value orientations using the centrally controlled mass media.

The party continued to suppress dissent in the 1950s but gradually with less brutality and tenacity. Resistance existed in Slovakia—as evidenced by Eastern Slovak farmers' noncooperation with agricultural cooperatives in 1950 and by strikes held in 1953 in response to currency reform—but, overall, Slovakia, the weaker third of the country in terms of education and economics, went along with the party as it was often very beneficial to do so. Indeed, for all the criticism laid upon communism, when Slovakia's development is compared with that of many other parts of the world, socialist Slovakia compares quite favorably. However, when Slovaks compare their lot with that of their now more affluent Austrian neighbors, they blame socialism for retarding their own progress.

1968 and Normalization

In the late 1960s, reformers, led by Slovakia's Alexander Dubček, attempted to transform Czechoslovak Stalinist socialism into "socialism with a human face." In 1968 Dubček oversaw the abolition of censorship, the rehabilitation of political prisoners, the reorientation of trade unions toward protecting workers, and the establishment of a pluralistic, democratic parliamentary system with greater involvement by broader groups of people in the political process. Most of the rapid pace of changes affected Prague primarily and the hinterlands, like Slovakia, secondarily.

The reforming effect never really had a chance to spread because it was stopped short by the Soviet-led Warsaw Pact invasion in August 1968. Then, with Moscow ultimately pulling the strings, another Slovak, Gustav Husák, led a "normalization" regime that turned back the reform process. Czechoslovakia returned to coercive compliance, to censorship, and to being one of the most dogmatically Marxist-Leninist countries in the Communist bloc. During this time, the Communist party attempted to placate the masses, as it were, by putting more resources into consumer needs. The standard of living went up because of this, particularly in Slovakia.

Normalization took Czechoslovakia into the 1980s. Protest and dissident activity were on the increase, and the economy and institutional reform was not. Husák's dogmatism pleased the Soviets in the 1970s, but in the 1980s, Mikhail Gorbachev's policies of perestroika demanded reform. The Communist party was largely stagnant and immovable in the face of internal and external calls for change in the 1980s. This situation ended in revolution in 1989.

Federalism

Of the 1968 reforms, one effort was not pushed back by normalization: "federalism" was the plan to create parity between the Slovak and Czech Republics and this would have effects in the 1990s. Slovakia had pushed for equal status ever since the Communist government had set aside demands for autonomy in the late 1940s. Despite the fact that capital investment in Slovakia appears to have been proportionally greater than in the Czech Lands (something the Czechs resented), Slovaks remained frustrated by disparate living standards, levels of development, and representation. Although largely initiated by reformists, on January 1, 1969, Czechoslovakia was federalized four months after the Warsaw Pact invasion. Federal institutions, however, had little power and served more as window dressing to show the Communist government's willingness to settle national issues between Slovaks and Czechs. However, when the 1989 revolution gave new impetus to arguing national issues, the federalist structures already in place gave Slovaks more even ground upon which to argue with the Czechs.

In autumn 1989, revolutions were astir in Eastern Europe's Communist bloc—Poland and Hungary had elected non-Communist governments, and East Germany had opened the Berlin Wall on November 9. On Friday evening, November 17, student demonstrators took to the streets of the Czech city of Prague, Czechoslovakia's capital city. The government's beatings of the students that night ignited countrywide indignation and thus began the celebrated "Velvet Revolution," which would see hundreds of thousands of people peacefully demanding that the Communist government give up its hold on power. Within six weeks, Václav Havel, a recently jailed Czech dissident playwright, would become president of Czechoslovakia.

Prague students, artists, and intelligentsia often overshadow the Slovaks' role in what Slovaks called the "Gentle Revolution," but it is interesting to note that a student protest took place on the streets of Bratislava on November 16, the evening *before* the Prague demonstration. Of course, the much smaller Slovak demonstration did not create the spark that the later one did, but it is a reminder that the revolution was not wholly a Czech affair. Indeed, within hours of the student beatings in Prague, Slovaks had begun to organize rallies in Slovak cities that took place that weekend and for the weeks that followed.

With the Communist party out of power, the new Czechoslovak government, after abolishing many Communist-era laws and drawing up a constitution reflecting Western capitalist democracies, was able to look at national questions again. The "hyphen war" was one of the first problems: Slovak legislators in the federal parliament argued for changing the official name of the country from Czechoslovakia to Czecho-Slovakia because they felt the hyphen helped demonstrate that the country was made up of two nations, that there was more than just the Czechs. The Czech legislators and media did not think this was necessary, and their resistance created friction before the name was finally changed and the hyphen inserted.

Most polls conducted in the early 1990s indicated that Slovaks were dissatisfied with the federal arrangement with the Czechs because they felt that Prague was continuing to hold most of the economic and cultural advantages for the Czechs. Many Slovaks thought a restructuring of the government, perhaps the creation of a confederation, would bring about greater autonomy for Slovakia. Notably, only a relatively small minority of Slovaks actually supported separation from the Czechs. Nonetheless, great differences had developed between the leading Czech and Slovak politicians. The Czech prime minister, Václav Klaus, wanted to introduce market economy principles quickly and was willing to scuttle social programs to do it; Slovak politicians in general were more wary. In 1992 Vladimír Mečiar was elected prime minister of Slovakia, and his unwillingness to go along with Klaus's measures, along with his strong public personality, put him at loggerheads with Klaus. Mečiar and Klaus both displayed strains of nationalism in their political actions and very quickly declared their differences unresolvable, and their political parties began the process of separating the country. No referendum was ever held in either the Czech or Slovak Republics probably because the politicians wanted the separation, and the polls indicated that Slovaks would not support it and the Czechs would probably not either. Thus political maneuvering and sparring personalities brought to reality a Slovak national independence.

The fact that the majority of Slovak citizens probably would not have voted for independence from the Czechs indicates that Slovaks had perhaps felt confident in their continued existence as a people and with this, an affinity for their Czech brethren, despite their economic and political differences. With independence, Slovakia was able to make its own decisions at last, but the society had, to some extent, become politically polarized. On the one hand, a populist prime minister, Mečiar, appealed to Slovaks' national sentiments and supported legislation that appeared to discriminate against the Hungarian minority. On the other hand, a splintered political opposition (which included Hungarian political parties) sought Westernization and to reform its markets while simultaneously conserving social programs, all to varying degrees.

Now Slovak sovereignty is something largely taken for granted by Slovaks, a way of being that is considered normal and unquestioned.

Subsistence and Economic Strategies

Agriculture

Archaeological finds indicate that Slovakia's first inhabitants farmed by burning forests and creating fields—the slash-and-burn method of cultivation. They used stone and wooden implements to grow wheat and barley and they bred sheep, cattle, goats, and pigs. Bronze and iron tools later replaced those of stone and, as food production increased, so did the population.

When Slavs came to the region in the first millennium, they used a two-field cultivation system in which one field was left fallow while the other was used for growing, using an iron share to till the soil. Fruit and vegetables were cultivated, as were flax and hemp for making clothing. People appear to have cultivated the soil in common within a commune-like setting (*občina*), although there appears to have been an emerging class of "landlords" by the seventh or eighth centuries.

When nomadic Hungarian tribes migrated to the region, they learned these agricultural methods and set up a system of serfdom that subjugated peasants to feudal landlords in a way that was characteristic of the political and economic systems typical of much of medieval Europe. In the lowlands, a three-field system was largely adopted (winter wheat was grown on one field, spring grain on another, and a third was left fallow), but in the highlands farmers continued using the two-field system, in some regions, into the twentieth century. Although some forms of communal ownership persisted in some areas (like the common use of forests and meadows), the *občina* gradually disintegrated into a stratified feudal system that remained in place until the nineteenth century. Slavic-speaking peasants tilled the soil, and the mainly German or Hungarian nobility managed and marketed the agricultural products.

Commercializing elements began to penetrate agricultural production in the nineteenth century, but feudal structures, which remained in place until the Hungarian kingdom's dissolution in 1918, hampered attempts to modernize agriculture in Slovak territory. This put the region behind other European agricultural developments. Large landowners held disproportionate shares of the land, and many Slovak peasant families, unable to live off their meager holdings, sought additional employment. Those unable to find other income sources often emigrated to work abroad.

With the founding of Czechoslovakia in 1918, a land reform program improved land distribution, and agriculture continued to be the backbone of the Slovak economy until World War II. After the war, however, the Communist regime attempted to collectivize farming and almost completely eliminated private agricultural landholdings. In 1948 there were an estimated 300,000 to 400,000 farms in Slovakia, but these had been cut to 108,000 twenty years later.[2] According to the Soviet model, farmers were either urged or, if necessary, forced to join agricultural collectives, and most land became state property. Large landowners lost their vast holdings, and hundreds of thousands of formerly private farmers became laborers for state agricultural cooperatives or were compelled to seek jobs in other areas of the widening economy.

With collectivization, central state plans regulated and determined agricultural output, the distribution of the means of production, and the sale of products. The goal was to distribute more fairly and functionally access to resources and to create a rational and societal agricultural plan. Ideally, this would have meant that farms, for example, would not produce too much of one crop and not enough of another. Prices would be controlled, wages set and guaranteed, and no one would be able to get filthy rich at anyone else's expense. To some extent, this worked out: no one was completely poor and no one was ridiculously wealthy in Slovak agriculture.

Corruption, however, was commonplace as some people used their positions for their own gain rather than for the collective good. Centralized planning also was too often inefficient and failed to respect local environmental conditions. For example, government officials might determine that all the farm collectives in one area of rural Slovakia should grow potatoes and so they would invest in the resources necessary to grow potatoes. This might work well for two-thirds of the given region, but it might be terrible for that other third—perhaps the land was better suited for some other crop or the people knew nothing about growing potatoes. Therefore, a region might end up only producing two-thirds of the food that it might otherwise have produced. With their guaranteed wages and the fact that they had no say in the decision to plant potatoes, farm workers did not feel accountable if their crop failed. Slovak farming also languished because the Communist government was continually trying to build up industry. They took more out of agriculture than they put in so that more investment could go to building factories.

After 1989 Czecho-Slovakia began a transformation to a market economy, and many collectivized farms began going back to private hands as restitution of pre-Communist property took place; other collectives became joint-stock companies. This complicated process has unsettled many agricultural workers. While a few people have become very rich and able to buy up land, many others have been displaced and impoverished in the new economy. The market has also meant that seed, fertilizers, and equipment have not always been available when needed because of price instability, lower subsidies, and less agricultural reinvestment.

Some Slovaks have faith in privatization and the market economy. They believe it will create the competition, accountability, and efficiency needed to revitalize agriculture. Other Slovaks see a rich class developing and taking advantage of the market economy while they slip into abject poverty. The poor tend to long for the days of the security of collectivized agriculture.

Industry

The Slovak people were primarily peasant farming people for most of their history, so it may seem surprising to say that from medieval times Slovak territory was one of the most productive manufacturing and mining areas in its region in East Central Europe. We must note, however, who was producing what in this territory: as rural Slovaks eked out a living in agriculture, town-dwelling Hungarian- and German-speaking populations were craftspeople, manufacturers, and miners. As the twentieth century began, Slovak territory was not as industrialized as significant parts of Western Europe, but a few large and many small factories existed and formed one of the most important regions of the Hungarian Empire's industrial base. Factories in Slovak territory produced more than half the paper and cellulose, more than a third of the textiles, and more than a quarter of the leather of the empire. However, only about 5 percent of the capital for this manufacturing came from Slovaks. The owners tended to speak and identify as German or Hungarian, not Slovak.

After World War I and the founding of Czechoslovakia, the Slovak industrial situation actually worsened. Many Hungarian and German industrialists withdrew their investments from Slovakia; some closed their factories and moved their machinery away. The Czech Lands were more industrialized and had greater access to European export markets so investors were reticent to invest in the more "backward" Slovakia. Czechs provided a safer bet with lower start-up costs and a more developed infrastructure. This created a crisis in the Slovak region for much of the 1920s and, just when the situation was improving, the 1929 Great Depression happened. In the 1930s some important armament companies were built in Western Slovakia, but by 1937, the industrial economy still had not returned to pre–World War I levels. Of all the Czechoslovak industrial production in the late 1930s, Slovakia accounted for only 8 percent. Some Slovak historians point to the lack of interwar Czech investment and industrial development in Slovakia as a key reason for why the Slovaks did not do more to resist the Nazis at the outset of the World War II.

German capital flooded into the country in the late 1930s, as Nazis and Slovak fascists engineered a break with the Czech Republic. In the "independent" Nazi-puppet state, Slovakia industry grew to unprecedented levels as it fed the German war machine. However, with the Slovak National Uprising against the Nazis in 1944 and then the Nazi plundering of the Slovak manufacturing facilities, the Slovak industrial economy was once again crippled at war's end.

Following the war, however, as the Czech and Slovak Republics were reunited, industrial growth in Slovakia expanded rapidly. From 1948 to 1989, Czechoslovakia's Communist government, following the Soviet socialist model of industrialization, nationalized all businesses and manufacturing concerns; that is, they were taken over and run by the state. The state concentrated on heavy industrial production. The machine and metalworking industry, for example, expanded by over 10,000 percent, and the chemical industries increased by over 8,000 percent.[3] By 1964 more people in Slovakia were working in industry than in agriculture. Slovakia, which had lagged far behind the Czech part of the country industrially, steadily increased its share through the decades so that, by the late 1980s, Slovakia was almost on par with the Czech Republic in per capita manufacturing production.

The ostensibly equalizing effect of this drive to industrialize, however, remained a source of friction between the Slovaks and Czechs. The aims and forms of industrialization in Slovakia did not meet the needs of the people of Slovakia. Centralized planning meant that important decisions concerning industrialization were not determined in Slovakia but instead in Prague or even Moscow. The government disproportionately located heavy armaments industries, polluting chemical production, and smelting in Slovakia. Slovakia ended up producing the raw materials or semifinished materials that were then shipped off to the Czech Republic where the goods were finished for consumption or export. Therefore the Czech Republic benefited from value-added production, while Slovakia had the heavier, dirtier industries. Some of these production sites were huge and employed massive numbers of workers in inefficient workplaces that lacked Western technological innovations, safety standards, and pollution controls. In 1989 the largest twenty companies in Slovakia employed almost a quarter million people.[4]

The Central Slovak town of Žiar nad Hronom provides a sad example of an economic and industrial strategy gone awry. Central planners in the 1950s wanted Czechoslovakia to be able to produce its own aluminum and planned a factory to do that in Žiar nad Hronom. The factory was huge by the 1970s and employed a very large percentage of the people in the town. Unfortunately, for reasons of technology, raw materials, and poor planning, the factory produced rather low-grade aluminum that could not be sold outside of Czechoslovakia and was inadequate for many needs within the country. Also, aluminum smelting produced a large amount of waste, and the planners did little to control the pollution of the area's earth, water, and air. Now the town suffers from an almost permanently gray atmosphere and high incidences of birth defects. The unprofitable, subsidized factory continues to function but still lays off its workers.

THREATS TO SURVIVAL

Many Slovaks, when they consider themselves as an ethnic group, see themselves as having been, for the longest time, the subordinates, the underlings, the little brothers, the peasants, the country cousins of their wealthier, urbanized, and sophisticated neighbors. They see themselves as having been exploited and even as the victims of a policy of cultural ethnic cleansing when the Hungarian government was trying to wipe out the Slovak language and its fledgling institutions less than 100 years ago. It is with bitterness that many Slovaks think about their first "independent" state— as a Nazi puppet during World War II.

Many resented that Slovaks seemed destined always to play second fiddle to the Czechs within the country of Czechoslovakia. Indeed many outsiders found it easy to forget about Slovakia as a place, reading "-slovakia" as a superfluous suffix to the word "Czech." Once in the early 1990s, when a U.S. newspaper reported on a Slovak separatist demonstration for independence, Slovaks might have been pleased to have received the news coverage, but unfortunately the paper headlined the article, "Czechs Protest."[5]

RESPONSE: STRUGGLES TO SURVIVE CULTURALLY

Now as the Slovak people can claim a nation-state as their own, it is ironic that some are saying the day of the nation-state is through. Just to the west of Slovakia, the European Union has been forming, tying nation-states closer together and breaking down economic and cultural borders between peoples. As Slovakia draws closer to these pan-European structures, it would appear that, even as Slovaks seek to exert their sovereignty and independence, their country needs to concede some of its sovereignty and independence in order to take part in the European community.

At the same time, large multinational corporations are becoming more and more powerful, and businesses are less and less beholden to national governments. These companies, mostly based in the West, are able to buy up local industries and often can dictate the terms of their residency in smaller and poorer countries like Slovakia. For example, when Slovakia's large Škoda automobile works needed capital to reinvest in its outmoded production facilities, the German company Volkswagen bought a controlling interest in the company. Now decisions about what cars to produce or whether to produce them is a decision made in Germany, by a German board of directors, and largely by German stockholders.

Fun Radio Bratislava is another case to consider. When idealistic students wanted to create radio "for the people" in the months following the 1989 revolution, they did not have the necessary money. A French media company, Fun Radio Paris, invested in a station for them, and now the station is one of the most popular in Slovakia. The DJs speak in Slovak and play an occasional Slovak pop song, but otherwise the station follows a strict generic corporate formula of European Top 40 pop and a slick, patterned, on-air style that one can hear anywhere.

Slovakia is dependent on loans from the World Bank and the International Monetary Fund because it needs capital to build its economy. These international organizations are largely controlled by the United States and Western European countries, and, through them, the United States and Western Europe can dictate fiscal policy within the Slovak economy. For example, suppose the Slovak government decided to raise the import tax of cigarettes coming into the country because they wanted to discourage Slovak citizens from smoking with high prices for cigarettes. U.S. and Western European tobacco companies would not like that because it would hurt sales in places where they are hoping to expand their market share. The companies might claim that the tax was an obstacle for free trade. Therefore they might pressure their governments and international loaning institutions to hold back money from Slovakia until the Slovak government removed these so-called free trade barriers.

The Slovaks now have Slovakia, a sovereign nation-state, which seemingly is not controlled by any other foreign government. However, because of Slovakia's relative size and poor financial condition, it often appears to be part of what could be called a neocolonial system. In other words, foreign powers or multinational corporations can dominate Slovak economics, politics, and culture.

FOOD FOR THOUGHT

Slovaks claim a heritage dating to the first millennium, and many state with pride that they have survived centuries of Hungarian and German domination, as well as Czech and Soviet manipulations in the twentieth century. Along the way, a Slovak national identity has developed as well as a Slovak cultural identity. Now, economic development is needed to make the Slovak nation more secure.

Questions

1. With sovereignty, can the Slovaks and their culture survive the influx of foreign corporate interests?
2. How are the Slovak language and culture in danger of being wiped off the map?
3. Does this mean that the Slovak people are "endangered" in the twenty-first century?
4. Is there any such thing as a national culture? Did you know there was a separate Slovak nation before you read this chapter?
5. How can Slovakia control industrial development by multi-national companies?

NOTES

1. M. Strhan, and D. Daniel et al., *Slovaks and Slovakia: A Concise Encyclopedia* (Bratislava: Goldpress, 1994).
2. Ibid.
3. Ibid.
4. Ibid.
5. *USA Today* (1991).

RESOURCE GUIDE

Published Literature

Bradley, John F. N. *Czechoslovakia's Velvet Revolution: A Political Analysis.* Boulder, Colo.: East European Monographs, Columbia University Press, 1992.
Johnson, Owen. *Slovakia, 1918–1938: Education and the Making of a Nation.* New York: Columbia University Press, 1985.
Kiliánová, G., and E. Krekovicová, eds. *Folklore, Folklorism and National Identification.* Bratislava: Slovak Academy of Sciences, 1992.
Kirschbaum, Stanislav. *A History of Slovakia: The Struggle for Survival.* New York: St. Martin's Press, 1995.
Leff, Carol Skalnik. *The Czech and Slovak Republics: Nation Versus State.* Boulder, Colo.: Westview Press, 1997.
Strhan, M., and D. Daniel, et al., eds. *Slovaks and Slovakia: A Concise Encyclopedia.* Bratislava: Goldpress, 1994.

WWW Sites

Guide to the Slovak Republic: People, Culture, Maps, F.A.Q., History, Economy
http://www.slovakia.org/

Slovakia Daily Surveyor. News, top stories, background information, essays, reviews, links
http://www.slovensko.com/

Slovakia: An Overview
http://www.slovak.com/overview/overview.html

Slovak Cultural Organization
http://www.matica.sk/

Slovak Radio. Listen to Slovak radio programs on Real Audio
http://www.slovakradio.sk/

Slovak News: Links to daily and weekly Slovak newspapers
http://nic.savba.sk/logos/news/list.html

Organizations

Slovak Canadian National Council
50 McIntosh Drive, No. 240
Markham, Ontario, Canada L3R 9T3
Web site: http://www.slovakcanada.ca

Slovak Information Center
406 East 67th Street
New York, NY 10021
Telephone: (212) 737–3971
Fax: (212) 737–3454
Web site: http://www.inx.net/~matica/

Chapter 11

The Tyroleans of Austria
Kelli Ann Costa

CULTURAL OVERVIEW

The People

Present day Tyrol, located in western Austria and sandwiched between Germany and Italy, was at one time much larger than it is now. Prior to World War I, during the first years of the twentieth century, Tyrol included the area now known as South Tyrol in northern Italy. This link between the north and south Alpine areas has been very important in today's Tyrol despite its split nearly 100 years ago. The people on both sides of the border remain staunchly "Tyrolean" whether they are officially Italian or Austrian. This notion of "Tyrolness" outweighing any political connection to a recognized country is what marks, and has historically marked, Tyrol as something separate and different from the rest of Europe.

Tyrol has been inhabited for thousands of years, but it became a thriving agricultural area only in the past five hundred. The harsh environmental conditions have helped enculturate a people who pride themselves on their ties to the land, their self-sufficiency, their loyalty to Tyrol, and their devotion to God. Tyroleans often say their location in the high mountains places them closer to God than other Europeans. Despite Tyrol's status as a breadbasket for Austria, its overwhelming beauty, and its current status as a tourist destination for skiing and hiking and other forms of vacation activities, Tyroleans are under increasing pressure from a number of sources to modernize, mechanize, and build. Land pressures have led to a loss of forests and farmland, and the increasing popularity of tourism has led to environmental degradation on a scale that makes recovery nearly impos-

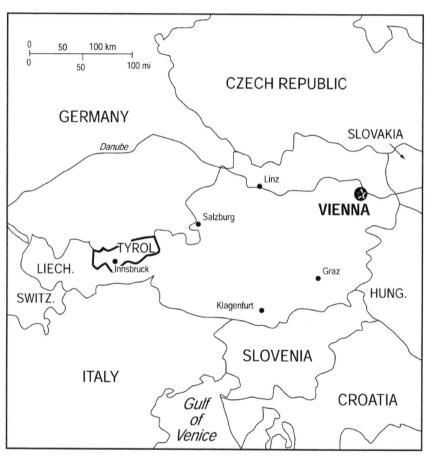

The Tyrol. Courtesy of Nighthawk Design.

sible. Traditional farming customs and materials are finding their way into museums and folktales, and once productive farms have been abandoned or converted into hotels. The people of Tyrol are rapidly becoming citizens in a modern world that rejects their traditions.

The Setting

Beginning in the last Ice Age and up until the present the Tyrol has been the crossroads of Europe. Located in the European Alps in western Austria, Tyrol has witnessed Neanderthal populations, the coming of modern man, Roman invasions, and both world wars. Its location, sandwiched between German Bavaria in the north, Switzerland in the west, and Italy's South Tyrol in the south, has provided Tyrol with myriad cultural influences as diverse peoples have moved between east, west, north, and south.

The Austrian Alps are divided into three chains: the Northern Limestone Alps, the High Central Alps, and the Southern Alps. These chains are separated by deep glacial valleys and river basins which include the Inn Valley where Innsbruck, the capital of Tyrol, is located.

About 10,000 years ago great Alpine glaciers covered much of Europe. Innsbruck was once covered by ice which may have been over a mile thick in places. Glaciers are unstable masses of ice which move at a constant, but slow, rate. The movement of the masses of ice formed the deep Alpine valleys. In the Alps glaciers formed a number of valley types: amphitheater-shaped "cirques," U-shaped valleys with steep sloping sides, and "hanging" valleys which feature high waterfalls.

As the glaciers receded at the end of the last Ice Age, the Tyrol's unique and complex landscape was formed. Remnants of these same glaciers are visible throughout Tyrol today in the high-altitude valleys where year-round skiing takes place. As Europe warmed, the vegetation of the Alpine areas developed. In mountains areas throughout the world, vegetation is influenced by several factors including soil, climate, and altitude. Many plants cannot grow at certain altitudes, and few can survive above the tree line.

Traditional Subsistence Strategies and Economic Opportunities

While passing through an Alpine valley, one is struck by the growth patterns on the mountainsides. Tree species (including spruce, fir, several pine species, larch, and birch) tend to succeed one another as the altitude increases. Sun-washed slopes that face the south are also most remarkable because of the amount of human influence on the vegetation. Many Alpine farms dot the landscape, but, in spite of their success, farming has led to mass deforestation and a necessity to formulate programs to replant huge areas of denuded land. In Tyrol, farming is practiced up to about 5,000

Local Tyrolean farmer tending a hay field by hand. His hay rake is made of wood by a local craftsperson. Courtesy of Kelli Ann Costa.

feet, but this depends on climate and location. In some areas farming can be done at somewhat higher altitudes. Alpine pastures, called "Alpen," are generally found above the tree line (about 7,000 feet) where cattle and sheep graze on summer pastures.

Today only between 10 and 12 percent of Tyroleans are full-time farmers; nevertheless, this number helps support a country where nearly 90 percent of the food is homegrown. In Tyrol many farmers have organized into cooperatives where high-quality dairy, beef, wool, lamb, and pork products are raised, produced, and marketed.

Austrians in Tyrol also depend on forestry, mining, industry, textile production, and tourism among other businesses for their livelihoods. In Tyrol, it is estimated that 60 percent of current income is directly tied to tourism.[1]

Social and Political Organization

Among the most significant historical events that influenced modern Tyrol were the rule of Maria Theresa in the eighteenth century and the Napoleonic Wars of 1792–1815. Maria Theresa, who came to power in 1740, ruled until 1765 during the Age of Enlightenment. She did not rule easily and was constantly challenged, even by those of her own family, the House of Hapsburg; nevertheless, she was a powerful leader who was known for her administrative and financial policies. She was also famous for her support of the arts. Maria Theresa welcomed a six-year-old Wolfgang Amadeus Mozart to her home at Schonbrunn Palace in Vienna where he played several compositions for her and her court. Maria Theresa, the wife of Francis I, duke of Lorraine, was the mother of Marie Antoinette, the queen of France and wife of Louis XVI, who was guillotined in October 1793. Maria Theresa's compassionate rule and love of Tyrol is evidenced in the beautiful Western Palace, the Hofburg she built in Innsbruck.

Austria was strongly opposed to Napoléon Bonaparte's efforts to be emperor of the world. In April 1792 France declared war on Austria, then ruled by Franz II. The war went badly for the Austrians who were unable to organize experienced troops against the war-hardened French and Bavarians who methodically attacked them. In 1804 Napoléon dealt Austria another blow after gaining the French throne. Several more victories forced Franz II to sue the French for peace and also to give up the crown of the Holy Roman Empire.

In Tyrol, mountain communities found themselves without any military support from the emperor as the war moved into the Alpine territories. At the time of the war with France, Tyrol was much larger than it is today and included what is now known as the South Tyrol (Sudtirol) of Italy. The mountain peasants organized under the leadership of the great Andreas Hofer, an innkeeper from South Tyrol, who led the poorly armed farmers to several victories against Napoleonic and Bavarian troops. Despite the victories, Hofer was betrayed, captured, and executed in Mantua, Italy, in 1810. Today he is remembered as the greatest single hero in Tyrolean history, and he is buried in the Hofkirche in downtown Innsbruck.

Another significant event that impacted the Tyrol of today was the breakup of the Austro-Hungarian Empire after World War I. The collapse of the Hapsburg monarchy in 1918 resulted in the reduction of the Austrian territories, including the ceding of the South Tyrol to Italy. To this day Tyroleans on both sides of the Brenner Pass bemoan their losses.

Imperial Austria

The Hapsburg dynasty was founded by Rudolf I in 1273. Prior to this, the land we now know as Austria was ruled from 976 to 1246 by the House of Babenberg, and by the king of Bohemia, Ottokar, between 1246 and 1273. During the reign of Rudolf IV (1358–1365), Tyrol was annexed to Austria as a "free and independent" territory.

Friedrich II (1440–1493) developed a system of powerful intermarriage that raised the Hapsburg monarchy to the highest level in all of Europe. Maximilian of Hapsburg, also known as the "Last Knight," was very fond of Tyrol and became emperor in 1493. He was an avid hunter and because of his love of the outdoors and his active lifestyle, he kept in constant contact with his subjects. Maximilian continued his predessessor's policy of selective marriage when he wed his first wife, Maria of Burgundy, the daughter of Charles the Bold, duke of Burgundy. Selective marriage helped to continuously increase territory for the Hapsburg monarchy.

> Let others war, thou, happy Austria, wed;
> What some owe Mars, from Venus take instead.

This short couplet was written to emphasize Austria's penchant at increasing lands without resorting to war.

Maximilian is responsible for one of Innsbruck's most famous architectural symbols: the Goldenes Dachl (Golden Roof) was erected in the late 1490s in honor of Maximilian's two wives, Maria of Burgundy and Bianca Maria Sforza.

The reign of Charles V (1519–1556) resulted in persistent rivalry between the Austrian crown and Francis I of France. Charles became head of the Holy Roman Empire during his reign. In 1556 Charles abdicated the throne to his brother, Ferdinand I, who founded the Austrian monarchy. During his reign, Austria acquired Bohemia, Hungary, Spain, Portugal, Sicily, Naples, northern Italy, the Low Countries, and Burgundy.

The next two hundred years were marked by war, including the Thirty Years' War (1618–1648), the League of Augsburg (1685–1697), the War of the Spanish Succession (1701–1714), the Battle of Blenheim (1704), the War of the Polish Succession (1733–1738), the War of the Austrian Succession (1740–1748), the Seven Years' War (1756–1763), and the Napoleonic Wars (1792–1815). All these conflicts, with their short interim peace times, brought change to the Austrian lands and a continual reshuffling of family alliances with foreign governments.

The following century (1815–1918) saw the Austrian monarchy begin to crumble and finally collapse. The Crimean War (1853–1856) strained an already weakened Austrian government, and defeats at Magenta and Solferino resulted in the loss of territory. The years from 1861 to 1865 witnessed a bloody civil war during the reign of Emperor Franz Josef I. In 1914 the chosen successor to Franz Josef, Franz Ferdinand, was assassinated in Sarajevo by a madman. Instead, Karl I succeeded Franz Josef I. The collapse of the empire was inevitable, and while World War I surged, Karl I was removed, and the House of Hapsburg came to an end.

Republican Austria

The First Republic of Austria was founded in 1919. Though it was a difficult transition to make—and doomed to fail with Adolf Hitler's Anschluss (annexation) prior to World War II—the First Republic adopted a federal constitution resembling Switzerland's. It remains a federal state with nine autonomous provinces: Burgenland, Carinthia, Lower Austria, Upper Austria, Salzburg, Styria, Tyrol, Vienna, and Vorarlberg. Autonomy does not necessarily indicate independence, although all provinces do exercise a great degree of self-determination.

Each province (called "Land") elects its government (the Diet) every four to six years. Depending on population, the number of elected officials numbers between thirty-six and fifty-six, much like the elected bodies in the United States. The Diet of Vienna has 100 elected members. The Diet is responsible for electing the provincial government which administers the Land. It makes its decisions by majority vote.

The Federal Assembly has two branches, like the government of the United States. The National Council has more than 180 members who are elected by all men and women over the age of twenty. The federal president, unlike the president of the United States, has the right to dissolve the National Council. The Federal Council has 54 members who are elected by the Provincial Diets. It is directly responsible for protecting the rights of the provinces.

The federal government in Austria consists of the chancellor, vice-chancellor, various ministers, secretaries of state, and other appointed officials. Currently (1998–1999) Austria is head of the European Union and retains its status as neutral country, established in 1955.

Religion and World View

Like the rest of Austria, the Tyrol is overwhelmingly Roman Catholic, which stems from Austria's long-term relationship with Rome and, until 1806, the Austrian emperor's status as Holy Roman Emperor. During the Reformation (the fifteenth and sixteenth centuries), Protestant nobles held much of the power in Austria, but little in Tyrol. The Counter-Reformation in the late sixteenth century brought Catholicism back into religious power throughout Austria where it has remained.

In Tyrol, Catholicism is wound up with many daily, weekly, and yearly rituals. There are processionals honoring saints, agricultural festivals (remaining from pre-Christian times) which give thanks to God, and Christian festivals and celebrations which are tied to Tyrol's connection with the land. An example of this would be the yearly Passion Plays which take place throughout Tyrol. Alpine Passion Plays have a particular twist in that the location of Biblical events takes place in the Alps, not in the desert of the Middle East. Tyroleans cannot separate themselves from their environment: their world view is Alpine in nature, grand on the one hand, dark and cold on the other.

As head of the Holy Roman Empire for nearly 600 years, the House of Hapsburg helped to entrench firmly a tradition of Catholicism throughout Austria. Challenges to this tradition by Turkish invaders and the Protestant Reformation were met head on, and the Catholic Church remains the major force in Austrian religion (fully 96 percent of Austrians claim membership in the Catholic Church).

In Tyrol, symbols of the Catholic faith are visible everywhere. Roofed crosses are located along roadsides and are a recognizable Tyrolean art form. They contain hand-carved figures of Christ, a tradition of wood-working that has been passed down for generations. Religious scenes are also painted in houses throughout Tyrol, and families often possess Christ figures that are family heirlooms. In many restaurants, inns, and other public areas, crucifixes are highly visible. Many families in Tyrol also have private chapels where they can pray, worship, and light candles. Figures of the Madonna are often dominant in these small chapels.

THREATS TO SURVIVAL

Demographic Trends

Austria's current population hovers around eight million with about 30 percent of the population in the cities of Vienna, Graz, Linz, Salzburg, and Innsbruck. Though by no means heavily populated, rural areas of Tyrol have experienced a steady increase in population density, especially since the late 1960s. Much like the urban exodus in American cities, rural Tyrol has seen many villages that were once farms and farmland turn into suburbs and bedroom communities in a few short years.

Land prices have skyrocketed in response to this and likewise so have property taxes. The rural poor are finding it more and more difficult to remain in villages and family homes because of the escalating suburbanization of some villages.

Current Events and Conditions

In spite of its idyllic location and breathtaking scenery, the Tyrol and the people who live there must confront a number of substantial—and very modern-day—difficulties. Foreign workers from Eastern Europe have recently made employment even more problematic for Austrians than usual. The recent Yugoslavian conflict has driven thousands of refugees across the border into Austria, and Austrians have been forced to find shelter, food, schooling, and, in many cases, jobs for them. Unemployment rates have risen sharply (12 to 15 percent) and ethnic prejudice is also on the incline.[2]

The people of Tyrol have been faced with enormous changes in their long history, but probably none more lasting than those that have occurred since World War II. Preindustrial Tyrol was a self-sustaining, economically independent province dotted with farmland and high mountain chains. Following the devastation of World War II and the years of Allied Occupation (ending in 1955), Tyrol found itself scrambling to modernize roads, water and irrigation systems, transportation, communication lines, and farming technology.

Villages in the mountains and valleys of Tyrol engaged in small-scale family farming prior to industrialization. After World War II, and especially since the late 1960s, fewer people have been engaged in small-scale farming, and a greater number of corporate or monoproduction farming operations have been developed. Village life had revolved around farms and their seasonal rhythms. Large-scale farms, now located on prime land, are separate from the small family farms. Many farmers found that their sons and daughters were not interested in carrying on the family business. The process of inheritance, in which farmland, animals, and dwellings are handed down from generation to generation, has become less and less the norm as more small farms stand abandoned or are sold off piece by piece to developers.

The landscape in rural Tyrol changes yearly as farmland decreases. In its place homes, hotels, resort areas, and roads are built. Over one thousand years of traditional independent rural farming has receded into the past and is now beyond recovery in many villages. However, many rural Tyroleans with the support of the provincial and federal governments, have taken steps to preserve the small farms that are left. The people of Tyrol have countered the loss of traditional life by tying the family farms to the burgeoning tourist industry. Though at first glance this may seem counterproductive, tourists seem to enjoy farm holidays in the participating farmsteads, and in many areas of Tyrol this strong effort to join tourist industry has reenergized traditional farming practices.

Environmental Crisis

Pollution is a major concern for Tyrolese due to the remarkably heavy traffic through the Alpine passes. Air, water, and noise pollution, as well as the effects of each of these, has made the Tyrol a target for environmental groups, and increases in a variety of industrial diseases are noted throughout the region.

Tourism, despite the economic advantages to the region, has resulted in a continuous loss of agricultural land throughout Tyrol. In some cases, as in Obergurgl in the Otz Valley, environmental degradation resulting from overbuilding has caused devastating damage to villages and traditional life. The daily crush of tourists in both urban and rural areas of Tyrol has also increased the stress of day-to-day living among Tyroleans.

Modernization, including road building, industrialization, and farming technology, has impacted Tyrolean life in myriad ways. As mentioned, increased travel has resulted in pollution of the air, waterways, and forests. Roads have also made previously inaccessible and pristine mountain areas open for development, tourism, and recreation. Industrialization has also had both good and bad impacts on Tyrol. The province depends on heavy industry for a good deal of its income, but this has resulted in many farms being abandoned as an entire generation of rural Tyrolese move from farming to wage labor. Modern farming technology, though undeniably responsible for increases in yield, has been detrimental to the landscape leaving a number of areas in Tyrol unable to support farming. Fertilization of fields has led to groundwater pollution and runoff in streams, which has steadily reduced water quality in many low-lying areas.

RESPONSE: STRUGGLES TO SURVIVE CULTURALLY

Thus far, tourism and the tourist industry seem to have been responsible—at least partially—for helping preserve many aspects of rural life. Paradoxically, the industry is also seen as responsible for the undeniable degradation of much of Tyrol, the overcrowding at many venues, and the increasing commercialization of rural Tyrolean life.

Tourism has been cited as both a cure and a curse for current problems in Tyrol. Many aspects of traditional Tyrolean life and material culture have been legislatively preserved because of the expectations of the tourist populations that descend on the area year-round. The tourist industry markets Tyrol as pristine, traditional, rural, and spectacular—anything less than the expected might prove economically devastating to the area.

Tyroleans for the most part have taken advantage of the tourist market. Seen as a way to preserve their lives, villages, and history and to participate in and prosper from the global economy, tourism has become a way of life for thousands of rural Tyroleans.

Some have saved their homes by developing guesthouses, guestrooms, and bed and breakfasts. The extra income generated by this often seasonal activity helps pay for the increases in taxes, while preserving the family home. While little can be done for many of the rural inhabitants, one strategy has been to reestablish communal areas that are protected from development. Many farmers have banded together into cooperatives to establish markets and power blocks in order to preserve farms and farm life.

The culture of Tyrol begins and ends with the peoples' ties to the land. Their current struggle to maintain their cultural heritage is constantly challenged by the perpetual motion of modernization and globalization: two factors the Tyroleans seem ill-equipped to battle. In many cases, they have been unable to preserve the land and have watched as development and environmental degradation increase at an uncontrollable rate. In some cases, Tyroleans have become clever legislators and have petitioned local, provincial, and national governments to move on their behalf to save the symbols of their long cultural heritage. The struggle simply to maintain their traditional way of life will continue into the future, some say with little success.

FOOD FOR THOUGHT

Unlike many endangered peoples, the people of Tyrol have never been faced with imminent destruction through forces other than war. What has challenged their way of life has been the unstoppable movement of modernization and the global forces that currently shape all our lives. They have witnessed their traditional and time-honored material culture commodified and marketed as memorabilia for tourists. They have watched their lands dwindle, space change, and magnificent environment permanently altered as "progress" has marched forth. The stress, strain, and tension of change have not passed over the rural populations of Tyrol. The people of Alpine Austria, no matter how remote the village, or how romantic the notion, have all been deeply affected by postmodern world culture. Communication systems, computers, and satellite dishes have worked in concert with the media and advertising to bring the Tyrol to the world. Likewise, these technological marvels have brought the world to Tyrol in ever-increasing numbers.

Questions

1. What do you suggest the Tyroleans do to preserve their land?
2. What environmental factors do you see as helping or hindering the people of Tyrol in their efforts to maintain their culture?
3. As a people who are culturally endangered (as opposed to physically endangered), how would you propose the Tyroleans organize politically to make themselves heard?
4. Do you see any parallels between the Tyrolean struggle for survival and the struggle of farmers elsewhere (for example, family farms in the United States)?
5. What steps can the tourist industry take to assist the people of Tyrol in their efforts to preserve their culture?

NOTES

1. Tirol Tourist Buro, interview with Innsbruck office, October 9, 1995.
2. Melanie A. Sully, *The Haider Phenomenon* (New York: East European Monographs Series, Columbia University Press, 1997), 13–21.

RESOURCE GUIDE

Published Literature

Allan, Nigel J. R., Gregory W. Knapp, and Christopher Stadel, eds. *Human Impact on Mountains*. Totowa: Rowman and Littlefield, 1988.

183

Cole, John W., and Eric R. Wolf. *The Hidden Frontier: Ecology and Ethnicity in an Alpine Valley.* New York: Academic Press, 1974.

Costa, Kelli Ann. "Image Brokering and the Postmodern Peasant: Material Culture and Identity in the Stubaital." Ph.D. diss., University of Massachusetts, 1998.

Crankshaw, Edward. *The Fall of the House of Hapsburg.* London: Papermac, 1981.

Eyck, F. Gunther. *Local Rebels: Andreas Hofer and the Tyrolean Uprising of 1809.* London: University Press of America, 1986.

Kann, Robert A. *A History of the Hapsburg Empire 1526–1918.* Berkeley: University of California Press, 1974.

Kuhebacher, E. *Tirol im Jahrhundert nach Anno Neun.* Innsbruck: Universtatverlag Wagner, 1986.

Netting, Robert McC. *Balancing on an Alp: Ecological Change and Continuity in a Swiss Mountain Community.* Cambridge: Cambridge University Press, 1981.

Sully, Melanie A. *A Contemporary History of Austria.* London: Routledge, 1989.

Ward, Martha C. *The Hidden Life of Tyrol.* Prospect Heights, Ill.: Waveland, 1993.

WWW Sites

A tourist-related site gives a substantial pictorial and informational overview of the whole of Austria as well as Tyrol. In English.
www.alpen.net/austria

This site offers up-to-date information on weather with many live-cam recordings throughout Tyrol. Also has a links page. In German.
www.tyrol.at

This comprehensive site is available in either English or German. Unlike many sites concerning Tyrol, this one goes beyond tourism, discussing such issues as regions within Tyrol, infrastructure, health and fitness, and cultural events. Also has access to live-cams and the interactive *Tirol Magazine.*
www.tiscover.com

Chapter 12

The Former Yugoslavians

Kathleen Young

CULTURAL OVERVIEW

The People and the Setting

Yugoslavia was pieced together as one country, from six separate republics—Croatia, Slovenia, Macedonia, Montenegro, Bosnia-Hercegovina and Serbia—in 1918. Currently, Yugoslavia is bordered by the nation-states of Italy, Austria, Hungary, Romania, Bulgaria, Albania and Greece. The climate and terrain are as diverse and conflicting as the people. Various groups have been pitted against one another and manipulated according to the changing interests of ruling powers. The breach between the Eastern world and the Western world was established early and complicated by the religious, linguistic, cultural, and economic differences that existed between the constituent parts of the former Yugoslavia. In most of the republics, city dwellers lived like city dwellers anywhere in Europe. They held jobs similar to people in any urban setting, listened to the same music, watched the same television and movies, wore the same fashions, and many, especially students, were as computer literate before the recent war and breakup of former Yugoslavia as most Europeans or Americans. People in the countryside tended to live more traditionally on farms or to work for mining companies, factories, or local industries. They also had access to modern communications and popular styles.

Slovenia was under Germanic rule from the eighth century (Hapsburg from the thirteenth) until 1918. It was the most economically prosperous, technologically developed, and ethnically homogenous republic. **Macedonia** was part of the Ottoman Empire until 1912 and part of Serbia until the

Courtesy of Mapcraft.

creation of Yugoslavia in 1918. Macedonia is ethnically mixed, with large numbers of Albanians. Macedonia is visibly multicultural, but many Macedonians fear that ethnic diversity may lead to a lessening of the national identity that has been distinctively Macedonian. **Montenegro** was the smallest republic in territory and population. Montenegrins along the coast may be Roman Catholic and culturally identify with Croatia or Italy in some areas, but most Montenegrins identified themselves on census forms as ethnically Serbian or Yugoslav. **Croatia** was an independent kingdom before union with Hungary from 1102 (and the Hapsburg monarchy after 1526) to 1918. Croatia, across the Adriatic Sea from Italy and similar to its Mediterranean culture and religion, Roman Catholicism, benefited from Western tourism. Croatia was the republic most centered on tourism.

Bosnia and Hercegovina, a medieval kingdom, was then part of the Ottoman Empire until 1918. It was part of the Nazi-sponsored Independent State of Croatia from 1941 to 1945. Bosnia and Hercegovina included a large Muslim population designated as a separate ethnic nationality within Yugoslavia after 1968. The capital of Bosnia-Hercegovina, Sarajevo, had a specific identity as the most cosmopolitan, literate, and multicultural European city in the republic.

Serbia was a kingdom before its conquest by the Ottomans after 1389 (and the Battle of Kosovo) and again in the nineteenth century. Kosovo is a province in Serbia, ceded to Serbia after the defeat of the Ottomans in 1912 through the Powers of the Protocol of Florence, 1913, leaving more than half of the population of Albania outside of the new Albanian state. The Serbs controlled the politic and the economy. Kosovo was given autonomy as a province in 1974. In 1989, the autonomy was revoked by Serbian leader Slobodan Milosevic. Even as the Serb-led Yugoslav army was consumed by war with Croatia and Bosnia-Hercegovina during the years from 1991 to 1996, Serbs and Kosovars lived separate lives, and Kosovo existed in a state of ethnic apartheid. As war in the former republics ended, Serbia faced war over what it considered part of its own republic and, central to its ethnic heritage, the province of Kosovo.

KOSOVO

The dissolution of the former Yugoslavia is often traced to the Serb annexation of the autonomous province of Kosovo in 1987. The annexation immediately raised fears throughout the other republics of increasing Serbian nationalism. As Serbia instituted a system of apartheid against the Kosovo Albanians, the other republics responded with calls for greater political independence. Serbia's restrictions on the non-Serb citizens of Kosovo set a precedent for distinguishing ethnic belonging from full citizenship, alarming the other republics.

The 1991 census showed a complicated ethnic design distinguishing

Former Yugoslavians in refugee camp. CIDA photo: Roger LeMoyne.

Muslims in Kosovo from Albanians, although most of the Kosovo Albanians were also Muslim. The Muslims in Bosnia-Hercegovina were considered an ethnic group, but the Muslims in the autonomous province of Kosovo were considered a separate nationality, Albanian, despite their assertion they had been living there as long as the Serbs.

Social, Political, and Religious Organization: An Historical Overview

Serbs and Albanians were living together and fighting together against the Turks at the battle of Kosovo in 1389. The battle of Kosovo Polje, the Field of Blackbirds, was one of the largest battles ever fought in Europe during the Middle Ages. The Turks left their enemy's bodies for carrion birds to scavenge, according to legend, hence the reference to blackbirds. Kosovo is etched in Serbian nationalist consciousness as a place of only Serbian torment and sacrifice. The day on which the ancient battle was fought, June 28, Saint Vitus Day (Vidovan), is celebrated each year and is the subject of heroic Serbian national ballads. On June 28, 1988, the year-long countdown to the sixth centenary of the Serbian defeat at Kosovo Polje began when the long-dead soldier Lazar's ancient coffin began a tour of every town and village in Serbia, drawing crowds of patriotic mourners.

Orthodox Serbs were not the only ones fighting the Turks at the Battle of Kosovo. Albanians, Croats, Bulgarians, and Hungarians experienced defeat together at Kosovo, but the Battle of Kosovo marks the end of the Serbian empire. Serbia remained under Turkish rule for 350 years, but it was never completely subdued. Islam was never widely accepted in Serbia, and most people remained faithful to the Serb Orthodox Church. The Turks had conquered Albania by 1468, and most Albanians converted to Islam while still maintaining their separate identity as Albanian.

Ottoman rule was ending in Bosnia by 1878. Serbia, Montenegro, Greece, and Bulgaria amassed troops and finally drove the Ottoman forces out of the Balkans in the Balkan Wars of 1912–1913. Kosovo, with its Albanian majority, did not go to Albania. France and Russia considered Serbia a friend and rewarded Serbia by transferring almost half the Albanian population to Serbia. The state of Albania was reduced to satisfy the Great Powers, leaving more than half of the total Albanian population outside the borders of the newly diminished state.

The Serbian victors in Kosovo massacred entire Albanian villages then looted or burnt anything that remained. European press reports estimated the number of Albanians killed at 25,000. From the end of the Balkan Wars to World War II, Albanians lived under Serb domination. The Albanian language was suppressed, Albanian land was confiscated, and mosques were turned into stables. Police harassment of Albanians was common—part of a documented Serb policy designed to pressure Muslim Albanians into leaving Kosovo.

During World War II a part of Kosovo was united with Albania under Italian occupation. Some Albanians collaborated with Nazi forces against the Serb population, continuing the cycle of retaliation, this time against the Serbs they considered their oppressors. The resentment of the Albanian Kosovars was so great that even the fascist Italian Nazis, who were hated invaders, appeared more compatible than the Serbs to many. Historians estimate that about 40,000 Serbs were expelled from Kosovo during World War II. Most did not return after the war.

Post–World War II

Yugoslavia fought a bloody civil war during World War II, resulting in a victory for the Communist leadership of Marshal Josip Broz Tito. For the first few years after World War II, Communist Yugoslavia and Communist Albania enjoyed friendly relations. The Yugoslav leader, Tito, established a multiethnic state in Yugoslavia, but to preserve Communist rule, he suppressed smoldering resentments by outlawing expression of ethnicity in any way that could be considered nationalistic by Communist authorities. The capital of Yugoslavia was still Belgrade, the capital of Serbia, but "brotherhood and unity" as Yugoslav was stressed in an attempt to balance a strong central government with brotherhood among the republics.

Yugoslavia struggled to balance centralist powers of the government in Belgrade, Serbia, with the sovereign autonomy of the five republics by continuing to revise its constitution. The first postwar Yugoslav constitution, adopted in 1946, defined Yugoslavia as a federal state of six sovereign republics. The territory of Kosovo was granted a degree of autonomy and allowed to send representatives to the federal legislature, but its internal affairs were to be defined by Serbia. The friendship with Albania ended in 1948 when Tito broke with Joseph Stalin, a move that most Yugoslavs welcomed but a move that pitted the Albanian Kosovars against Albania. During Tito's clash with Stalin, Albania supported the Soviet Union. Yugoslav and Albanian border guards clashed along the Kosovo-Albania border. The Yugoslav secret police heightened the persecution of the Albanians in Kosovo. As Serbs persecuted and feared Albanian-Kosovars, the Kosovars harassed Serbs in turn. Serb-Kosovars reported feeling pulled to Serbia proper for economic reasons and pushed out of Kosovo by the alleged Albanian harassment.

New Yugoslav constitutions adopted in 1963 strengthened Serbia's control over Kosovo by conditioning autonomy on the will of the Serbian government. As Serbs moved into power in the government of Kosovo they usually lived in state-owned property. Albanians were forced to buy their own land and build their own houses. The traditional extended family organization, the *zadruga*, persisted among Albanian-Kosovars long after urbanization and industrialization caused its erosion throughout the rest of Yugoslavia. Brothers stay together in the *zadruga* system, effectively sharing property and work, while women marry into the family, and all family members stress the general prosperity of the group as an economic unit, rather than individual nuclear family interests. The *zadruga* is functional in a mainly agricultural society where large families offset the death toll.

A woman in the *zadruga* system enhanced her security in her husband's house by having a son right away. If a woman failed to produce a son she was insecure because she and her daughters would leave the family without a son and she would never have a daughter-in-law to share her domestic duties. Demographic figures from 1979 show Albanian Kosovars had the highest population growth rate in Europe.[1] The *zadruga* contributed to the escalating Albanian birthrate even as it lowered their standard of living compared to the rest of Yugoslavia. The greater degree of urbanization of the Serb population is associated with the demise of the *zadruga* system for the Serbs and the decline in their birthrate. The abortion rate was higher among Serbs than in the rest of Europe whereas Albanian women rejected abortion as self-defeating based on familial, cultural, and religious norms.

Swelling numbers of young ethnic Albanians under the age of twenty-five, unemployed and without access to education, fueled dissent. Demonstrations broke out in Kosovo in 1968 in which Albanians demanded a separate republic and access to education. In response, the government established an Albanian-language university. Yugoslavia's third constitution was revised and revised again between 1968 and 1974 when it was implemented, and Kosovo was then defined as an autonomous province and as a constituent member of the federation. Kosovo was unofficially granted the status of the republics with the exception that Kosovo was not given the right to secede from the federation of Yugoslavia, a right held by the five republics. The Albanian-language university established in Pristine, Kosovo, became the center of Albanian national identity in Kosovo. When it opened the rest of the world up to its students, the students saw the disparity between their freedoms, including access to information, and those of the rest of the world.

Students demonstrated in 1981 for better living conditions, an extraordinary event in a Communist country. The demonstration of thousands of students inspired construction and factory workers to take to the streets in protest throughout Kosovo. Retribution by the Serb government was immediate and harsh. The Yugoslav army was sent to Kosovo, where they killed Albanians and arrested them for "verbal crimes," any complaint made by anyone at anytime. Prison sentences for complaining were substantial. The press, local governments, and schools were purged of Albanians. Few Albanians held jobs in comparison with Serbs. Approximately 30,000 Serbs left Kosovo (according to Yugoslav government estimates) because of alleged Albanian retaliation to Serb properties, but critics suggest the Serbs left because the Yugoslav government's economic policy toward Kosovo was one of resource extraction. Wealth, in the form of minerals, was extracted from Kosovo for the benefit of the other republics with very little ever coming back in the form of increased prosperity or economic opportunities.

Threats to Survival

Both sides grew increasingly hostile and wary of each other in the 1980s. Albanian women stopped going to government-run hospitals to have their babies, fearing Serbian infanticide of Albanian babies. Albanians were convinced Serbs would kill their children in order to reduce the high Albanian birthrate. Serbs, a numerical minority in Kosovo, held the social and political power as ethnic isolationism became further entrenched and each side grew more suspicious of the other.

Serb-Kosovars lodged complaints in the Yugoslav Federal Assembly of the alleged genocide against Serbs in Kosovo. These accusations asserted that the escalating Albanian birthrate constituted willful genocide against the Serbs. In a formal memorandum, Serbs claimed the Albanian-Kosovars had made war against Serbs by their escalating birthrate, cultural differences, and physical presence in Kosovo. Serbs complained about Tito's concessions to Albanian ethnic nationalism by making the province of Kosovo a "constituent part" of Yugoslavia, on the same footing with Serbia during the revision of the constitution in 1974. All of this added to Serbian resentment, which, after Tito's death in 1980, eventually contributed to the emergence of a virulent nationalism in Serbia.

From the Albanian perspective, they were not Serbs but they were citizens whose ancestors had established their right to live in Kosovo and maintain their ethnic identity. In 1987 peaceful Albanian demonstrations for republic status were met by Serbia banning all public meetings. It was during this time that Serbian nationalism was mobilized by the words of Slobodan Milosevic.

In April 1987 Milosevic was attending a meeting in Kosovo when a crowd of Serbs and Montenegrins tried to push their way into the meeting. When the local police used force to prohibit the mob's entry, Milosevic commanded the police to let "his" Serbs through, and the crowd became electrified. Belgrade's official press service reported that citizens spontaneously sang the national anthem and shouted they would never give up Kosovo. Milosevic immediately became identified as the savior of the Serbs living outside the borders of Serbia. Critics charge Milosevic adopted Serbian nationalism for his own personal advancement.

Milosevic, leader of the Communist party in Serbia, also found it expedient to espouse support of Serbian Orthodox Christianity in 1989, aligning nationalism with the Serbian religion. In order to stroke Serbian nationalism, this reportedly nonreligious Communist leader brought the Serbian Communist party and the Serbian Orthodox Church into a kind of alliance. The church-state alliance worked to draw the Russian Orthodox and Greek Orthodox churches together to support Serbia, which in turn solidified ties among the governments of Russia and Greece and Serbia. At the same time, a merging of the interests of Serbia with the specific character of the Serbian Orthodox Church added religious fervor to nationalism.

General strikes erupted throughout Kosovo in 1989. The federal government arrested Albanian leaders and protestors of any sort. Renewed police violence, demonstrations against violence, demonstrations met with violence, and violent demonstrators plagued daily life. The escalating oppression of Albanian-Kosovars was sealed when the government revoked Kosovo's autonomy. Apartheid resulted. Albanian-Kosovars relied on barter and exchange, sent their children to Albanian language schools in neighbors' homes, and shunned all things Serbian. Students strove to maintain an underground university system and continue their education. Education became a radical act of resistance and protest.

War in the Last Decade of the Twentieth Century

Milosevic was elected president of Serbia with 65 percent of the electorate's support in 1990. The republics of Yugoslavia, including Serbia, passed new constitutions in 1990. Albanian police officers in Kosovo were then suspended from their jobs and replaced with 2,500 Serb policemen imported from Belgrade to Kosovo. When thousands of Albanian children in segregated schools became sick and hospitalized in the spring of 1990, it was rumored that Serbs were poisoning the Albanian children. A United Nations toxicologist reported finding substances used in chemical weapons in the blood and urine of the children. Some Albanian parents attacked Serb houses, and the Serb government immediately transferred another 25,000 policemen to the area. Laws allowed the police to keep anyone in jail for three days for questioning without filing charges and imprison anyone for up to two months for committing the crime of insulting the "patriotic feelings" of Serbs. In response to mounting human rights abuses, Albanians turned to passive resistance, following the model of nonviolence espoused by the Indian leader Mahatma Ghandi.

Conditions deteriorated in all ways, and thousands of Albanians left to find work in other areas of Europe. The Serb war against Bosnia worsened the situation for Albanians in Kosovo as Albanians suffered from the anti-Muslim fervor of Serbs and the hardships resulting from the economic sanctions against Serbia by the international community. A man who would be charged with war crimes in Bosnia, "Arkan," was elected to represent Kosovo in the Serbian assembly—a man who called the majority Albanian community in Kosovo tourists, not citizens.

The Bosnian war was negotiated to an end with the Dayton Accords, but Kosovo was left out of the discussion. Disappointed Kosovars watched Western diplomats congratulate Milosevic on his peace-making efforts. Albanian Kosovars continued their practice of passive resistance until the events that unfolded in 1997 challenged that policy.

The country of Albania collapsed into chaos in March 1997. The government had invested in a pyramid scheme which ultimately left everyone in the country bereft of their savings. Police stations were looted, and in this state of anarchy, Kosovo was flooded with weapons from Albania. The ethnic majority, Albanian Kosovars, now had access to weapons, a serious concern for the Serbs. Suspected members of the newly formed Kosovo Liberation Army were arrested and charged with "hostile association," a charge they never denied.

Current Events and Conditions

War Escalates in Kosovo

One year after the fall of Albania, in March 1998, a Serb policemen was murdered. Serb police then attacked the village of Drenica and killed 100 Albanians. Albanian students put pictures of the brutalized corpses of men, women, children, the elderly, and babies on the World Wide Web within hours of the massacre. They begged students in the West to not forget them, to watch and not turn away from the gruesome pictures. The use of sophisticated technology in a country with the lowest standard of living in Europe highlights the contradictions in warfare around the world today: transportable high-tech equipment used in the basest, most brutal human conditions.

The massacres of Albanians continued over the summer along with retaliation and the mobilization of the Kosovo Liberation Army. Cell phones were carried from village to village as Kosovar Albanians struggled to keep the world informed of their situation. Refugees streamed into Albania, further weakening the social fabric of that collapsed country. Serbs lined the borders of Kosovo with land mines in order to keep the Kosovars from fleeing. An estimated 270,000 Albanians fled to the hills fearing the continuing attacks on villages and increasing militarization of the Serb police. In the fall of 1998 NATO authorized air strikes against Serb military targets, and Milosevic agreed to withdraw his troops. By the winter of 1998, the U.S. State Department was proclaiming that Serbs were committing "crimes against humanity" in Kosovo.

Negotiations to end the Serb crimes against humanity were fashioned in Rambouillet, France, in early 1999. The peace plan proposed by the United Nations was rejected by both Serbs and Albanian Kosovars. The political blueprint called for NATO troops to be placed in Kosovo to oversee peace and protect the combatants from each other. Serbia rejected the presence of foreign troops on its soil. A United Nations force, similar to the peacekeepers in Bosnia, may have been accepted, but the West insisted on a NATO force to avoid the situation that occurred in Bosnia when the peacekeepers were forced to stand by idly and watch Bosnian women and children being killed. For their part, the Kosovo Liberation Army (KLA) refused to comply with the Rambouillet mandate that they lay down their weapons and disarm. There had been too many instances in Bosnia in which the Muslims had disarmed and put themselves under the protection of the United Nations; for example, in Srebenicia where 8,000 boys and old men were murdered by Serbs while in a United Nations–protected safe haven. As the negotiations continued, Serbia sent 40,000 troops to the border of Kosovo, exploiting the break in diplomacy to further what appeared to be preparations for an all-out occupation of Kosovo. Fearing a bloodbath, knowing the far superior military strength of the Serb army and with knowledge of the atrocities committed in Bosnia, the Albanians agreed to the stipulations of the Rambouillet treaty. Hundreds of thousands of ethnic Albanians were hiding in the hills; thousands more were displaced; and more than 2,000 civilians had been killed by this time. The KLA signed the accord.

NATO threatened Serbia with bombing if it refused to sign, but NATO had threatened before and the powers in Belgrade had no reason to believe action would be taken against them this time, despite the NATO rhetoric, and they refused. It seemed inconceivable that Yugoslavia (Serbia and Montenegro), a sovereign nation, would be attacked and bombed by NATO forces over what was a conflict with what it deemed was a secessionist terrorist organization, the KLA. Kosovo had never been a separate republic like Bosnia; this was strictly an internal matter, they reasoned, and not within the legal mandate of the NATO countries. Russia was still a nuclear power and a staunch Serb ally. The world would not hazard World War III over Kosovo, so Serbia reasoned.

Response: Struggles to Survive Culturally

The United States and NATO Enter the War

On March 24, 1999, NATO bombed strategic targets in Kosovo, and the Serbs immediately initiated what came to be called Operation Horseshoe. Moving in the shape of a horseshoe, soldiers went from village to village killing or burning everything in their path, forcing those who could run to run for their lives. Operation Horseshoe was so effective that many analysts conclude it must have been planned in advance of the NATO bombing. To many, it looked as if the NATO bombings were to blame for the extraordinary events that followed. Three days after the start of the bombing, 25,000 Albanian Kosovars were fleeing in terror.

Within a few weeks, 800,000 Albanian Kosovars were running for their lives. Some may have left in fear of the bombs, but those interviewed said they left because of the Serb forces going from door to door. Those in the city reported that one day they were listening to music, going about their business, watching events unfold, and the next day the Serbs broke into their houses and told them they had five minutes to leave or be killed. One man reported protesting his mother was ill and it would take that long just to get her ready to go. The Serb soldier shot her in the head and laughed, he said. Those that could crammed onto buses and trains; others walked. Thousands and thousands left. Border guards took their identification papers and any money they had before letting them out of the country, destroying any proof they ever existed.

When satellite technology showed pictures of mass graves, Serbs began to move the remains and burn their victims, leaving families no way of ever knowing what had happened to their missing relatives. Another common means of disposal was to throw bodies in a well or water supply. Reports of Serb soldiers engaging in gang rapes and abductions of young women circulated. The genocide of ethnic Albanians and the humanitarian catastrophe was well under way by April 1, 1999. By May 20, 1999, one-third of the entire population of Albanian Kosovars had been expelled from Kosovo. The refugee crisis overwhelmed Macedonia and Albania, threatening to undermine the weak economies of both countries and flood the rest of Europe with refugees and asylum seekers from Kosovo.[2]

The International Criminal Tribunal for the Former Yugoslavia, conceived to prosecute war crimes in Bosnia, indicted Milosevic for crimes against humanity on May 27, and NATO escalated its strikes on Serbia. On June 2, 1999, Milosevic capitulated to the terms of NATO, and within ten days Serb troops began pulling out of Kosovo. A Russian convoy entered immediately and took over the Pristina airport, terrorizing the Albanian Kosovars with their presence since the Russians had supported the Serbs and were rumored to have fought with them in some instances against the KLA. The next day, the first NATO peacekeepers moved in, and American marines followed as peacekeepers within days.

The tensions remained. Kosovo remained "cleansed" or destroyed in large part, but the refugees began to return and rebuild. Between mid-June, when the NATO troops were deployed, and mid-August 1999, more than 755,000 Kosovars returned to Kosovo. Most of the returnees, 714,000, came from refugee camps in neighboring countries; the rest returned from countries in Europe, North America, and Australia, where they had sought refuge. Over 12,000 refugees were flown into the capital city of Pristina by the United Nations Internal Organization of Migration in the first week of August 1999, and thousands more made the trip home overland, through Macedonia, Albania, Bosnia-Hercegovina, and Montenegro. The summer of 1999 was a summer of mass migration for Kosovars who, for the most part, had rarely traveled before. Most had nothing to come back to but the opportunity to build a new life on the ruins of the old.[3]

The situation reversed for Serbs in mid-June with the deployment of NATO troops. There were an estimated 20,000 Serbs in Pristina, Kosovo, before the war. By mid-August the United Nations High Commission of Refugees reported only 2,000 Serbs left in the capital city and increasingly violent attacks on the Serb population by Albanian Kosovars on the rise. Some Albanian Kosovars used the same tactics the Serbs had used against them and forced Serbs to sign over their property and possessions and leave. At the time of this writing, most of the Serbs left in Pristina are the elderly or those incapacitated in some way and unable to flee. The only housing that remained after Operation Horseshoe was usually Serb owned; Albanian homes had been destroyed. As winter approached, the remaining

Serbs, in what housing remained, were in a precarious situation. Ethnic cleansing continues and the mass migrations continue; only the ethnicity changes. Close to 200,000 Serb refugees from Kosovo fled into Serbia and Montenegro when the Albanian Kosovars returned. Again, the departure was abrupt and fearful.[4]

In those areas of Kosovo where Russian peacekeepers dominate, tensions are particularly high and peace is tenuous. Albanians have fought with the Russians and continue to resent their presence, while the Russians continue to guard Serb housing from homeless Albanians Relief organizations fear the winter snow will come before housing is available for thousands of Albanians who find themselves home but homeless. Thousands of Roma (Gypsy), caught between embittered Serbs and Albanians, are homeless in Kosovo and the surrounding areas. Approximately half a million refugees from Croatia and Bosnia-Hercegovina are still displaced; many live in camps in extremely difficult conditions. Misery has no preference for ethnicity and rarely does it ennoble.

It is doubtful peace will come as swiftly or as completely as the exodus of Albanians occurred. It is doubtful that Albanians, traumatized and displaced in their Kosovo homeland, will uniformly prevail over the impulse to retaliate. The political issue of autonomy for Kosovo remains unsolved. Like the culture of the Muslims in Bosnia, the people will carry some of their customs with them, but for most there is nothing to go back to, only the present experience of displacement with other refugees a long way from home and in what is left of the homeland.

BOSNIA-HERCEGOVINA

Social, Political, and Religious Organization

The phrase "ethnic cleansing" was introduced into common usage with the independence of Bosnia-Hercegovina from the former Yugoslavia in 1992. There were three primary ethnic groups in Bosnia-Hercegovina prior to 1992: Bosnians whose ancestors had converted to Islam centuries ago and who were considered an ethnic group known as Bosnian Muslims; Bosnian Croatians; and Bosnian Serbs. Most of the Croatians were nominal Roman Catholics, and the Serbs had ties to the Serbian Orthodox Church. The power and the weapons were in the hands of the Serbs, and, as a result, hundreds of thousands of Bosnian Muslims and Croats were killed, tortured, raped, starved, expelled, and forced to flee when Serbs and the army of the former Yugoslavia attacked civilians from rural villages to the capital city, Sarajevo. Within a few years, the unique way of life of Bosnian Muslims that existed prior to the war had been extinguished, and Europe revisited the memories of the Jewish Holocaust of World War II with the euphemism "ethnic cleansing."

Ethnic cleansing takes many forms. For example, Serb soldiers took over an elementary school, raped the little girls, and sent them home to tell their parents that if the family was not gone in twenty-four hours, they would do it again.[5] People were put on trains, reminiscent of the boxcars Nazis used to haul Jews to gas chambers, and were expelled or never seen again. Ethnic cleansing ranges from the mass slaughter of civilians to calculated attempts to inflict emotional damage on a scale wide enough to break down an entire community. For example, during the two-year siege of Sarajevo, a Serb sniper shot at a woman on the street, purposefully shooting her in the knee to cripple her, and then just as purposefully shot her eight-year-old son in the head so she would watch him die in front of her.[6] After such purposeful wounds to the soul, Bosnians asked how the injured could stay and live next door to those who had committed such crimes. To leave (and there was no way out for many), however, would be to acquiesce, to give in, to ethnic cleansing.

The Yugoslav army used genocidal methods as a tactical or planned form of warfare intended to "cleanse" an area of the targeted population and then either destroy or take their houses and all their possessions. More than 250,000 people were killed between 1991 and 1996, 70 percent of them were women and children.[7] It was a war in which soldiers, especially Serb soldiers, fared much better than the civilian population. Most of the victims were Bosnian Muslims who, prior to the war, lived much like everyone else in Europe, watching the same films, listening to the same pop music, wearing similar fashions, and never imagining the horror to come.

Bosnian Croats were also tortured, raped, abused, and killed by Serb forces and for a time in parts of Bosnia, Croats also brutalized and killed Muslims in similarly gruesome ways. In the area of west Hercegovina, near the formerly tourist shrine town of Medjugore, a Bosnian Croat named Mate Boban created a Croat state within a state, and in April 1993 Bosnian Croats killed hundreds of Bosnian Muslims, culminating in the demolition by the Bosnian Croats of the famous medieval bridge of Mostar on November 9, 1993. Eventually, the government of Croatia assumed the position that the Croat-Muslim conflict was playing into the hands of the Serbs, and a three-way war would be suicidal for both Croats and Muslims.

In every war, victims sometimes retaliate by committing atrocities, and there were indeed occasions when Bosnian Muslims killed unarmed Croats and both killed innocent Serbs, but no group as a whole can match the victimization of Bosnian Muslims, and Serbia has the distinction of being the first European country since World War II to have committed genocide, according to the United Nations. While the world watched, Serbia and Serbs in Bosnia engaged in genocide, the willful targeting of a population for mass destruction, and they succeeded. The Bosnia-Hercegovina that existed prior to 1992 has disappeared, and with it has gone a way of life, a cultural ethos that will never be the same.

In this area of southern central Europe, Bosnia-Hercegovina, like some of the other republics of the former Yugoslavia, had never experienced prior international recognition as an independent European country of the modern age. But Bosnia-Hercegovina did not share in the ethnic or religious homogeneity of some of the other republics of the former Yugoslavia. For example, more than 90 percent of Slovenia, another of the Yugoslav republics trying to free themselves from the communism and oppression of Serbia, was made up of people declaring themselves to be Slovenians. There was no singularly pervasive national identity of "Bosnia-Hercegovinian." In comparison, people living in the capital city of Sarajevo considered themselves as broadly European and sophisticated urbanites, not ethnic nationals.

The idea of living in a democracy in an independent Bosnia-Hercegovina frightened many of the Serbs living in Bosnia because they could not feel certain that democracy, the will of the majority, could guarantee their safety and protect their civil rights in an area where they were in the minority. They had no guarantee and no reason to trust that the tyranny of the majority would not be directed against them if they were in the minority in an independent Bosnia-Hercegovina.

In the Bosnia-Hercegovina of the early 1990s, 40 percent of the population were ethnic Muslims (meaning that generations ago some of their relatives had converted to Islam, regardless of whether they were religious in the present; in fact, most of the younger generations were completely secularized), 32 percent were Serbs, 18 percent were Croats, and the rest called themselves Yugoslavs or were in that ambiguous category of "other."[8] Those claiming to be "other" on official census forms included people of mixed marriages (Muslim-Orthodox-Roman Catholic); Gypsies, who continually remain underenumerated in the census; and individuals who refused to be identified by any government designation. The ethnic census was for government purposes; people of the younger generation in the 1990s paid little or no attention to the ethnic ancestry of their friends and neighbors prior to the war.

The 1991 census evidences a complicated ethnic design that distinguishes Muslims in Kosovo from Albanians, most of whom are also Muslim. Muslims in Bosnia-Hercegovina were recognized as an ethnic group, but the large numbers of Muslims in the autonomous province of Kosovo were considered a nationality, Albanian, even though, typically, most had been living there for generations. The 1991 census also records a significant number of Gypsies (30,000) in Kosovo but does not record the number of Gypsies in Bosnia-Hercegovina. All attempts at ethnic distinctions for census purposes in the former Yugoslavia hopelessly confused the issue, showing, in fact, how arbitrary a government ethnic census can be.

For example, in the 1931 census, the term "Yugoslav" was employed for both Serbs and Croats, but this forced a superficial unity on people who spoke different dialects, used different alphabets, had different family interactions, and saw the world through different religious and cultural lenses. It was subsequently dropped, and in the period following World War II, the designations of the newly formed republics (with the exception of Bosnia and Hercegovina) were used. That meant that Croats had Croatia and Serbs had Serbia, but the people of Bosnia-Hercegovina were in contention about the governance of their newly independent republic. The Muslim population of Bosnia, especially in the cities and surrounding urban areas, was committed to a multicultural, multiethnic, pluralistic country. How could they maintain that commitment, they asked, when one segment of the population, Bosnian Serbs backed by the Yugoslav army, not only feared democratic pluralism but also wanted to destroy them, cruelly and completely.

Paradoxically, even though ethnic designation in the former Yugoslavia was so arbitrary from one republic to another that it was meaningless, it actually was not meaningless because ethnicity became a deciding factor in determining who lived and died, who was "cleansed" from an area and who remained after the war. People whose families lived in Bosnia-Hercegovina for generations did not always call themselves Bosnians; they were most likely to call themselves Croats if they were Roman Catholic and Serbs if they were Orthodox Christians. The war in the former Yugoslavia demonstrates that religious affiliation is often viewed as an ascribed, not freely chosen, aspect of ethnicity and not necessarily an indication of faith, participation, or registered membership in any specific church.

The history of Bosnia's Muslim population shows that their religion, as an ethnic identification, may have spared them from the nationalism that made even nonwarring Serbs complicitous in genocide and even may have influenced practicing Roman Catholic Croats to be tolerant of government and military policies and practices that made ethnicity, not citizenship, a criteria for national belonging. Like a virus, ethnonationalism spread among the Serbs and Croats, manifesting itself in the virulent destruction of non-Serbs by the Bosnian Serbs, but Bosnia's Muslims, for the most part, remained immune. Faced with genocide, they tried to defend themselves, and some individuals were less immune to retaliatory aggression than others. Their avowed disinterest in violent ethnonationalism did not result in any immunity to the genocide perpetrated against them, however.

Bosnia was part of the kingdom of Croatia from the ninth century to the eleventh century, and then it was conquered by the Magyars (Hungarians) in the twelfth century, but for the most part it was left alone by the Magyars who administered from a distance. During this time, in the middle of the twelfth century, feudal Bosnia embraced a religion that was denounced as heretical by both Eastern (Serbian Orthodox, a regional or nation-based Christianity) and Western (Roman Catholic) Christian churches. Adherents of this religion denounced as heretical were called Manicheans. They stressed the human aspect of Jesus, inspired by the teaching of Mani, a reformer and prophet born in Babylon in A.D. 216. By the tenth century a unique, neo-Manichean sect called Bogomils had taken root in the area of Bosnia-Hercegovina.

In the early 1300s, the area or principality south of Bosnia, called Hum or Hlum (later Hercegovina), was claimed by Hungarian and Serbian powers until it was conquered by the Bosnians in 1325. Bosnians and Hercegovians fought together against Serbs, Croats, Hungarians and Venetians under the leadership of Ban (the ruler or governor) Stevan Tvrtko I who founded the independent kingdom of Bosnia-Hercegovina in about 1377. The kingdom fell when the Serbian army was defeated in Kosovo in 1389 and the entire area was surrounded and eventually conquered by the Ottoman Turks.

The Bogomils had been a challenge to the political and religious authorities surrounding them. Bosnia's Bogomil Christians had distinguished themselves from both the Roman Catholics and Eastern Orthodox Christians, and eventually that separation, and the ensuing harassment suffered by the Bogomils, contributed to their conversion to Islam. Islam became a religion of refuge from the persecution of the Bosnian Bogomils. The religion of the Bogomils seemed similar in many ways to Islam; both had austere beliefs and both were considered heretical, even threatening, to the Orthodox Christians and Catholics.

Religion had been used to manipulate local populations by the various powers trying to conquer the area since the first Slavic tribes had established themselves. In 1415 the Islamic Turks offered the Bogomils military protection, secure title to their lands, and freedom to practice their religion—if they counted themselves as Muslims and did not attack their Ottoman forces. The Bogomils could not refuse and Turkish rule brought about wholesale conversions to Islam. Such voluntary conversions occurred in huge numbers partly because of the political and economic advantages gained by joining the state religion and the Turkish promise that the Bogomils could be Muslims in their own Bosnian way. Bosnia became a Slavic state within the Ottoman Empire—a state in which Bosnian Bogomils enjoyed special autonomy and status. The Turkish influence left a particular stamp on the culture, and it has been estimated that, by the end of the of the seventeenth century, three-quarters of the population of Bosnia had officially converted to Islam.

Bosnia's remaining Christians, with Russia's support, joined the Serbs in a war against the Turks in 1875. It was during this time that Austro-Hungarian armies invaded and occupied Bosnia. The conundrum of political maneuvering intensified when Russia declared war on Turkey on April 24, 1877. On March 3, 1878, the two parties signed the Treaty of San Stefano which somewhat enlarged Serbia and Montenegro and made both fully independent. The Treaty of San Stefano virtually annihilated Turkish control of Bosnia, but there was still disagreement concerning the disposition of the Balkans generally. Russia agreed to another Congress to reconsider various aspects of the Treaty of San Stefano.

Threats to Survival

The Congress of Berlin in 1878 gave additional territory to Serbia and handed Bosnia and Hercegovina over to Austria to administer. The powers participating in the Berlin Congress—Russia, Britain, France, Germany, Italy, Austria-Hungary, and the Ottoman Empire—also reached a settlement to the Russo-Turkish War of 1877–1878, officially marking the end of the Turkish-Ottoman power in this area of the Balkans. Serbia benefited from the Congress in territory but complained about Austria-Hungary's right to administer Bosnia and Hercegovina, although that right did not include the formal right of annexation.

Austria annexed Bosnia-Hercegovina in 1908, which brought Europe to the brink of war. Serbia reacted with violent threats against the incorporation of Bosnia-Hercegovina into the Hapsburg empire. Serbia wanted Bosnia-Hercegovina to be autonomous so Serbia could annex the area. Russia's relations with Serbia and Austria were challenged by Serbia's staunch demand for intervention to stop Austrian influence in the area. Russia sided with Serbia, a tradition of occlusion between the two countries that would strain world relations in the war in Bosnia in the 1990s as it strained Austro-Russian relations during this time and led to World War I.

The start of World War I is attributed to the assassination by a Serbian Bosnian of Archduke Francis Ferdinand, the heir to the Hapsburg throne, on June 28, 1914, at Sarajevo, the capital of Bosnia. World War I finally led to World War II, the horrors of which were revisited in the form of genocidal ethnic cleansing in the war in the 1990s in Bosnia. The resolution of World War II did end Austria-Hungary's administration of Bosnia-Hercegovina, and the area became part of the kingdom of the Serbs, Croats, and Slovenes in 1918. The fate of Bosnia-Hercegovina was sealed to the fate of Yugoslavia, and ultimately was placed under Serbian hegemony.

In 1941 Bosnia-Hercegovina was incorporated into a Nazi puppet state until the Nazi Ustasha enforcers (as the Nazi forces in Croatia and Bosnia were called then) were forced to retreat in 1944. Some of the worst battles with the heaviest civilian casualties during the war took place in Bosnia-Hercegovina with Serbs specifically targeted for annihilation and suffering. There were concentration camps and forced expulsions of Serbs from these areas. After the genocidal world war that engulfed all of Europe and brought about the self-immolation of Yugoslavia, the country started over.

The emphasis was not so much on rebuilding as on fashioning a brand new country, under the direction of the Communist government headed by a Croat-Slovene called "Tito."

The Communists under Tito considered linking Bosnia-Hercegovina with either Croatia or Serbia or annexing parts of the area to both Croatia and Serbia, but neither option seemed feasible after the wartime killings. The borders were drawn to balance the political interests of collectivist Yugoslavia with the competing reality of the separate ethnicities within Bosnia-Hercegovina. As a result, part of Bosnia-Hercegovina was carved out of the Dalmatia, along the Adriatic Coast across from Italy, while the rest of the Dalmatian coast was assigned to the Republic of Croatia, giving it the shape of a croissant, almost wrapped around Bosnia-Hercegovina with an excessively long border, compared to other European entities. As a result, some Croats, like some Serbs, came to regard the borders as artificial and intentionally designed to mitigate their powers as republics.

Tito's collectivist Communist paradigm began to collapse after his death in favor of ethnic nationalism. State relations with the Catholic Church in Bosnia-Hercegovina were complicated in 1981 by the alleged appearance of the Virgin Mary to six children in Medjugore, resulting in the eventual pilgrimage of nearly 10,000 religious tourists from all over the world nearly every day until the start of war in the area in 1992. At first, the Communist-Socialist state of Yugoslavia responded to the phenomenon of the proclaimed apparition of the Virgin Mary by arresting the local priest. When the government realized that the influx of tourists would bring hard currency into the country, officials considered the possibilities of building hotels and leading state-sponsored tours. Medjugore opened Yugoslavia up to tourists in unprecedented numbers in June 24, 1981, but visas were required.

Tourism declined sharply when Medjugore came under Serbian aerial attack and all of Bosnia was plunged into siege at the start of the war on Bosnia in 1992. The Croatian police who patrolled the area found unexploded artillery shells in the village, and the rumors spread that Medjugore was under divine protection. The international press reported that some religious devotees credited the Virgin Mary with protecting the town against the Serbian onslaught. Certainly, Medjugore fared better than many other cities in Bosnia. The Virgin may indeed have been a better refuge than the United Nations and the European Community ever were, according to the sardonic comments of some Bosnians and Croats, particularly in areas that were hit hard by the Serbs.

If Croats were associated with a tradition of Catholicism, and Serbs associated with Serbian Orthodoxy (a national Christianity), emergent ethnonationalism in Bosnia-Hercegovina was complicated by the population's religious mix prior to the war. Three nationalist parties gained prominence in the 1990 elections: the Muslim party of Democratic Action (SDA) the Croatian Democratic Union (HDZ), and the Serbian Democratic party (SDS), who shared power under President Alija Izetbegovic, a Muslim.

Bosnia's Muslims and Croats voted in favor of sovereignty and independence for the republic on March 1, 1992, nine months after Slovenia and Croatia had committed to independence. Over 63 percent of the electorate voted; however, the SDS, led by Radovan Karadzic, boycotted the referendum. Bosnian Serbs began fighting other Bosnians shortly before the recognition of Bosnia-Hercegovina by the United States and the European Community in April 1992. Their leader, Karadzic, cited two immediate reasons for offensive acts: the absence of real guarantees to Serbian minorities living in a Muslim-dominated Bosnia-Hercegovina and the refusal of Serbs to accept minority status anywhere in the former Yugoslavia, regardless of constitutional guarantees. Using this logic, offensive acts become defensive acts.

The European Community favored ethnic cantonization, or breaking up Bosnia into different regions based on the ethnic identity of the majority who happened to be residing in the area. Ethnic cleansing seemed to be rewarded as a profitable landgrab and anyone—Serb, Croat, or Muslim— who favored a multinational community or a community based on citizenship, not on ethnicity, was abandoned. The tragedy that unfolded in Bosnia-Hercegovina was matched by conflicting and mismanaged policies toward Yugoslavia by the international community and the United States. In the early stages of the Yugoslav crises, the United States, under the Bush administration, sided with Belgrade in the hopes of preserving the unity of the Yugoslav state, even with full knowledge of the repression and mistreatment of the minority populations. The non-Serb populations of Croatia and Bosnia complained that the policy of the U.S. government, in the early 1990s, placed a higher value on stability, even on preserving the repressive communism of the Serbian regime in Yugoslavia, than on democracy and human rights. Croats and Bosnians were confused by what they saw as a betrayal of the democratic ideals of the United States when it supported a unified, if repressive, Communist Yugoslavia.

By late autumn 1992, more than 100,000 Bosnians, mostly Muslim Slavs, were dead or missing, and the world was shocked by ethnic cleansing, systematic rape, and internment camps. All sides have been accused of perpetrating atrocities. According to a U.S. government report on human rights abuses, however, although Croats and Bosnian Muslims sometimes retaliated and targeted Bosnian Serbs, their acts of terror and abuse pale in comparison to the sheer scale and calculated cruelty of the killings, beating, rapes, and violations of every conceivable sort committed by Serbian and Bosnian Serb forces.

There was no physical threat to Serbia. There is no credible argument of "self-defense" in the systematic shelling of civilian populations and the forced starvation of masses of people caused by the siege waged by Serbian forces. The Serb army alone had both the means and the will to commit the crimes against humanity the world was forced, reluctantly, to face. Genocide was occurring again in Europe.

Women and children, professional people, the well educated, the old, and the most vulnerable were the primary targets of Serb military action. Abuses of non-Serbs took almost every conceivable form of torture, humiliation, and killing, in ways designed to do the most damage to the individual, the family, and the community. The atrocities and ethnic cleansing dwarfed anything seen in Europe since the Holocaust. By 1993 Bosnian Serbs, aided by the Serb-dominated army of the former Yugoslavia, had captured about two-thirds of Bosnia and had driven out or killed most of the non-Serb populations. The ancient way of life established by the Bogomils, and maintained through their conversion to Islam, a way of life unique to Bosnia, had disappeared.

The Bosnian Serbs held a referendum in May 1993 and voted to reject the ethnic cantonization proposed by the Vance-Owen plan. According to the plan, drafted by Cyrus Vance and Lord Owen, the Serbian share of Bosnia would be reduced to about 43 percent, and Croats and Muslims would govern their own cantons. The Serbs rejected the plan that would have required them to relinquish captured territory and refused to be governed by democratic law. Serbian officials explain these offenses as defensive measures taken to protect their country and their ethnic group.

The United States and the European Community decided to accept the outcome of the Bosnian Serb's referendum and to let the Bosnian Serbs keep all of the territory they had captured by 1993. The United Nations designated six safe havens in Bosnia, and on May 22, 1993, voted to protect the United Nations' peacekeepers guarding the havens with air power, if necessary. U.S. Secretary of State Warren Christopher had two weeks earlier objected to the plan, saying it would essentially put the Muslims into ethnic ghettos and thus reward ethnic cleansing by Serbian nationalists, but he reversed himself and abdicated to the Serb conquest. Spokesmen for the Bosnian Muslims also objected to the plan initially. Bosnian Serbs then specifically targeted one of the areas designated a safe haven—the Muslim enclave of Gorazde—for continued shelling, forcing the Muslims to change their stance and accept the UN plan or witness more mass deaths. The Bosnian Muslims were forced to concede to ethnic cleansing.

The UN military powers were said to be preparing a plan to defend the six designated havens and deter possible Serbian aggression, aggression they feared would be intended to draw American air power and, thus, involve the United States directly in the war. According to critics, the United States, in 1993, had a policy designed to avoid U.S. military involvement, even to the point of minimizing or ignoring Serbian atrocities and attempts at genocide.

It was during this time that Croats and Muslims, former allies who endorsed ethnic cantonization in order to end the war, began to fight each other in some areas for the domination of specific areas of Bosnia-Hercegovina advanced by the Vance-Owen Plan. It was a plan that rewarded the landgrab policies of the strongest and most brutal, and sadly Croats and Muslims in some areas of Bosnia followed suit. As Croats and Muslims responded by fighting each other over territory, the situation for civilians continued to deteriorate disastrously. The Vance-Owen plan was finally abandoned in June 1993. Bosnia's Muslims were then pressured by both Serbs and Croats to agree to a three-way division of Bosnia-Hercegovina, although the borders and particulars of the division were not clearly delineated. Within a few months during 1993 the tenor of the international response to the war had changed, and any hopes for an internationally brokered peace settlement preserving Bosnia as an independent multiethnic country shared equally by Serbs, Croats, and Muslims were extinguished.

After the Vance-Owen plan was relinquished by the United Nations, Bosnia's Croats and Muslims agreed to end hostilities in early 1994. Bosnia's Serbs remained recalcitrant and continued to engage in acts of war and terrorism. A massacre in the Sarajevo marketplace on February 5, 1994, killed sixty-eight people waiting in a line for bread. The Serbs alleged the Muslims did this to themselves in order to gain international sympathy, but evidence showed the mortar shell was launched from Serb-occupied territory. The gruesome pictures of the bodies and body parts, shown immediately on CNN, drew more condemnation of the brutality from the international community. One of the most moving pictures from the war shown in the Western media was one of Vedran Smailovic, a member of the Sarajevo orchestra, dressed in formal attire playing classical music on the street where the massacre had occurred in honor of the dead. His bravery and the use of his art as a means of resistance, as well as an act of mourning, touched many.

Response: Struggles to Survive Culturally

By the summer of 1994, Croats and Muslims had agreed to the UN brokered peace plan, calling for a three-way division of the country in which the Bosnian Serbs would keep about 50 percent of the country. The plan would require the Serbs to give back some of the territory they had captured, since they were controlling about 70 percent of Bosnia by then. There had to be some incentive for the Serbs to stop the killing and let people return to what was left of their homes. The incentive seemed to come from Slobodan Milosevic's withdrawal of support for the Bosnian Serbs.

By mid-summer 1994, President Milosevic of Serbia and spokespersons for Russia were openly critical of the Bosnian Serbs. Milosevic declared Serbia would no longer support the Bosnian Serbs, but he refused to allow international monitors at the borders of the former Yugoslavia to guarantee the blockade. On August 29, 1994, Bosnia's Serbs spurned the pressures of the international community and rejected the proposed peace plan. Bosnia's Serbs defied the world and embarked on an even more openly visible genocide of Bosnia's Muslims.

Bosnian Serbs seized a UN safe haven, Srebenica, a neutral territory under the protection of UN forces, and on June 14, 1995, began to massacre all the Muslims in Srebenica. Muslims had been encouraged to come to Srebenica from anywhere in Bosnia, lay down their weapons, and be protected by the UN. The UN forces abandoned them when Serb forces came to massacre the refugees. Over 8,000 boys and old men were slaughtered by Serbs under the auspices of UN protection forces. An estimated 20,000 Muslim women and children were forced to leave while their sons, fathers, and grandfathers—all unarmed—were murdered. Srebenica is now known as the site of the single worst war crime committed since the end of World War II.

FOOD FOR THOUGHT: WITNESSING THE THREAT TO SURVIVAL

The United Nations and the United States had knowledge of the mass slaughter and the expulsion of thousands of others before, during, and after the abandonment of the safe haven to the Serbs. It was not a spontaneous bloodbath but all carefully planned, the result of a calculated chain of Serbian command that correctly recognized that the international community was willing to let Serb aggression run rampant, as long as it did not exceed the borders of the former Yugoslavia. In retrospect, Srebenica changed everything, and bloodbaths and ethnic cleansings continued to change the political landscape in what was left of Yugoslavia.

The following month, August 1995, the Croat army "took back the Krajina." Fearing minority status, regardless of guarantees from the Croatian constitution, the Serbs who live in the area of Western Croatia known as the Krajina had seceded from that republic in 1991. The Serb-dominated Krajina, the center from which attacks on all of Croatia were launched, was an area where the non-Serb civilian population suffered terribly. Richard Holbrooke, an American diplomat, had given his approval, encouraged, and vouched support for the 1995 Croatian offensive that ultimately, from the Croat perspective, took back part of their country used illegally to harbor paramilitary troops who terrorized, bombed, and shelled the rest of the country. In a matter of days after the Croat offensive on August 4, 170,000 Serbs left or were driven out. The government of Croatia, especially the president, Franjo Tudjman, is criticized for not doing enough to protect Serb civilians and for allowing atrocities and ethnic cleansing to occur. The government of Serbia, especially Slobodan Milosevic, is criticized for not coming to the rescue of the Serbs in the Krajina area of Croatia, or even of tacitly allowing their expulsion.

Croats and Muslims joined forces in September 1995 and advanced on Serb strongholds in Bosnia. NATO then commenced air strikes on specifically targeted Serb armaments, a significant and surprising change in NATO policy. As the Serbs started to lose ground and Croatia and Bosnia started to take back parts of their countries, U.S. emissary Richard Holbrooke intervened and initiated a peace effort that would allow the Serbs to keep what they had occupied by force, halt the Croatian and Bosnian offensives, and accept all the ethnic cleansing previous committed.

On November 21, 1995, the leaders of Croatia, Bosnia, and Serbia signed an agreement, the Dayton Accords, that confirmed the sovereignty and independence of Bosnia-Hercegovina. Half of Bosnia became known as the Federation, combining Croatian and Muslim areas, and the Republika Srpska took the rest. All sides may have considered it an unjust agreement, but this time, conflicting conceptions of justice were laid aside for a tenuous break from war and a hopeful, if tenuous, peace.

The Dayton Accords allowed the soldiers to go home, but few of the refugees returned. Over half a million dead, hundreds of mass graves, three million refugees, tens of thousands of raped and tortured women and children, traumatized men, and broken destitute families are the spoils of this peace—these are the victors of the Dayton Accords. How does the world assess the cost-benefit analysis of stopping genocide? How do non-Serbs forgive and live without fear among their Serbian neighbors? Before these questions could be fully considered, the world was forced to turn its attention to Kosovo and another ethnic cleansing undertaken by forces of the Serb army.

Questions

1. What roles do religion and language play in establishing a person's identity in the former Yugoslavia? How do they affect the way in which you see the world and how the world sees you?

2. How does the *zadruga* system work to perpetuate an Albanian ethnic identity? Why do the Serbs feel threatened by the *zadruga* system?

3. Kosovo has been treated as a colony within Yugoslavia, used primarily for resource extraction to benefit the industrial development of the other republics. How was this similar to other colonizations in Europe?

4. How do ethnic groups survive ethnic cleansing?

5. What is the role of the media, especially the Internet, in alerting the world to

holocausts? Can you think of possible future effects of increased use of the media in hostile situations?

NOTES

1. Miranda Vickers, *Between Serb and Albanian: A History of Kosovo* (New York: Columbia University Press, 1998), 172–173.

2. KFOR, "Facts and Figures": http://www.kforonline.com/resources/facts.htm.

3. UNHCR, "UNHCR Begins Organized Repatriation of Kosovar Refugees," press release (June 28, 1999); Human Rights in Kosovo OSCE, paper: http://www.osce.org/kosovo/reports/hr/index.htm.

4. KFOR, "Chronology of Events": http://www.kforonline.com/kfor/chronology.htm.

5. United Nations Commission on Human Rights testimony before the United States Congress (U.S. Government Printing Office, 1993). See also "Bosnia-Hercegovina: Rape and Sexual Abuse by Armed Forces," *Amnesty Action* (Spring 1993); "Yugoslavia: Women Under the Gun," *Amnesty Action* (Spring 1993); Beverly Allen, *Rape Warfare* (Minneapolis: University of Minnesota Press, 1996).

6. Zlatko Dizdarevic, "A Letter from Sarajevo: One Thousand Days of Solitude," *Time* (December 12, 1994), 33.

7. See Norman Cigar, *Genocide in Bosnia* (College Station: Texas A&M University Press, 1995); Richard Holbrooke, *To End a War* (New York: Modern Library, 1999); David Rieff, *Slaughterhouse* (New York: Simons & Schuster, 1995); Michael Sells, *The Bridge Betrayed* (Berkeley: University of California Press, 1996); Nader Mousavizadeh, ed., *The Consequences of Appeasement* (New York: Basic Books, 1996).

8. See "The Dying City of Sarajevo," *The New York Times* (July 26, 1992); Peter Maass, *Love Thy Neighbor: A Story of War* (New York: Alfred G. Knopf, 1996); Thomas Cushman and Stjepan G. Mestrovic, eds., *This Time We Knew* (New York: New York University Press, 1996): Zlatko Dizdarevic, *Sarajevo: A War Journal* (New York: Fromm International, 1993); Dzevad Karahasan, *Sarajevo, Exodus of a City* (New York: Kodansha International, 1994); Barbara Demick, *Logavina Street* (Kansas City: Andrews and McMeel, 1996.

RESOURCE GUIDE

Published Literature:

Kosovo

Anzulovic, Branimir. *Heavenly Serbia. From Myth to Genocide.* New York: New York University Press, 1999.

Judah, Tim. *The Serbs. History, Myth and the Destruction of Yugoslavia.* New Haven, Conn.: Yale University Press, 1997.

Malcolm, Noel. *Kosovo: A Short History.* New York: New York University Press, 1998.

Vickers, Miranda. *Between Serb and Albanian: A History of Kosovo.* New York: Columbia University Press, 1998.
Vucinich, Wayne S., and Thomas Emmert. *Kosovo, Legacy of a Medieval Battle.* Minneapolis: University of Minnesota Press, Minnesota Mediterranean and East European Monographs, 1991.

Bosnia

Bringa, Tone. *Being Muslim the Bosnian Way.* Princeton, N.J.: Princeton University Press, 1995.
Cigar, Norman. *Genocide in Bosnia. The Policy of "Ethnic Cleansing."* College Station: Texas A&M University Press, 1995.
Cushman, Thomas, and Stjepan G. Mestrovic. *This Time We Knew. Western Responses to Genocide in Bosnia.* New York: New York University Press, 1996.
Helsinki Watch. *War Crimes in Bosnia-Hercegovina.* New York: Human Rights Watch, 1993.
Holbrooke, Richard. *To End a War.* New York: Modern Library, 1999.
Honig, Jan Willem, and Norbert Both. *Srebenica. Record of a War Crime.* New York: Penguin, 1997.
Judah, Tim. *The Serbs.* New Haven, Conn.: Yale University Press, 1997.
Mousavizadeh, Nader, ed. *The Black Book of Bosnia. The Consequences of Appeasement.* New York: Basic Books, 1996.
Rieff, David. *Slaughterhouse: Bosnia and the Failure of the West.* New York: Simon & Schuster, 1995.
Silber, Laura, and Allan Little. *Yugoslavia. Death of a Nation.* New York: Penguin USA, 1996.
Stiglmayer, Alexandria, ed. *Mass Rape. The War Against Women in Bosnia-Hercegovina.* Lincoln: University of Nebraska Press, 1994.
Tanner, Marcus. *Croatia. A Nation Forged in War.* New Haven, Conn.: Yale University Press, 1997.

Films and Videos

Calling the Ghosts (video), written/produced by Mandy Jacobson and Karmen Jelinic. New York, N.Y.: Bowery Productions, distributed by Women Make Movies, 1996. Women survivors of Omarska Detention Camp describe the camp and the situation in Bosnia and Herzegovina. Their release and recovery process are also described.
Peter Jennings Reports: "How the U.N. Failed in Bosnia."
We Are All Neighbors (video), produced and directed by Debbie Christie. Granada Television. Chicago, Ill.: Public Media/Films, Inc. Video, c. 1993. Series: *Disappearing World: War.* Credits: Anthropologist Tone Bringa. In a Muslim/Catholic village near Sarajevo, rumors fly and suspicions spread. When Catholic Croats assert control, Muslim businesses are attacked, villagers are arrested and harassed, and homes are threatened. Three weeks later, neighbors who had been close friends for fifty years no longer speak to each other,

and the peaceful coexistence between Croats and Muslims disintegrates into mutual distrust and fear.

WWW Sites

Human Rights Watch
http://www.hrw.org/campaigns/kosovo98/photo.shtml

Society for the Anthropology of Europe
http://h-net.msu.edu/~sae/

Glossary

Capitalism: an economic system that originated in Europe where everything, including land, labor, and people, is a commodity to be exchanged on the market for profit.

Clan: a group of people who assume kinship based on a common ancestor.

Culture: way of life characteristic of a group of people including shared behaviors, beliefs, art, material culture, and mode of production.

Diaspora: settling of a dispersed population outside their homeland.

Egalitarian: equal access to resources for all members of a culture.

Enculturation: the process of learning one's own culture.

Ethnic Group: a group of people who think of themselves as being alike because of common ancestry, real or fictitious, and are seen in this way by others.

Genocide: willful targeting of a population for mass destruction, ethnic cleansing, and pogrom.

Identity: Individual and/or group recognition of a specific condition or character.

Matriarchy: Female dominated society.

Nation: A collective culture and identity; associated with a specific political state.

Nationalism: A devotion to one's own nation.

Patriarchy: Male dominated society.

Polytheism: A belief in many deities, gods, and/or goddesses.

Glossary

Race: a cultural construction of a group of people as a distinct kind of people with common habits and/or traits.

Stratification: severe restricting of access to resources, which creates a class system.

Subsistence: how people obtain the necessities of life, especially food production, from the environment.

Transhumance: the seasonal movement of livestock from warmer, lower pastures in winter to higher, cooler slopes in summer.

General Bibliography

Bodley, John. *Victims of Progress*. 3d ed. Mountain View, Calif.: Mayfield Publishing, 1990.

Clark, Robert P. *The Franco Years and Beyond*. Reno: University of Nevada Press, 1979.

Foucault, Michel. *Two Lectures*. In *Power/Knoweldge; Selected Interviews and Other Writing, 1972–1977*. Edited by Colin Gordon, 78–108. New York: Pantheon Books, 1980.

MacDonald, Sharon, ed. *Inside European Identities: Ethnography in Western Europe*. Oxford, England: Berg, 1993.

Nadel-Klein, Jane. "Reweaving the Fringe: Localism, Tradition, and Representation in British Ethnography." *American Ethnologist* 18 (1991):500–517.

Smith, Valene L., ed. *Hosts and Guests: The Anthropology of Tourism*. 2d ed. Philadelphia: University of Pennsylvania Press, 1989.

Vickers, Miranda. *Between Serb and Albanian: A History of Kosovo*. New York: Columbia University Press, 1998.

Wilson, Thomas, and Estellie Smith, eds. *Cultural Change and the New Europe: Perspectives on the European Community*. Boulder, Colo.: Westview Press, 1993.

Wolf, Eric R. *Europe and the People without History*. Berkeley: University of California Press, 1982.

Index

About the Editor and Contributors

DAVID BLOOMBERG graduated from Stanford University with a B.A. in history and international relations.

KELLI ANN COSTA is an assistant professor of Anthropology and Women's Studies at Franklin Pierce College in Rindge, New Hampshire. She is the author of the forthcoming title, *The Brokered Image: Material Culture and Identity in Tyrol*.

LORING M. DANFORTH is professor of Anthropology at Bates College in Lewiston, Maine. He is the author of *The Death Rituals of Rural Greece* (1982), *Firewalking and Religious Healing: The Anastenaria of Greece and the American Firewalking Movement* (1989), and *The Macedonian Conflict: Ethnic Nationalism in a Transnational World* (1995).

SUSAN M. DIGIACOMO is a visiting professor in the Department of Sociology and Anthropology at Middlebury College in Middlebury, Vermont, and is an adjunct professor in the Department of Anthropology at the University of Massachusetts at Amherst. Fluent in Catalan, she has published both English translations of work by Catalan anthropologists and Catalan translations of English-language anthropology.

JEAN S. FORWARD is a lecturer in the Department of Anthropology at the University of Massachusetts at Amherst. She has published articles focusing on the original peoples of North America and environmental/educational issues. Her fieldwork focuses on the role of education in the maintenance of identity among the Mi'kmaq in Boston and in Nova Scotia, as well as the Scottish Gaelic communities in Scotland and Nova Scotia.

JOSEPH S. JOSEPH is an assistant professor of International Relations in the Department of Social and Political Sciences at the University of Cyprus.

KYRIACOS C. MARKIDES is professor of sociology at the University of Maine at Orono.

SUSAN PATTIE is a senior research fellow at the University College in London. She is the author of *Faith in History: Armenians Rebuilding Community* (1997).

THOMAS TAAFFE is pursuing his Ph.D. in cultural anthropology at the University of Massachusetts at Amherst. He has been working in Northern Ireland for several years, primarily studying the role of the news media in the conflict and under the changes produced by the Good Friday Agreement.

RICHARD WALLACE is a graduate student in anthropology at the University of Massachusetts at Amherst. He is focusing on Eastern Europe and is currently completing a Fulbright in Croatia.

LINDA WHITE is on the research faculty of the Center for Basque Studies at the University of Nevada at Reno. She is the co-author of the *Basque-English English-Basque* dictionary and has translated several books on Basque topics. She also specializes in Basque language and literature with an emphasis on Basque women writers.

KATHLEEN YOUNG is an assistant professor at Western Washington University in Bellingham, Washington.

Recent Titles in
The Greenwood Press "Endangered Peoples of the World" Series

Endangered Peoples of Southeast and East Asia: Struggles to Survive and Thrive
Leslie E. Sponsel, editor

Endangered Peoples of the Arctic: Struggles to Survive and Thrive
Milton M. R. Freeman, editor

Endangered Peoples of Oceania: Struggles to Survive and Thrive
Judith M. Fitzpatrick, editor

Endangered Peoples of Latin America: Struggles to Survive and Thrive
Susan C. Stonich, editor